Public Violence in Canada, 1867-1982

Violence is commonly equated with acts resulting in personal injuries or property damage. This definition covers a wide array of actions – the manufacturer polluting the environment, a schoolyard tussle, revolution – not all of which are conventionally recognized as violence, or of equal significance. Judy Torrance introduces the concept of public violence to denote acts widely considered to be violent and of importance to society. Public violence differs from related concepts like political violence in explicitly recognizing that the subject matter is socially constructed.

Historically most public violence in Canada has been associated with the frontier, wartime, elections, job-related conflicts, or conflicts involving ethnic and religious groups. Analysis of violent incidents and cross-national comparisons suggest that the Canadian experience resembles that of other western democracies, although there are some exceptions. The differences between Canada and the United States are especially marked.

Torrance considers various theoretical approaches to violence. Theories stressing the breakdown of values in crowds and in anomic or marginal populations offer some insight into cycles of violence. Discontent theories focus our attention on a society's stress points and on the motivations of the violent. Solidarity theories, using the concepts of risks, rewards, and resources, discuss group mobilization, cohesion, organization, and membership. They also stress that violence is an interaction, and that government is often one of the parties involved. Torrance analyses the contribution of all these theories to an understanding of violence in Canada. She also discusses the importance of cultural heritage in legitimizing violence and norms governing violent conduct, as well as in promoting the myth of Canada as the peaceable kingdom.

Judy Torrance is at present living in Ottawa and carrying out research on several projects.

Public Violence
in Canada,
1867-1982

JUDY M. TORRANCE

McGill-Queen's University Press
Kingston and Montreal

© McGill-Queen's University Press 1986
ISBN 0-7735-0590-3

Legal deposit 1st quarter 1986
Bibliothèque nationale du Québec

Printed in Canada

Canadian Cataloguing in Publication Data

Torrance, Judy Margaret Curtis.
  Public violence in Canada, 1867–1982
  Bibliography: p.
  Includes index.
  ISBN 0-7735-0590-3
  1. Violence – Canada. 2. Violence – Canada –
History. I. Title.
  HN110.Z9V58 1986   303.6'2'0971   C85-099973-1

Contents

Figures and Tables

Preface

Canadians have long assumed that their society is relatively free of violence, particularly in comparison with that of the United States. They see themselves living in a "peaceable kingdom" where problems are resolved without resort to violence. According to this idea, Canadians may be identified by their aversion to bloodshed. They "have found a better way for the solution of [their] troubles" in patient compromise, and they consequently provide a model meriting "the most earnest attention of other countries." These are the words of George Brown in the Confederation Debates over one hundred years ago (Mackenzie, 1882: 301). Today the same sentiments are still expressed, often almost word for word. Kilbourn (1970: xi), for example, voices the hope that Canada "might be a guide to other peoples who seek a path to the peaceable kingdom." Similarly, Prime Minister Pierre Trudeau, in his Dominion Day message of 1972, proclaimed that Canadians have the "opportunity to demonstrate to [themselves] and to the world the benefits of a society guided by the principles of tolerance and understanding" (*The Globe and Mail*, 30 June 1972).

This enduring piece of nationalist rhetoric merits careful examination; for it would indeed be a wondrous thing if Canadians had found "a better way." But it is no easy matter to assess. Canadians know very little about the violence that has taken place in their country, as it has been largely ignored by the academic community, at least until recently.

There are three specifically Canadian reasons for this academic neglect of violence. First, the imagination of historians has been captured not by violent struggles, but by the heroic feat of constructing and holding together a nation against improbable odds. As Mealing (1965: 216) writes: "Nation-building is our great theme ... When Canadian historians write of conflicts, except for that between English and French, it is to emphasize the compromises that prevented them from becoming destructive." Second, nationalism among academics has caused them to stress the differences between Canada and the

United States, one of the most obvious of which is the lesser role played by violence in Canadian history. "In Canada," Underhill (1960: 12) notes, "we have no revolutionary tradition; and our historians, political scientists, and philosophers have assiduously tried to educate us to be proud of the fact." And third, not only is Canadian violence relatively less significant than that of the United States, it is absolutely so in the sense that it has rarely affected the structures of power. Given the tendency of historians to "concentrate on political history as seen from the top, [so that] the only protests which matter are those which produce some rearrangement of power" (Tilly, 1979: 86), it is not surprising that the usually ineffective record of Canadian violent protest groups should have been all but forgotten. Finally, a non-specifically Canadian reason for the inattention to violence can be found in the once prevailing theoretical approaches in the social sciences which emphasized consensus over conflict and dismissed violence as anti-social and aberrant behaviour.

Much of this began to change in the sixties. Violent events in the United States (assassinations; the long, hot summers of black rioting; student and anti-war protests) reawakened an interest in the subject among American scholars. Their interest spilled over into Canada, stimulated further by the shock of the events of October 1970 (the FLQ's kidnapping of James Cross and the murder of Pierre Laporte). Concurrently two academic trends fostered the growing attention to violence. Historians were increasingly attempting to reconstruct the life experience of everyday people, including their experience with violence of less than regime-shattering proportions – history from the bottom rather than from the top. As well, Marxists and other conflict theorists were arguing that society is better characterized as a process of struggle, confrontation, and violence rather than one of consensus and conflict-regulation.

As a result of these influences, there are now a number of works on violence in Canada. Books and articles have been devoted to such events as the Riel rebellions, the 1918 anti-conscription riots, the Winnipeg General Strike, and the October crisis of 1970. There have been some attempts to trace the incidence of Canadian violence, some thoughts on the role of violence in Canadian society, and studies of particular kinds of violence (see, for instance, Frank and Kelly [1977] on collective violence in Ontario and Quebec, 1963-1973; McNaught [1970, 1975, 1975a]; and Jamieson [1968] on industrial conflict). Without the work of these scholars and others in the field, this book could not have been written.

The scholarly work of the Canadians, however, pales in contrast to the explosion in the literature on violence largely emanating from the United States. So much has been produced over the last twenty years that yet another book on the subject is not going to be greeted with great fanfare. Nevertheless the present study does fill a gap. Canadian undergraduates have no general text on violence that uses extensive data and examples drawn from their own country, even though work from around the world has shown the importance of studying violence in relation to a particular society. To understand a country's experience with violence, we must take into account its history, its culture, and its political, social, and economic structures and institutions.

As the actual amount of violence in the United States and Canada has declined during the seventies, so too has interest in the subject. This is natural but, to my mind, unfortunate. During the peak years, students of violence tend to be passionate and partisan, pressed for time, and overly concerned with finding practical solutions to immediate problems. Periods of relative peace, by contrast, facilitate a deeper and more dispassionate exploration of the issues. The present work takes advantage of this opportunity to place Canadian violence in its proper social context, while at the same time it brings to the reader's attention the major theories on violence potentially applicable to this country. These theories have all been developed outside Canada and, as we shall see, they often fail to explain one aspect or another of the Canadian experience. When this occurs either the logic of the theories must be questioned or the special features of Canadian society past and present must be searched for what renders the theories inapplicable. In the process the weak points of the theories become evident and our understanding of Canada is deepened.

Major cross-national surveys on the incidence of violence establish one incontestable fact: countries vary in their levels of violence. Many explanations have been offered for this variation. After a historical survey of Canadian violence (chapter 2) and a discussion of ways in which violence may be classified (chapter 3), I examine some of these explanations as they apply to Canada. They may be expressed simply as follows. The incidence of violence varies according to:

- how people define and perceive violence (chapter 4);
- the extent to which they live within cultures, or embrace ideologies, that encourage the resort to violence (chapter 5);
- the extent to which societal norms are crumbling (chapter 6);
- the number and kinds of reasons people have for being angry (chapter 7);
- the way people are organized and how profitable they judge a resort to violence (chapter 8);
- and the behaviour of the government and its agents (chapter 9).

The object is not to discredit one theory in favour of another. As will become evident, I find, in general, some theories better founded or more powerful than others, and, with reference to particular incidents, some explanations to fit better than others. My tone is often critical as the limitations of the theories are tested. Nevertheless, I believe that, singly or in combination, each has something to offer. Thus I have set up no straw men for gleeful demolition – such as might be found, for instance, in a chapter on mankind's supposed innate disposition for violence.

Violence is a subject that refuses to be confined within conventional academic disciplines. In the pages that follow I shall discuss the ideas of economists, historians, lawyers, philosophers, political scientists, psychologists, and sociologists, as well as non-academic authors. A political scientist by training, I have often found myself brashly venturing into others' preserves. In helping me find my way, I have to thank my friends – above all George Torrance – and two anonymous readers for McGill-Queen's University Press. For help in preparing the manuscript for publication, I should like to thank the copy-editor, William Barker. I have not always followed everyone's advice, and the responsibility for the end result remains on my own head. My family has helped create this book by continuing to provide me with material and emotional support – despite my periods of inattention and bad temper.

This book has been published with the help of a grant from the Social Science Federation of Canada, using funds provided by the Social Sciences and Humanities Research Council of Canada.

Public Violence in Canada, 1867-1982

CHAPTER ONE

The Concept of Violence

Violence is among the most inconsistently defined concepts found in social science literature. This inconsistency is surprising because it is a robust and overt form of behaviour and not an abstraction like "legitimacy." Furthermore, there is a widely used basic definition of violence: "physical injury to people and their property." However, when we come to particular cases – does this incident constitute violence? should that incident be included? – we find a wide penumbra of disagreement.

There is one obvious reason why the concept of violence should be so shadowy. Not unnaturally, academic and governmental interest in violence tends to rise and fall with the incidence of violence in society. Much research consequently takes place in the midst of crises and seeks only to find practical solutions to current problems. Empirical research is devoted to answering such questions as: Is there more violence now than then or here than there? Has the cycle peaked? Who are the violent? Why are they acting in this way? And what will satisfy them? In the urgency to come to grips with the problem, philosophical speculations on the meaning of violence are pushed to the sidelines.

Another reason for the inconsistent definition of violence is that, as Eckstein (1964: 12) points out, the study of violence is at a theoretical crossroads. Violence is "one of the great synthetic subjects of social science," of interest to a number of disciplines, and capable of being illuminated by many theoretical approaches among which, he suggests, are theories of social force, of political competition, of social deviance, of social instability, and of war. Yet these diverse approaches, while claiming the same subject matter, often fail to meet at the crossroads; for each tends to define violence in terms of the particular injurious behaviour with which it is concerned. For example, an analyst of social deviance might treat violence as something that occurs following the breakdown of norms against injuring others, with the result that those injurious acts used to maintain a society's norms are simply excluded from the discussion.

A third reason why we are not sure what is and what is not violence is that the word is used inconsistently in everyday speech (see chapter 4). Because violence is heavily freighted with negative connotations, people tend not to apply it to those with whom they sympathize, while pinning it with alacrity on those they despise. Social scientists are no different in this regard. They often simply ignore the injurious acts of the favoured party or, if the favoured party is admitted to be violent, they then demand that all actions against that party be tarred with the same brush and be termed "violence" as well. In neither case is Camus's (1960: 85-6, 90) admonition being followed:

When violence answers violence in a growing frenzy, ... the role of intellectuals cannot be ... to excuse from a distance one of the violences and condemn the other. This has the double result of enraging the violent group that is condemned and encouraging to greater violence the violent group that is exonerated ... [Rather, their] role is to clarify definitions in order to disintoxicate minds and to calm fanaticism, even when this is against the current tendency.

In order to set about clarifying definitions, let us first look at some examples to be found in the literature. Most theorists accept as a point of departure the basic definition of violence as "physical injury inflicted on people or their property." Yet few accept it without qualification. Some find it too broad and argue that it includes acts that should not properly be called violent; others consider it too narrow.

Among the former are those who say the basic definition should be narrowed to include only those acts which are intentionally harmful. Skolnick (1969: 6) defines violence as "the intentional use of force to injure, to kill, or to destroy property," while Graham and Gurr (1969: xxx) call it "behavior designed to inflict injury to people or damage to property." Sometimes intention is used to differentiate one type of violence from another. Bowen and Masotti (1968: 13), for instance, define civil violence according to "the intent of those engaged in it to strike out at the animate or inanimate representatives of the civil order."

Another way of narrowing the basic definition of violence is to say that only injurious acts which take place in a certain manner, or under certain conditions, or of a certain magnitude should be called violent. Wolin (1963: 16-17), for example, argues that violence (1) "denotes an intensification of what we 'normally' expect a particular power to be" (it is the "unexpected intensity" of the act that makes it violent); (2) alarms us because of its "eruptive or unpredictable quality"; and, (3) "implies that an unusual amount of destruction will accompany a designated act." Similarly, Johnson (1966: 8) defines violence in terms of its disruptive and disorienting characteristics, and MacCallum (cited in Nardin, 1973: 95) requires that the action be sudden and produce radical change in the person or thing harmed.

Both these ways of narrowing the basic definition of violence bring us closer to the way the word is used in everyday speech. We probably do not call things violent unless we discern behind them an intention to do harm and unless we are somewhat shocked by them. However both cases create methodological problems. Each requires us to look into the minds of either the perpetrators or the observers of an incident and ask what were the motivations of the former and the reactions of the latter. Pity the poor researcher merely trying to make a count of violent events if they are to be defined in this way.

Furthermore, many theorists argue that, rather than trying to narrow the definition, we should be seeking to expand it. One line of reasoning suggests that if we confine our definition to cases of physical damage, we unduly emphasize the destructiveness of certain segments of the population while glibly ignoring the everyday oppression inflicted upon them. According to Skolnick (1969: 5):

Less dramatic [than overt violence] but equally destructive processes may occur well within the routine operation of "orderly" social life. Foreign military ventures come quickly to mind. Domestically, many more people are killed or injured annually through failure to build safe highways, automobiles, or appliances than through riots or demonstrations. And as the late Senator Robert Kennedy pointed out, the indifference, inaction, and slow decay that routinely afflict the poor are far more destructive than the bomb in the night. High infant mortality rates or rates of preventable disease, perpetuated through discrimination, take a far greater toll than civil disorders.

Nevertheless, attempts to expand the basic definition of violence have also run into criticism. The U.S. National Commission on the Causes and Prevention of Violence (1970: 73), for example, considers "group violence as the unlawful threat or use of force by any group that results or is intended to result in the injury or forcible restraint or intimidation of persons, or the destruction or forcible seizure of property." This is an unusually large definition. Currie (1971: 455) argues that it serves an ideological rather than an analytic purpose, since it is used to discredit acts that the Commission finds "particularly disturbing," such as sit-ins or the locking up of military recruiters, and "to justify severe responses by authorities."

The dilemma of theorists, then, is that if they expand the definition of violence they can be accused of seeking to attach the reprehensible connotation of "violence" to acts they disapprove of, while if they narrow the definition they can be accused of refusing to recognize the harmful and reprehensible conduct of those to whom the physically violent are responding. On balance, however, the charge of ideological bias would seem to be more appropriate against those who would expand the definition of violence. For in these cases the theorists would generally use "violence" to replace other perfectly adequate words. This can be seen if we look more closely at some of the suggested extensions of the definition of violence.

First are the theorists who argue that it is inappropriate, both analytically and for humanitarian reasons, to consider only physical assaults while ignoring other forms of injury to people. Included in this group are those making the general point that harmful actions can be non-physical, as in the case of insults, and can have non-physical consequences, such as damage to the psyche. The group also includes two other, more elaborate approaches. According to one, the essence of violence is not brute harm; rather it lies in the idea of violation. Any act should be called violent if it infringes upon or disrupts the integrity (other words used are autonomy, inherent structure, nature, being, action, constitution, pattern of existence, and essence) of some individual or even, occasionally, some thing – a right, a contract, or a constitution. Such violation may or may not be physical in nature (Garver, 1969; Wade, 1971; Harris, 1973). According to the other elaborated approach, we should not confine our definition of violence to cases where the agent is an identifiable individual (personal violence). Instead we should include cases where physical and non-physical damage occurs as a consequence of some situation or institution (structural, institutional, system, or regime violence). Barrington Moore (1966: 103-4) provides one instance of this latter usage when he writes: "The prevailing order of society always grinds out its tragic toll of unnecessary deaths year after year ... To dwell on the horrors of revolutionary violence while forgetting that of 'normal' times is merely partisan hypocrisy."

Nardin has examined these concepts of violence in detail. His analysis suggests, for example, that the idea of violence as violation is culture-bound since it "only makes sense within an individualist conception of man," and that the concept of structural violence turns on some notion of avoidable harm which again "will vary from one cultural context to another" (1973: 96, 110). Structural violence also raises sticky questions, familiar to lawyers, of foreseeable knowledge and the limits of responsibility. My major objection to these concepts is that they so extend the meaning of violence that it becomes virtually synonymous with injustice, wrong-doing, or disruption of the established order. We can recognize that there are many forms of conflict and harm without calling them all violence. If we fail to distinguish among them, we end up with a notion of violence far removed from everyday usage, as in the contention of Harris (1973: 112) that Gandhi's civil disobedience campaign was violent since he sought to disrupt "an essential part of government, its administrative machinery."

The second way that the definition of violence is extended is to include events in which no physical injury is done although the threatened use of violence is clearly present. Is there any essential difference, asks Rubenstein (1970: 173), between these two scenarios?

(A) Armed peasants surround the palace. Their leader breaks into the throne room, kills the king and promulgates a new constitution. This we call a "violent revolution." (B) Armed peasants surround the palace. Their leader is granted an audience with the king. The king counts up the number of peasants and the number of his troops and promulgates an amended constitution. This we call "peaceful change."

As well, Nieburg (1969: 127) points out that "peaceful demonstrations" are designed to demonstrate the protesters' strength and commitment. Military coups are also almost invariably included in lists of violent events even though they can be quite bloodless. And many authors include the physical occupation of another's property (land seizures, sit-ins) and interference with another's freedom of movement (kidnappings, incarceration) within their definition of violence. In all these cases, there are no physical injuries but only because the victims or the authorities make no resistance. Violence is not yet on the stage but everyone is aware of its presence in the wings.

Against the argument that threatened violence cannot be logically distinguished from violence itself, Walter (1969: 13) cogently notes that the former is a viable technique of power, but violence tends to destroy those against whom it is directed (you cannot compel a dead man to obey you, although admittedly you can use his death as an example to others). Another point is that not all violence neatly fits the threat-resisted pattern. Such a model is often apposite, especially when we study the process by which individual incidents develop, but it must be remembered that violence can be used for non-threatening purposes, such as to punish or gain revenge, to destroy, to defend oneself, and to express frustration. The most obvious point is that our subject is violence. Thus we must not lazily assume that all coups, demonstrations, and sit-ins are within our field, but rather must single out those with bloody outcomes in order to distinguish their particular causes and consequences and to contrast them with the non-violent variants.

Finally, the third way of extending the meaning of violence lies in seeing it as a means of getting one's own way over the opposition of others. In such usages, violence is melded in with the concepts of coercion, force, and power. As Arendt (1969: 43) observes, these concepts may be taken to be synonymous because they are all seen as "the means by which man rules over man." The argument carried to its logical conclusion produces such statements as "*every* political act, whether by private parties or by agents of the state, is violent" (Wolff, 1969: 608). According to Wolff (1969: 606), the distinction between the uses of force that result in bodily injuries and those that do not is "not sufficiently sharp to be of any analytical use" and "usually serves the ideological purpose of ruling out, as immoral or politically illegitimate, the only instrument of power that is available to certain social classes."

Wolff correctly notes that the fairly common definition of violence as unjustified force is a confused concept whose use in practice will probably depend on the user's socio-economic standing. Yet Nardin (1973: 81) equally correctly argues that to equate violence and force is to undermine the notion that some uses of power are indeed legitimate or justified, while others are not. "The result may be good rhetoric, but it is disastrous for both political philosophy and empirical research." In any event, there are many definitions of power, force, coercion, and violence that do not revolve around the notion of legitimacy.

Power, for example, can be defined quite simply as the ability to get things done. Power rests on different bases. Among these is *consensus*, which involves people co-operating to achieve some object. Other means of power come into play when the object can only be achieved over the resistance of others. *Coercion* entails the threat or actual application of punitive sanctions to overcome the resistance. A sanction need not involve physical injury; it may take the forms of ostracism or withdrawal of benefits. Another means of overcoming resistance is *force*. This is the physical overpowering of a person either by personal physical strength or through the use of weapons. *Violence* is the actual infliction of physical injuries. Coercion or force may or may not involve violence (that is, result in physical injuries). Violence may or may not be used in the service of power.

A domestic example may make these distinctions clearer. A parent confronted with a recalcitrant child at bedtime may choose to threaten:

1 Get upstairs right now or there'll be no television for you tomorrow.
2 If you won't go up on your own, I'll pick you up and carry you to bed.
3 Do as you're told or I'll spank you.

These are all expressions of non-consensual power, where the speaker is seeking to obtain something over the resistance of another. The threat of undesirable consequences makes (1) a case of coercion, as is (3) where the threat of pain is held up, thus making it a case of coercion through violence if the threat is carried out. The threat in (2) is one of force; the child is to be physically overpowered although violence is not present since no physical hurt is involved.

There is nothing sacred about this particular set of definitions. It can be adapted at will providing the result is well thought out and coherent. For many purposes it may be unnecessary to go into such detail. Yet the set just given (or some variant of it) does enable us to think precisely about violence and the various means of power. In particular, it shows that power and violence are not the same thing even if the two often appear hand in hand. There can be power without violence, and there can be violence unrelated to power (in self-defence, for example).

The various attempts to expand the basic definition of violence all force us to think about the subject. They remind us that a man's soul can be bruised as readily as his body, that we can be hurt by systems or institutions as much as by other people, that legitimate powers engage in physical violence and also compel obedience in other, equally unsavoury ways. But such expanded definitions also raise difficulties, the chief of which to my mind is their confounding of concepts which, while related, are none the less useful to keep distinct. Thus, in this book violence is simply defined as the infliction of physical harm on people or their property.

This unelaborated basic definition has a number of advantages. Unlike some of the other definitions we have been considering, it is not culture-bound (though cultures may vary somewhat in their concepts of people and property); it is readily observable to an outside observer – we can tell when it has taken place; and it need carry no normative judgment or partisan bias if used carefully. It is also closer than some of the extended definitions to everyday speech, although, as we shall see in chapter 4, the correspondence is far from precise. At least the basic definition gives us a yardstick against which to gauge the extraordinary variations in the usage of "violence" in common language.

Before leaving the problem of definition, some specific points should be noted. First, although I speak of physical damage, I would count as violence cases in which physical pain is inflicted even if no enduring physical injuries result. Second, I would include within the definition such self-inflicted injuries as suicide and the destruction of one's own property. And third, a curious consistency in all definitions of violence is the unquestioned way in which we lump together damage to both people and property. Without thinking we equate the stone thrown at a man with the stone thrown through his shop window. It seems that our possessive individualist assumptions have so much rendered a man's replaceable property an extension of the irreplaceable man himself that injury to either is automatically taken to be an expression of violence.

A UNIFIED CONCEPT OF VIOLENCE?

The basic, unexpanded definition of violence still offers us an enormous field of inquiry. We have to consider an array of behaviour ranging from a cuff on the ear to torture and death on the battlefield. Players inflict injuries on one another in sporting events. Parents "discipline" a child. Police or soldiers "restore order." Criminals meet with capital punishment. There are assassinations and arson, child abuse and coups d'état, suicides and sedition, vendettas and vandalism.

Can we include within one discussion all forms of violence, from child-beating to revolution? Another question, already partly dealt with in the discussion on definitions, is whether there is some attribute of violence unique to it that justifies exclusive attention to it and not to some larger category of behaviour. In practice, theorists who give a positive answer to the first question (yes, we can subsume all forms of violence under one theory) usually end up with a negative response to the second (no, violence is only one type of a larger group of behaviour). Two examples will make this clearer.

First, Gurr (1970: 36) argues that "the primary source of the human capacity for violence appears to be the frustration-aggression mechanism." To Gurr, violence in its several manifestations can be interpreted in terms of this common underlying mechanism.[1] However, he also makes the point that frustration does not invariably result in violence and cites (1970: 33-4) psychological studies showing that frustration may also express itself in regression, evasion, avoidance, innovation, apathy, and so on. Attention is thus diverted away from violent behaviour in itself. It is merely one case of the broader category of behaviour resulting from frustration.

Second, Nieburg (1969: 45) claims that his theory of violence operates "at all levels of human action, from interpersonal to international." But, as with Gurr, this comprehensiveness is achieved by downgrading violence from being a subject in itself to being one aspect of a larger category. According to Nieburg (1969: 56), there is a bargaining dimension in all human relations. The threat or use of violence is simply a means of bargaining and as such is analogous to the other rewards and punishments that govern all social interactions. Unless we consider violence as a part of this larger category, he argues (1969: 5), we tend to end up with a perspective that denies the functionality of violence and sees it instead as "erratic, exceptional, and meaningless."

The argument, then, is that we should not write books about violence, but rather ones with such titles as Conflict, Frustration, Deviance, and Bargaining in which only one chapter would be devoted to violence. However, many theorists deny that there is any conceptual unity behind the various manifestations of violence and say that we can only treat together particular subgroups of violent behaviour. The question then is how do we divide up the subject matter? And how do we identify those incidents for analysis that we can justifiably regard as important?

Probably the most widely used subcategory of violence is "political violence." This is not simply the special phrase of political scientists eager to join other theorists of violence. Rather political violence is said to have a conceptual unity because of the monopoly of legitimate violence attributed to the modern state or because such violence can destroy, disrupt, or be a symptom of the breakdown of the necessary consensus on which political

1 However, in a subsequent analysis Gurr and Bishop (1976: 96) conclude that "there is no empirical basis here for contending that 'violence' is a unitary phenomenon: quite the contrary."

power rests. Political violence is very often treated as an aberration, a disease of the polity, and the opposite of "normal" politics whose business it is to resolve disputes in a non-violent fashion.[2] However, as we shall see, violence both by and against governments can play a part in "normal" political relations. Thus, when we find political violence defined in terms of disruption, illegitimacy, and a challenge to the regime, we are dealing implicitly with pejorative labels and not necessarily with descriptions of fact. The revolutionary, for instance, sees his violence as constructive – as a means of excising the rotten wood so that a new and, to him, better structure can be built.

A closer look at those events called "political violence" makes us ask whether even the subset of political violence is all of one piece. Gurr (1970: 3-4) defines political violence as "all collective attacks within a political community against the political regime, its actors – including competing political groups as well as incumbents – or its policies." For some this definition may be too narrow. Why, for instance, are only collective acts included? Surely the lone assassin has an impact on the political system when he attacks political actors. More importantly, why are acts of violence by the regime excluded? For others, however, Gurr's concept is too broad. He argues (1970: 5) that the differences between a riot and a revolution seem to be ones "of degree, not kind." Yet factor analytic studies of politically violent events come to a different conclusion. They show two distinct dimensions: violence of an unplanned nature, usually called "Turmoil," and violence of an organized nature, labelled "Internal War" or "Revolution." Sometimes a third dimension is found, "Subversion," comprising acts of a conspiratorial nature. The authors of such studies (Rummel, 1966: 71; Bwy, 1968: 228; Morrison and Stevenson, 1971: 364) emphasize that incidents associated with the different dimensions usually occur independently of one another and arise out of different conditions.

Another common subcategory of violence is "collective violence" – violence carried out by a group of people. This concept is used frequently by those interested in collective behaviour, including such events as panics, bank runs, disaster behaviour, and various kinds of organized social movements. Treating violence in this context stems from nineteenth-century theorists, such as Le Bon, who discussed crowds in terms of irrationality, suggestibility, and the throwing off of restraints. Skolnick (1969: 330-9) argues that present-day collective behaviour theorists retain many of these nineteenth-century assumptions. They typically treat riots as distinct from normal social

2 Gurr (1970: 4), for example, writes: "Some common properties of political violence encourage attention to it rather than more general or more specific concepts. Theoretically, all such acts pose a threat to the political system in two senses: they challenge the monopoly of force imputed to the state in political theory; and, in functional terms, they are likely to interfere with and, if severe, to destroy normal political processes."

life, irrational, inappropriate, and resulting from the breakdown of social control. While recognizing that collective behaviour theories may be helpful in analysing how an incident develops, Skolnick objects to their tendency to overlook the role of the authorities, both as a precipitant and as a participant in destructive behaviour, to play down what is often the purposefulness and rationality of the rioters' behaviour, and to neglect the political dimensions of that behaviour.

Others use the concept of collective violence, not to lay stress on a particular way in which violence can develop, but simply to differentiate "significant" events from the mass of "petty" acts of violence. The rationale for this procedure is that if social scientists were to deal with every occasion on which one person harmed another they would never stop counting and get on with the analysis. Yet how can one determine significant events on the basis of number alone? The problem becomes manifest in the analysts' arbitrary specification of the number of people it takes to constitute a collectivity. Some choose 15, others 20, 50, or even 100. Evidently the number selected (information on which is generally buried in a footnote on coding procedures) must profoundly affect the subject matter of a study. Anyway, we may well question whether the number of participants can reliably indicate the seriousness of an event: from the perspective of a victim, it matters little whether he or she is struck down by one hand or many.

Another subcategory is "criminal violence." This concept reflects everyday usage as well as an academic subject area. Often criminal violence is distinguished from political or collective violence in order to mark those incidents in which violence serves private, non-political motives. The distinction is carried over into the division between "political" prisoners and "ordinary" criminals. These are valid distinctions in theory, but their application may be controversial. First, what may be a crime in one community may not be regarded as such in another. The Inuit, for example, are said to have regarded as a murderer any person who contributed to an individual's starvation, but not necessarily one who killed a newborn infant or aged parent (Hagen, 1977: 4). Second, one person may believe a particular act of violence to be motivated by selfless ends where another can see only criminality. The situation is not made any clearer by the mixed motives that characterize many incidents. In this context, to label an incident "political" is to justify and ennoble it, while to call it "criminal" is to belittle and condemn it. Third, violence carried out for private, criminal motives may well have political consequences, for example, the murder of a political figure by a burglar or the rising level of street crime that produces a demand for law and order reform.

Thus, each of these subsets of violence can be questioned on various grounds. Like the overall concept of violence in general, they subsume acts that are not patently all of one kind and distinct from other events. The only apparent common denominator, and it is common by definition, is that someone or something gets hurt in the process.

To some this is a trivial matter. Whether or not there is violence is merely "a matter of the weapons that are chosen by conflict groups to express their hostilities" (Dahrendorf, 1959: 212). Tilly (1978: 177) also sees violent and non-violent collective actions as being "basically similar," with the reaction of the authorities often being the determining factor. On another tack, we have already cited Wolff's (1969: 606) claim that the distinction between violent and non-violent force is "not sufficiently sharp to be of any analytical use." In effect, these theorists would urge us not to write books about violence at all; we should forget it as a subject for study. This opinion is generally held by theorists who view society in terms of conflict rather than consensus. Violent conflicts, they say, are not necessarily representative or the most unpleasant or the most important of social conflicts. The shadow must not be confused with the substance; the relatively rare occasions on which violence erupts are insignificant compared to the continuing class struggle at the heart of our society. Studying violence is a waste of resources. More than this, given the tendency to concentrate on the violence of rebels (as in the academic interest and government commissions on the subject inspired by the 1960s ghetto violence in the U.S.), it is actively pernicious because it leads to prescriptions for minor adjustments in the status quo and the maintenance of existing agencies of social control.

I believe the strictures of the conflict theorists are overstated. They are helpful in reminding us that non-violent coercion is a fact of life and that authorities routinely employ violence for their own ends. Yet some conflicts are violent while others, ostensibly similar, are not, and it is surely valid to inquire why this should be so. Furthermore, the conflict theorists assume answers to some as yet unanswered questions: we cannot know if violent conflicts are similar to other conflicts in their causation and process unless we study them. Also, in dismissing violent civil conflicts as uninteresting, the conflict theorists do not give us reason to ignore the many other kinds of violence that arise out of different contexts.

Nevertheless the main reason for studying violence and not dismissing it as a trivial conflict variant is ultimately a moral and philosophical one. This is the belief that social relations, even ones involving conflict, are better when conducted without violence. Admittedly violence may have beneficial results – as when it is used to overthrow tyranny – but we can still prefer nonviolent change or, failing this, require that violence be balanced by resultant good. Be this as it may, violence remains, to my mind, the ultimate social evil because it corrodes our trust in others and undermines our willingness to co-operate. When people raise their hands against each other, they deny the possibility of consensus and threaten the social structures that have been erected against the original Hobbesian state of nature. As Johnson (1966: 10) puts it: "Violence tends progressively to inhibit and ultimately to extinguish the union of men into a ... [society], regardless of the principles – coercive and/or consensual – which may have been operating to maintain that ... [society]."

It is the belief that violence worsens social relations that unites the several manifestations of violence – from child abuse to revolution – under a single conceptual heading. And yet as a subject matter it remains unwieldy. Some principle is needed to determine which incidents are most important to our analysis. It is here that the concept of "public violence" may be useful.

PUBLIC AND PRIVATE VIOLENCE

Public violence comprises those incidents that are widely regarded as having a significant impact on society or an important part of it. Private violence covers the incidents to which no such significance is attached. Naturally what may be "significant" or "important" to one person may not be so to another. Assessments of violence nevertheless do tend to fall into patterns. The incidents which are agreed generally to be significant usually display certain attributes. One such attribute is that the violent are acting on behalf of a group to remedy injustice. Violence that is not considered to be socially or politically significant – private violence – is typically the work of individuals acting on their own behalf. Besides motivation, other characteristics distinguishing public and private violence relate to the participants, the victims, the cause, and the impact of the violence. They are listed in figure 1.

"Civil conflict," "collective violence," and "political violence" are similar to "public violence" and tend, by and large, to denote the same events. Unlike the former concepts, however, "public violence" is not defined by objective criteria. Rather, the concept stresses that the incidents of violence that academics feel called upon to study are those that their society has determined to be important. Such an approach raises a number of interesting issues. Why do some incidents attract greater attention than others? What has happened when an incident that is significant by some objective criterion, such as the numbers involved, is dismissed as insignificant by public opinion, or vice versa? How and by whom is the decision made that an incident is public or private? What are the consequences for the participants? What role do the actors' social or political standings play in the process? Do some countries accord public status to violent incidents less readily than others, thereby giving the impression of having less violence simply because less is recognized? Do we anticipate that some groups' violence will be private rather than public?

Another distinction between the framework proposed here and analogous concepts such as political violence is that there is no hard and fast line dividing public from private violence. Rather it is better to think in terms of a

FIGURE 1
Public and Private Violence

Private Characteristics	Public Characteristics
Violent act on their own behalf.	Violent act on behalf of a group.
Violent motivated by personal animus, greed, hell-raising; have no motive; have no intention of changing society.	Violent motivated by a desire to rectify perceived injustices; act deliberately to change or maintain some social arrangement.
Violent are labelled criminals or insane.	Violent see themselves and are seen by others to be rebels with a cause.
Causes of the violence lie in the individual, not society.	Causes of the violence lie in social arrangements.
Violence not regarded as a threat to public order or requiring any more than routine police work.	Violence regarded as a threat to public order.
Victims are isolated individuals.	Victims are members of a recognized group.
Violence widely regarded as routine, unavoidable, and trivial.	Violence widely regarded as extra-ordinary, avoidable, and significant.
Violence affects only the parties involved.	Violence affects the interests of non-participants.
Violence passes unrecorded outside of crime statistics.	Violence is widely reported in the mass media, commented on by prominent individuals, and recorded in history texts.

continuum along which incidents may be placed according to how closely they approach the ideal types of public or private violence. Thinking in terms of a continuum permits the examination of the usually unprecedented and not easily defined incidents that share public and private characteristics. It also helps in recognizing that different groups may locate the same event at different places on the continuum.

A further advantage of the continuum is that all varieties of violence can be embraced by it. While I shall concentrate on public violence, private incidents are not automatically excluded from consideration. This is important given the earlier argument concerning the philosophical and moral unity behind all acts of violence. It also raises some inherently interesting questions: What is the ratio of public to private violence? Is it constant over time and space? Does the incidence of private violence vary directly or inversely with the incidence of public violence? If there is a relationship between the two, how can it be plausibly explained?

As we shall see in chapter 4, people in their everyday speech have as many problems defining violence as academics do. What they call violence may not be considered as such when judged by the basic definition of violence: behaviour resulting in injury to people and damage to property. Alternatively what they consider to be non-violence may in fact be violence. Thus, we must first determine whether an incident is in truth an act of violence before considering its public or private status.

For many purposes it is unnecessary to distinguish between public violence and concepts such as civil conflict. They may be used interchangeably. I merely suggest that the notion of public violence has some advantages. First, it helps us sidestep the difficulties experienced by those who have used objective criteria to single out important events. And second, it raises lines of inquiry that have been scarcely explored. Let us turn now to consider those violent incidents in Canada that have been considered to be public.

CHAPTER TWO

An Overview of Canadian Public Violence[1]

THE FRONTIER

By the time of Confederation, the agricultural frontier lay in the West. The earlier, eastern pioneers had experienced their share of violence – the 1837 rebellions, the Shiners of the Ottawa Valley, and other assorted commotions. The West, however, was opened up more or less peacefully under the guidance of the North-West Mounted Police.[2] This peacefulness is remarkable given the inevitable conflict with the aboriginal inhabitants, the disruption and weakening of such established institutions as family, schools, and churches, and the need on the part of a heterogeneous and mobile population to develop fresh modes of thought and practice in the new surroundings (Clark, 1962: 3-19). The exceptions to the general pattern of orderly development were the two Riel risings.

1 This chapter is primarily about the public violence that has taken place within Canada since Confederation. Private violence, pre-Confederation incidents, and international warfare differ in many ways from the conflicts under study, but the restriction on the subject matter is an artificial one dictated by my own interests and knowledge. While the analysis in later chapters covers the period from 1867 to 1982, some more recent incidents are mentioned in this chapter.

Another proviso concerns the completeness of the following account. Given the limited historical work of direct relevance, anyone claiming to have produced an exhaustive catalogue would be a fool. We are still waiting for the patient combing of primary sources that would make such a claim justifiable. In the meantime, a wide reading of secondary sources must be relied upon.

The account that follows is based on the work of many people, but I should acknowledge my heavy reliance on the work of G. Stanley (1961) and S. Jamieson (1968) in particular. The text includes references to many of the specialized studies that have been made of the various incidents. Where no reference is given, further information can be obtained from the appropriate editions of the *Canadian Annual Review* and *Canadian News Facts*.

2 Referred to herein as the NWMP and popularly known as the Mounties. In 1904 the force became the Royal North-West Mounted Police (RNWMP), and in 1920 its name was changed again, to the Royal Canadian Mounted Police (RCMP), reflecting its new responsibilities across the country.

The first Riel rising occurred in 1869-70 when the Hudson's Bay Company (HBC) passed jurisdiction over the western territories to the Dominion of Canada. At the time this vast area was sparsely populated by whites, French-speaking half-breeds (the Métis), English-speaking half-breeds, and Indians. Some small settlements had developed, such as the one at Red River, with a population of 11,000, about half of whom were Métis, and which was the centre of the Riel rising. Here farms had been established, many of them on narrow strips of land stretching back from the rivers in accordance with the French-Canadian pattern. The economy, however, was largely based on the fur trade. The annual buffalo hunt was by necessity a community enterprise, and the Métis had developed a sophisticated organization to undertake it. The Métis also had a tradition of political activism; they had earlier united under Riel's father in armed protest against the HBC monopoly.

The immediate origins of the rising lay largely in the inhabitants' fears for their future status. They had not been consulted or offered reassurances, and foresaw their distinctive culture being crowded out if there was to be large-scale immigration from the east. What they knew of Canada and the Canadian government was scarcely reassuring: government surveyors, already at work, seemed to threaten their land titles; a governor and council, largely appointed from the outside, was to be thrust upon them; and a small Ontario group, known as the "Canadian party," had rendered themselves obnoxious to the community through their noisy agitation against HBC rule.

Organized resistance to the new order evolved from secret meetings and small gatherings to large assemblies. By October 1869 a Comité National des Métis had been formed, steps were taken to block the entry of the prospective governor, William McDougall, and a muster of men was begun. Louis Riel rapidly assumed the leadership of the resistance. Then 25, he was educated, eloquent in French and English, and a gifted politician and administrator. After rebuffing McDougall, he seized Fort Garry and set about extending support for the movement. On 1 December, McDougall decided to force his way in, but Riel's men successfully resisted the attempt and took a number of prisoners. A week later Riel announced the formation of a provisional government, declaring it "the only and lawful authority now in existence."

The government in Ottawa, under Sir John A. Macdonald, sought to mollify opinion at Red River by sending out spokesmen to explain Canadian intentions. The Canadian case was presented at mass meetings in January. The residents drew up terms for their entry into Canada, and delegates were selected to bring these to Ottawa. At this point the irrepressible Canadian party again entered the scene. They organized a raiding party, and two men were killed when it came in contact with Riel's forces at Kildonan. Riel had Thomas Scott, a member of the raiding party, executed to discourage further unrest. The execution raised a furore in Ontario. However, the negotiations between the western delegates and Ottawa went smoothly. With the exception of an amnesty for all involved in the resistance, an issue not finally settled until 1877, the delegates' terms were by and large accepted. They were embodied in the Manitoba Act which provided for provincial status, separate schools, linguistic guarantees, and tax exemptions. At the same time a military expedition under Colonel Wolseley left for Red River and after a laborious trek of three months reached Fort Garry on 24 August. Riel quietly slipped across the American border for a while. The incident was over, although by some accounts undisciplined brawling by Ontario militia resulted in the death of a Métis.[3]

The Red River rising is an example of essentially non-violent resistance directed against government policy. It was non-violent primarily because the physical remoteness of the settlement rendered an immediate governmental resort to coercion impossible. It is none the less a tribute to the federal government's restraint that it resisted strong Ontario pressure to avenge Scott's death and managed not to provoke the inhabitants into prolonging their revolt or resisting the advance of the Wolseley expedition. Riel also deserves credit for the discipline he imposed on the armed Métis and for his efforts to secure co-operation and maintain harmony among the diverse elements of the settlement. Such violence as did occur was the result of breakdowns in discipline and unity within each side: on the Red River side, the challenge of the Canadian party and Riel's subsequent exemplary execution of Scott; on the federal government side, McDougall's unauthorized attempt to seize power and possibly some members of the Ontario militia taking the law into their own hands. There was no official violence between the two sides. The resistance is also noteworthy for its success in changing government policy. Again the political astuteness – the awareness of what was possible and what was necessary – of both the federal government and Riel deserves tribute.

The Northwest Rebellion of 1885, the second Riel rising, illustrates the great potential for tragedy when such astuteness and restraint are lacking. The 15 years between the two incidents saw the opening up of the Canadian West. A territorial government was in place, and the NWMP, established after the first Riel rising, policed the area. The Indian population signed treaties and for the most part retired to reservations. White settlers entered the newly surveyed lands; between 1881 and 1891, the non-Indian population grew sevenfold to some 50,000. Schools, churches, banks, and newspapers were established. The Canadian Pacific Railway (CPR) line was nearing completion.

Discontent, however, was rife. White settlers were in economic straits as a result of a general economic decline, the collapse of the land boom, and poor

3 W.L. Morton (1967: 145) blames the death of Elzéar Goulet on the Ontario volunteers. However one of their number, Sam Steele, vigorously denied the militia were involved (1972: 34-5).

harvests. They had as well a number of particular grievances, including tariffs, land use policy, control of natural resources, and the territorial form of government. The Indian population, whose economy had been undermined by the disappearance of the buffalo, was also affected by the depression as the federal government cut back on its subsidies. The half-breeds, many of whom had emigrated from Manitoba to set up their own communities, were again troubled by the land question – the amount to which they were entitled, the difficulty in securing legal title, and the survey system.

By 1884, the different elements of the population were beginning to co-ordinate their agitation. In May, whites and half-breeds jointly invited Riel to give his assistance to their cause. Riel was then in Montana, where he was working as a schoolteacher after a period of drifting that had included spells in Quebec mental asylums. He heeded the call and set about organizing the burgeoning protest. Co-operation among the groups reached a highpoint the following December with the forwarding of yet another petition to Ottawa. Thereafter the coalition gradually crumbled, and Riel moved to more extreme forms of action, seeking to recapture his success of 1870. On 19 March a provisional government was proclaimed in the Métis settlement of Batoche. The call went out for their Indian brothers to take up arms.

Open hostilities with the government followed shortly after. On 26 March a predominantly Métis force clashed with a NWMP column near Duck Lake in an attempt to secure police hostages. The police managed to retreat at the cost of 10 dead on the field and two others mortally wounded. On the 30th, Indians under Poundmaker pillaged the HBC and other buildings at Battleford, where they were joined by the Stonies who had already killed their farm instructor and a white settler. At Frog Lake on 2 April, Big Bear tried unsuccessfully to stop his men from shooting nine whites and taking three prisoners. They then went on to Fort Pitt, where a police scout was killed, more prisoners taken, the police forced to retreat, and the fort pillaged and set on fire. A series of minor outbreaks and the pillaging of other HBC posts followed.

Towards the end of April the North Saskatchewan valley was in the hands of the insurgents. Around a thousand men were in arms, about half of them Métis. They had few modern weapons, and there was little orchestration behind the revolt. Nevertheless, the situation was extremely serious. There were numerous other Métis settlements not yet involved, and the Indian population of the the prairies numbered some 20,000. In an effort to localize the rebellion, the federal government, once again under Macdonald's leadership, rushed gifts and missionaries to the wavering Indian bands. The settlement of the Métis land claims was also speeded up. However, the main thrust of the federal response was the military suppression of the rebellion. Nearly 8,000 men were mobilized under General Middleton. The force was divided and moved northwards from three points along the CPR line. After a month of campaigning the soldiers captured Batoche. Riel gave himself up on 15 May,

Poundmaker a week later, and Big Bear finally in early July. A number of participants escaped across the American border. Those in government hands – Indians, half-breeds, and whites – were brought to trial. The two whites were found not guilty. Eleven Indians were condemned to hang for murder, of whom three were later reprieved; Big Bear and Poundmaker were also briefly imprisoned. Eighteen Métis were sentenced to prison on treason charges. Riel, after refusing his counsel's advice to plead not guilty by reason of insanity, was convicted of high treason and, after various appeals, executed at Regina on 16 November.

The second Riel rising, unlike the first, involved fighting between government forces and rebels, and as such can be classified as a rebellion. With some 200 dead, it was by far the bloodiest incident in Canadian history: 38 government soldiers and around 140 rebels lost their lives in battle; the remainder of the deaths resulted from attacks on civilians and judicial executions.[4] A good deal of property was destroyed; the HBC, for example, entered a claim of over $52,000 for losses sustained at Fort Carlton alone. The cost of the military expedition was put at $5,000,000.

Why should the second Riel rising have been so much more violent than the first? Part of the explanation lies in the failure of Riel's political grasp. By 1885 he was convinced of his prophetic mission and tended to rely on charisma and divine intervention to win the day (Flanagan, 1979: 182-6). His objectives were unclear or beyond the capacity of the government to grant. Having failed to secure hostages in the Duck Lake clash, his tactics proved confused, and the lack of organization behind the revolt was soon revealed. He alienated significant segments of western opinion, thus enabling the government to move against the isolated groups of Métis and Indians who took up arms rather than forcing it to deal with a united community. He failed to control his Indian allies and misjudged the fear and revulsion that his incitement of the Indians would arouse. By openly attacking government forces at Duck Lake, he provided the government with the justification for mounting a military expedition against him. He also failed to take into account the changed circumstances since 1869, particularly the virtual completion of the CPR line, which enabled the government to turn swiftly to a military solution rather than a negotiated settlement.

Most commentators feel that the chief cost of the 1885 rebellion was not its violence but the exacerbation of French-English conflict that resulted from the decision to hang Riel. Here again the contrast with the first rising is marked. In 1885, with some justification, Macdonald's government was on the

---

4 Few commentators agree on the number of deaths occasioned by the Northwest Rebellion, mainly because the number of Métis casualties is uncertain. My figures are based on Morgan (1886: 156). Flanagan, in a recent book on the rebellion (1983: 1), gives lower figures: "It is safe to say that about a hundred men lost their lives in all engagements together."

defensive about its western policy, and consequently chose to interpret the incident as the product not of discontent but of the machinations of a rational and devious individual. Riel was the government's scapegoat. The government was able to focus attention on Riel because it had him in its hands and because it had been able to end the rebellion militarily rather than by dealing with western grievances in a negotiated settlement. However, Macdonald misjudged the depth and persistence of opinion in Quebec that turned Riel into a political martyr. The real tragedy of 1885 was that the original grievances of the westerners were lost sight of in the battle-lines that formed in Central Canada over the question of Riel's fate.

WARTIME

In addition to the violence of the battlefield, wartime in Canada has been the occasion for various incidents on the home front. These have grown out of protests against involvement in the war and the imposition of conscription. An early manifestation of French-Canadian resistance to Canada's involvement in what some regarded as imperial entanglements occurred in 1900 when a Montreal crowd rioted in protest against the sending of recruits to the Boer War.

During the First World War there were recurrent incidents of low-level violence. In July 1915 a Montreal recruiting meeting was broken up with cries of "we don't want conscription," and recruiting posters at the offices of the pro-government newspapers *La Presse* and *La Patrie* were torn down by rioters singing "O Canada." Other recruiting meetings also ended in disturbances. In April and May of 1917 troops passing through the province were pelted with rotten vegetables, ice, and stones, and pro-government papers were again attacked. After conscription was introduced in August, the violence intensified. On the night of 29 August, a meeting of some 7,000 in Montreal ended with one man shot and four policemen seriously injured. At the same time a plot was uncovered to dynamite the house of the owner of the pro-conscriptionist *Star* and subsequently to assassinate Prime Minister Borden and other government leaders. In the ensuing election, speakers for the Unionist government were howled down and subjected to rotten eggs and other missiles.

The culminating round of violence came in Quebec City on the Easter weekend of 1918. For five days large crowds assembled. Newspaper offices were attacked, and the building that housed conscription records was burned. Some 700 troops were sent in to restore order, and more followed. The soldiers opened fire on two occasions. The first, on Sunday afternoon, was a minor affray that left three injured, but on Monday night there was a serious incident. According to the official version, the troops were responding to sniper fire. Four civilians were killed and around 70 were injured seriously enough to seek out a doctor. Sixty-two arrests were made by the soldiers.

During the Second World War, conscription evoked a far less violent response, but there were some incidents none the less. Disorder followed various meetings in the campaign to get out the Quebec No vote in the 1942 conscription referendum (A. Laurendeau, 1973: 66-72), and there was a 1945 draft riot in Drummondville in which an angry crowd of some 1,000 participated (Beck, 1968: 245).

Among anti-war violence, we can also include the violent demonstrations that took place in Canada against American involvement in Vietnam. Jackson, Kelly, and Mitchell (n.d.: 296-7) list eight such incidents for Ontario between 1965 and 1975. Another incident was the 1982 bombing of the Litton Systems plant, just outside of Toronto, which manufactures the guidance system for the Cruise missile. Ten people were injured, and damage was estimated at $3.8 million.

A second type of violence during wartime involves attacks by civilians and returned veterans against "shirkers" and "enemy aliens." During the First World War, there were some ugly incidents of this nature: in a tense atmosphere partly induced by hysterical anti-German propaganda, those passionately committed to the righteousness of Canada's participation struck out at various targets. There was an anti-German riot in Victoria. Veterans attacked foreigners in Toronto and Winnipeg. In Vancouver in 1917 a brief general strike was held to protest the shooting death of a prominent union leader resisting the draft,[5] whereupon several hundred veterans attacked union men and property.

The third major type of violence occurring during wartime involves members of the armed forces. Most of this violence consisted of brawling, which has taken place in times of peace as well as war. Such violence is usually considered more private than public in nature, although the drunken V-E day riot in Halifax was sufficiently disruptive of public order to be placed squarely in the public category. There have also been occasional breakdowns in discipline. I have already mentioned the incident attributed to the Ontario militia at Red River. The most serious case, however, occurred outside Canada, in the Canadian demobilization camps in the U.K. at the end of the First World War. Protest against restrictions in the camps and the slowness of repatriation produced disturbances in several camps that left seven men dead (D. Morton, 1980). As well, in the Second World War, conscripted troops at Terrace, B.C., mutinied at the prospect of being sent overseas and set up anti-tank guns to prevent any movement in or out of the town. The government skilfully defused the situation by granting the men leave (Pickersgill and Forster, 1968: 251-6).

5 This was not the only death of its kind. The uncle of one of the early FLQ activists was killed in resisting conscription during the Second World War (Morf: 1970: 62). However, we have no figures on how many men lost their lives in this fashion.

During wartime, governments commonly assume larger powers, not the least of which is censorship of communications. Reports of internal opposition to the war effort tend to be suppressed lest they persuade others in the country to follow the example or encourage the enemy. The Terrace mutiny, for example, was kept out of the press. For this reason, we have little record of wartime violence. Another reason is that violent resistance, brawling soldiers, and attacks on minorities do not square with the myths of wartime: the myths of our soldier heroes; of democracy in mortal combat with barbarism; of a united people at home matching the sacrifices of the men on the battlefield. The incidents we have been considering in this section call the national mythology into question. Consequently they have been consigned to oblivion for the most part. We still await a history of the resistance to Canada's war efforts.

ELECTIONS

Elections have provided a remarkably persistent, if little-recognized, forum for Canadian public violence. The first post-Confederation elections carried on the violent traditions established in earlier years. We hear of a family feud in Kamouraska, Quebec, which led to rioting that made polling impossible (Beck, 1968: 7); of Alexander Mackenzie being chased from a rowdy meeting by a "howling mob" (Waite, 1962: 12); and of the militia being called out in Montreal in 1872 to keep order during Cartier's election campaign (D. Morton, 1970: 409). Typical of this early violence was D'Arcy McGee's experience:

When McGee tried to hold a series of three meetings early in August [1867] in each of the Montreal wards, he managed to speak in the face of considerable opposition at the first meeting, but was assaulted by an egg-throwing crowd at the second, and managed to speak only with the aid of police protection at the third ... Two weeks later ... he was pelted with stones, and soon found it was virtually impossible to hold a public meeting in Montreal ... McGee complained that his friends were receiving threats that their homes and places of business would be burned if they gave him their votes ... When McGee's victory was announced, [his opponent's] supporters attacked McGee's committee rooms ... apparently under the impression he was inside. (Senior, 1978: 123-5)

The institution of the secret ballot in the 1870s removed the possibility of directly affecting the vote through intimidation, but the practice of intimidating candidates, seeking to keep known supporters away from the polls, and disrupting meetings has been carried on. Besides the use of violence as a deliberate means of influencing the outcome of the election, another element has been the violence erupting between rival groups, stimulated by the heightened passions of the campaign (and, often enough, further inflamed by alcohol).

The extent of election violence has declined during the twentieth century, although apparently somewhat more slowly in the province of Quebec than in other regions. Nevertheless it remains a noticeable component of Canadian public violence. Frank and Kelly (1977: 148), for example, note the concentration (five times the average rate) of incidents of collective violence in Ontario and Quebec between 1963 and 1973 during federal and provincial campaigns.

The reasons for this persistent tradition are not hard to determine. Apart from the general atmosphere of conflict and abnormal excitement during campaigns (see figure 4), the outcome of elections has often been of material importance because of patronage considerations. Elections also draw public attention towards contentious issues. Perhaps most importantly, party political divisions have coincided with other lines of social and economic conflict. For example, a fight in 1935 between Conservative and Liberal supporters in rural Ontario turns out to have been more of an old-style Orange-Green riot than anything else (Bull, 1936: 270). Similarly, in Sorel, Quebec, the bitterness and issues from the preceding year's industrial conflict were carried over into the civic election of 1938, during which there were numerous battles and one man fatally shot (Jamieson, 1968: 503). This is the only known instance of a death in post-Confederation election violence; injuries, if numerous, were rarely serious. Elections, in short, have often served as an outlet for intergroup hostility which has turned to violence as campaigning mobilizes and polarizes opinion.

ON THE JOB

That the workplace should be a locus of violence is not surprising given the material and psychological needs that can be satisfied or threatened there. The workplace also serves to bring people together physically and to provide them with joint interests. As well, the Canadian industrial system is structured in such a way as to promote conflict. There are the struggles among employees for jobs, among employers for profits, and, most importantly, between employers and employees. All these conflicts tend to be seen in terms by which an advantage gained by one side is considered to be at the expense of the other. Further exacerbating the situation are the conflicting norms existing within the workplace. Concepts such as the rights of property and the sanctity of contracts, on the one hand, and of unfair practices and a just wage, on the other, may not only collide but harden the confrontation. Then the conflict changes from one of material advantage to an issue of principle, thereby attracting outside interest and interference.

The most common form of job-related violence occurs during strikes. One study reports "approximately" 300 violent strikes between 1900 and 1974 (Jamieson, 1979: 142). Another gives a figure of 227 for the years 1910-66

(Latouche, 1971: 181). Frank and Kelly (1977: 152) find 87 incidents between 1963 and 1973 in Ontario and Quebec. Strike violence, then, is far from exceptional. However, it must be remembered that the great majority of strikes are settled without resort to violence. During the turbulent decade, 1957-66, for instance, there were 84 violent strikes (Jamieson, 1968: 403), but this figure still represents less than 3 per cent of all the strikes that took place.

The classic place for strike violence is the picketline around company property: police and company guards strive to permit free entry into a plant while strikers try to prevent the entry of strike-breakers and non-striking workers. Occasionally, in isolated communities (for instance, in the Cape Breton coalfields in 1923 and at Asbestos, Quebec, in 1949) the picketline is extended around the town itself as strikers search incoming vehicles for strike-breakers. Picketline scuffles rarely result in serious violence, although some exceptions can be noted: in the 1925 strike against Besco in Nova Scotia, a clash between company guards and picketers resulted in the death of a picketer; in 1959, during the lumberworkers' strike in Newfoundland, a police officer was killed by a picketer; and in 1977 in Montreal, security guards at a flour mill shot and wounded eight picketers who had stormed company property.

Damage to company property is another feature of violent strikes. For example, in the above-mentioned 1925 Nova Scotia strike, "it was estimated that $300,000 worth of goods were looted from company stores. Buildings worth $200,000 were destroyed and two mines were damaged by flooding" (Bjarnason, cited in Jamieson, 1968: 202). The 1958 strike at the Murdoch-ville coppermines in Quebec saw dynamite explosions on company property, in one of which a striker was fatally injured. A teamsters' strike in 1959 resulted in an explosion and fire at a struck plant at Milton, Ontario.

Rather more rarely, violence during strikes has taken the form of attacks against prominent individuals from both labour and management. In Vancouver, 1903, an organizer for the United Brotherhood of Railway Employees was murdered while picketing. In 1938 at Blubber Bay, B.C., an International Woodworkers of America organizer was allegedly so badly beaten by police that he had to be hospitalized; imprisoned while still weak from his wounds, he died a short time later. On the other side, an American manager was kidnapped and taken across the border during the Quebec textile workers' strike of 1937. And there have also been repeated examples in that province of the homes of executives being attacked with everything from stones to bombs.

In terms of loss of life, however, the most serious strike violence has occurred either when strike-breakers have been attacked or when police have moved in to break up an illegal demonstration or parade. There are two noteworthy cases of violence involving strike-breakers. In 1906 sawmill workers in Buckingham, Quebec, attacked strike-breakers attempting to bring logs downriver under the protection of police and company guards. In the ensuing riot, two strikers and a detective were killed and others on both sides were seriously injured. The other case involved pulpwood cutters in Kapuskasing, Ontario, in 1963. When their property was attacked, non-striking workers opened fire and killed three strikers. Among examples of illegal demonstrations, there is a notorious case that occurred in Estevan, Saskatchewan, in 1931. Striking coalminers clashed with police, leaving three dead, 23 injured, and $60,000 worth of property damage (Hanson, 1974: 51). Also, there was the 21 June 1919 incident during the Winnipeg General Strike when RNWMP charged through a crowd and opened fire. Two men died and 30 were injured.

It is evident that the province of Quebec has had a notable history of strike violence. The tradition reached a peak in the late sixties and early seventies when the province's unions entered a particularly militant and radical phase. There were a number of serious incidents. An armed takeover of the Domtar mill at Windsor in November 1968 left damages of $100,000. In October 1971 a demonstration by 10,000 people at the strike-bound *La Presse* in Montreal resulted in one person dying of a heart attack, 160 injured, and some 60 arrested. The following May, unionized workers took over the town of Sept-Iles for two days in protest against the imprisonment of their leaders. A 75-man emergency unit of the Quebec Police Force was flown up from Montreal and used tear gas to regain control. Prior to this there had been property damage, 34 injuries, and a death when a man was hit by a car that ran into a crowd of demonstrators.

The role of militia and police forces in strikes deserves special mention. The militia or regular soldiers intervened in a total of 33 strikes, most of them before the First World War in areas where police forces had not been established (D. Morton, 1970: 407). Given that the soldiers and police often came from different class backgrounds than the striking workers,[6] and that before the Second World War they were required to maintain laws clearly favouring employers, it is no wonder that they should have been unpopular in union circles. They were regarded as being used as indirect agents of the employers to intimidate the workers and mislead public opinion. Such sentiments have occasionally caused police and soldiers to abandon any semblance of impartiality and brought them into violent conflict against the strikers. For example, when 300 of the "best" citizens of Sarnia, Ontario, bloodily evicted sitdown strikers from a plant in 1937, the local police did nothing to protect the strikers. Indeed, after their eviction, the police arrested them for trespassing and took no action against their assailants (Abella, 1974:

6 For the social classes from which the militia drew its recruits, see D. Morton (1970: 415-16, 424); for the NWMP, see Macleod (1976: 86).

98-9). Blubber Bay in British Columbia in 1938 was said to be "under a police dictatorship" employing "terrorist tactics" (cited in Jamieson, 1968: 505). During the 1949 Asbestos strike in Quebec, many of those arrested by provincial police were badly beaten, and several were threatened with further arrest unless they returned to work (Jamieson, 1968: 331). Special police forces, whether those maintained by large corporations or constables sworn in for the occasion, were particularly mistrusted by striking workers. The arrival of CPR police during a strike by freighthandlers at the Lakehead, Ontario, in 1909 was blamed for an ensuing riot by most commentators, from the local chief of police to the federal deputy minister of labour (Morrison, 1976: 155). The appearance of special constables on the streets during the Winnipeg General Strike resulted in a disturbance in which one of their number was badly beaten.

Yet the record of police and military interventions in strikes is far from being entirely one-sided. The reason for the enrolment of the Winnipeg "specials" was that the local force was ready and willing to strike alongside the other workers and had only remained on duty at the behest of the Strike Committee. Provincial police officers and Mounties may have provoked violence in some cases, but in many others they have acted with bravery, impartiality, and common sense to head off or curtail violence on the part of the strikers. In most cases when the militia was called out there was no real violence. And while there were examples of the militia acting partially and provocatively, there were also cases of strict neutrality, the maintenance of a low profile, and good-humoured relations between soldiers and strikers (D. Morton, 1970: 424-5; Frank, 1976: 177-8). The most violent occasion on which troops have been called out found them largely uninvolved in the violence. This was the night of 7 October 1969 after the Montreal police force had come out on strike. Demonstrations, vandalism, and looting resulted in the death of one Quebec Police Force officer, dozens of civilian injuries, and property damage estimated in the millions.[7]

Job-related violence is also found in unionization campaigns. Many of the violent strikes we have been considering were fought over the issue of union recognition. But in addition to strike situations, there have been cases of violence, and more often threatened violence, directed against union organizers. For example, in the Saskatchewan coalfields in 1920, a One Big Union organizer was kidnapped, driven across the U.S. border, and promised "a real reception which would start with tar and feathers" if he ever returned (Hanson, 1974: 41). Unionization campaigns have also involved violence between rival unions. The best known case is the campaign against competing

7 Exhibitions of hooliganism have also accompanied the police strikes that have occurred in the Maritimes. Even though they have been minor in comparison with the Montreal incident, they nevertheless form a depressing commentary on human nature.

unions waged by members of the Seafarers' International Union under Hal Banks during the late fifties and early sixties. The Norris Commission listed 75 examples of violence and intimidation. Another example is the 1974 riot that followed the refusal of a contractor at the James Bay construction site to fire workers belonging to a rival union. The cost occasioned by the resulting delays and in making good the damage was placed at $35 million.

Job-related violence also involves the unemployed. Canada has experienced recurrent, acute bouts of unemployment, and until recent years government programs have been rudimentary and inadequate to meet the basic needs of the unemployed. These programs were typically structured so as to bring the unemployed together at one spot, thus enabling the men to confirm and give active expression to their grievances. During the thirties, married men in Vancouver had to line up for their food and tokens at a central location; only after a series of riots on the grounds did the authorities start dispensing relief to the married unemployed at their homes. The single unemployed were dealt with in special camps set up across the country, and these too were the sites of repeated disturbances.

Radical political parties and unions sometimes have taken an interest in organizing the unemployed. In Vancouver before the First World War, there were protest meetings and demonstrations organized by the Industrial Workers of the World and the Socialist Party, at least one of which ended in violence (Jamieson, 1968: 146). During the thirties, the Communist Party through its affiliate the Workers' Unity League was active among the unemployed. There were a number of disturbances in Vancouver, including riots when police evicted relief camp strikers from a store in April 1935 and from the post office in May 1938 (39 injured, 22 arrests, and property damage of $30,000). The best known incident occurred in 1935 during the On to Ottawa trek when the men decided to ride freight cars eastwards from Vancouver in order to present their grievances directly to the federal government. The government ordered the trek halted at Regina and on 1 July had the leaders of the movement arrested. In the three-hour riot that followed, a city policeman was killed, over 200 were injured, some 130 arrested, and $20,000 worth of property damaged.

The period of high unemployment beginning around 1980 has also seen a few incidents though to date they have been different in character from those of the Great Depression. Typical recent incidents have occurred in the small towns of Quebec and have involved the community as a whole fighting to keep open local industries or to secure new ones. At Grande Vallée in October 1983, protests were directed against the provincial government after it declined to give assurances that the local sawmill would reopen. Members of the town council resigned as a gesture of support. During the protests, provincial property was damaged, the administrative offices of the mill were destroyed by fire, and its manager attacked (*The Globe and Mail*, 12 October

1983). The desire to protect local livelihoods also lay behind the March 1984 destruction of a helicopter belonging to the International Fund for Animal Welfare by the seal hunters of the Magdalen Islands (*The Globe and Mail*, 12 and 13 March 1984).

Canada's most famous case of job-related conflict is the Winnipeg General Strike of 1919. The preceding year in Winnipeg had seen individual unions defeated by intransigent employers, but also a notable success against the municipal government when workers in other unions came out in sympathy with the civic workers. The general strike was an attempt to repeat this success, this time on behalf of workers in the building and metal trades who had become deadlocked with employers over the issues of higher wages and union recognition. On 15 May almost the entire city work-force walked off the job. The strike lasted six weeks, but ended in failure. The general strike itself was non-violent, in no small measure because the Strike Committee sought to prevent open clashes that would serve as a pretext for violent repression. Yet it deserves mention in a history of Canadian public violence for two reasons. First, it was the backdrop for a few isolated incidents that have already been mentioned. Second, it shows how those fearful for their economic and political position perceived violence to exist where in fact it did not (see chapter 4). In middle-class Winnipeg and in government circles, there were many who saw the strike as the opening round of an attempted re-enactment of the Bolshevik revolution.

ETHNIC AND RELIGIOUS GROUPS

Canada has two "founding nations": the French and the English. To this basic division, immigration from around the world has added over the years many other distinctive elements. The resulting heterogeneity of the population has produced violent conflict between groups, as well as between a government and a particular group resisting assimilation or contesting the existing structures of Canadian society. The two Riel risings on the western frontier could be included in this latter category.

Some of these ethnic incidents involved job-related grievances. Lack of solidarity among groups of workers with different backgrounds produced several violent incidents. Irish and French-Canadian dockworkers in Quebec City clashed during the 1870s partly over the latters' willingness to accept lower wages. In one riot in August 1878, two men were killed and 15 others injured. Japanese fishermen in British Columbia were attacked in the early 1900s when they accepted a contract from the canneries ahead of other groups. Newly arrived immigrant groups, eager to secure employment and unfamiliar with Canadian practices, have been attacked when they accepted jobs as scabs; for example, the 1914 assaults on Italian and Asian strikebreakers during the Vancouver Island coalminers' strike. Sometimes immigrants have been attacked because they were seen as competitors for jobs in a tight market. After the First World War "aliens" were assaulted on the grounds that they were taking jobs away from returned veterans. And on occasion immigrant workers have themselves resorted to violence, partly because of their unfamiliarity with Canadian strike procedures and the violent traditions of their homelands (see Morrison's [1976] analysis of the Lakehead freighthandlers' strike of 1909).

Violence between groups has not been confined to job-related grievances. Xenophobia has prompted attacks on relatively powerless groups, distinctive in their ways or appearance from the general population. Such violence is generally considered more private than public in nature, involving isolated assaults by a handful of thugs against individuals. However there have been a few cases of widespread participation in general attacks on a minority community. Asian immigrants have been particularly victimized. When an outbreak of smallpox in Calgary in 1892 was traced back to a Chinese laundry, a mob forced the Chinese community to take shelter in the NWMP barracks. More serious incidents of anti-Chinese rioting occurred in Vancouver in 1887 and again in September 1907. These incidents were not confined to the West where the Chinese population was concentrated: Halifax had an anti-Chinese riot in 1919.

Some anti-minority violence can be attributed to the efforts of extreme right-wing movements to stir up prejudice. A. Laurendeau (1973: 71-2) suggests the Montreal rioters who smashed the windows of Jewish shopkeepers in March 1942 were from Adrien Arcand's blackshirt organization. In Toronto during the sixties and early seventies, the Edmund Burke Society and the Western Guard became involved in several unsavoury incidents.

Intergroup violence has also stemmed from struggles between more evenly matched groups. Conflicts between ultramontane and liberal Catholics in Quebec resulted in a riot in 1875 when members of the former group prevented the burial in sanctified ground of an excommunicated liberal, one Joseph Guibord. Orange-Green riots were frequent in the nineteenth century. Between 1867 and 1892 there were 22 such clashes in Toronto. These were mostly minor skirmishes resulting from parades marching through rival territory. No lives were lost, and, apart from Orangemen wrecking Cosgrove's Hotel, an Irish-Canadian centre, on four occasions, there was little property damage. The two major incidents were the Pilgrimage or Jubilee riot of 1875 and the Rossa riot three years later. In the first incident between 6,000 and 8,000 people were involved, and the entire city core was out of control for a number of hours, but even so little damage was done (Kealey, 1976: 26-32). In Montreal, however, the 12 July 1877 parade resulted in a riot in which one Orangeman was beaten to death. The following year feelings ran so high that the parade was banned. The militia was called out (as they were on four other occasions of Orange-Green conflict) to enforce the ban, but were not used.

This was fortunate since their impartiality and discipline were open to question: the train returning them to Sherbrooke was decorated with orange colours, and, when a crowd of bystanders threw stones at it, a few shots were fired from the train, one of which wounded an elderly onlooker (D. Morton, 1970: 413-14).

Orange-Green rioting is one example of immigrants carrying on the disputes and customs of the homeland in their new environment. Cultural background also contributed to the reign of terror carried out by the Donnelly family against their fellow Irish immigrants in the Lucan area, north of London, Ontario, during the 1860s and 1870s. The Donnellys employed traditional forms of violence – fist fighting, animal mutilations, arson, and wrecking – to intimidate their economic competitors and those who would take them to court. They eventually met their end at the hands of a drunken mob of vigilantes. Another example, also involving the Irish, is the activity of the Fenians which led to Canada's major case of assassination: the shooting down of D'Arcy McGee in an Ottawa street in 1868. More recent examples of immigrant groups violently continuing the disputes of the homeland include Americans organizing and participating in various anti-Vietnam war protests, Eastern Europeans reacting to the visit by Premier Kosygin, bombs placed at various embassies, three Armenian assaults (two of them fatal) on Turkish diplomats, and, within the Toronto Sikh community, disturbances in one of which two men were killed.

Groups have also turned their anger against the government when faced with what they considered to be discriminatory policy. An early and relatively minor case was the Caraquet affray in New Brunswick, 1875, when the militia arrived with two nine-pounder cannons to subdue Acadians rioting against the province's Common Schools Act which was intended to put an end to separate schools. In Vancouver harbour in 1914, Sikhs on the SS *Komagata Maru* violently repelled an attempt to serve deportation orders on them.

Various groups of native Indians have occasionally protested government policy. Usually Canadian governments have avoided being drawn into a violent confrontation, and the protests have been mostly peaceful; for example, the closing of roads through reservations in British Columbia and the occupation of a park near Kenora, Ontario. However, a 1974 demonstration on Parliament Hill resulted in injuries when police repulsed an attempt to enter the Centre Block, and in 1983 Indians in Quebec clashed with provincial game officers over fishing rights. Given the grievances of Indians, they have been involved in surprisingly little violent protest. In contrast are the two most prolonged campaigns of violence in Canadian history: that of the Doukhobors and that of the Front de libération du Québec (FLQ).

The Doukhobors immigrated to Canada from Russia at the turn of the century, settling first in the prairies, with a majority moving on to the interior valleys of British Columbia in 1908. This religious sect enjoins pacifism, a communal way of life, and individual obedience to one's own conscience rather than to the dictates of some external authority, such as a church hierarchy or the state. These views have brought them into conflict with Canadian authorities. At various times they have disputed governmental demands that they keep their children in schools, register their lands in the names of individuals, report vital statistics, pay their taxes, take out naturalization papers, swear an oath of allegiance, or register under the National Resources Mobilization Act of the Second World War. In addition, much conflict among the Doukhobors has caused them to split into groups of varying willingness to accept the sterner tenets of the sect. The most militant and intransigent became known as the Sons of Freedom. Animated by a millennial enthusiasm, they emerged shortly after the sect arrived in Canada. At first they engaged in "amiably bizarre happenings" (Woodcock and Avakumovic, 1977: 223): setting off on pilgrimages to destinations unknown even to themselves, freeing their farm beasts, handing over their money to any bewildered official they could find. There were also signs of times to come. On occasion the early Sons of Freedom discarded their clothes in order to live as Adam and Eve had done. They also lit fires in which they burned their own possessions and also the property of less high-minded Doukhobors in order to encourage the latter to follow their own course of renouncing the material temptations of this world.

The burning of nine schools between 1923 and 1925 marked the shift among the Sons of Freedom to a more aggressively militant campaign. Thereafter outbreaks of violence succeeded each other every few years. Two types of targets remained: the property of governments and other politically or economically powerful agencies, and the property of other Doukhobors. The Sons of Freedom were protesting against a hostile government and against any tendency among their wavering co-religionists to allow themselves to be assimilated by the wider materialist society. "Mass nude demonstrations expressed the solidarity of protest. The ritual burning of one's own house or that of another Doukhobor, accompanied by stripping and singing, still expressed renunciation of material things." At the same time a small minority turned to secret acts of destruction against targets within and without the community. Known as "black work," "there seems little doubt that it was approved by the movement in general and gave prestige to those who performed it" (Woodcock and Avakumovic, 1977: 312).

Governmental authorities at first tried to humour the Doukhobors, but by the interwar period they had swung to repression. The Criminal Code was amended in 1931 to make nude parading punishable by three years' imprisonment. The federal government tried to deport the leader of the sect. The provincial government set up special facilities to permit the mass jailing of men, women, and children. Children were forcibly parted from their parents and placed in a boarding school. Yet repression seemed only to harden the resistance. During the 1950s conciliation was tried, and over the long run this policy can probably be regarded as successful. Efforts are currently underway to reconcile the differences within the community.

Between 1958 and 1962, however, there was an unparalleled outburst of terrorism, "a desperate last-ditch action against a process of inevitable change." At this time about 600 of the Freedomites took an active part in nude demonstrations and the burning of their own homes. A further 200 formed "a black élite belonging to a few families among whom, in the forty years of continuous incendiarism from 1923 to 1962, a tradition of destructive action had grown up." This total group of 800 were a minority forming "less than a third of the twenty-five hundred people who identified themselves as Sons of Freedom and less than a twentieth of the whole Doukhobor population in Canada" (Woodcock and Avakumovic, 1977: 333). The great campaign at the turn of the sixties saw heightened terrorism including major sabotage and an indifference to human life spreading beyond Doukhobor regions. A lake ferry at Kelowna was attacked along with railway and power lines, bombs were planted in hotels and the bus depot at Nelson, the Nelson court house was bombed, and an attempt was made to blow up the annex of the jail. Fellow Doukhobors also continued to serve as targets; for example, in August 1961 a whole village was destroyed and 40 people narrowly escaped with their lives.

By 1962 most of the active terrorists had been captured. Led by the women, 1,400 Freedomites trekked over the mountains to camp around the jail near Vancouver where the terrorists were detained. Woodcock and Avakumovic (1977: 355) speak of the "extraordinarily rapid" assimilation the Sons of Freedom then underwent, once they "were exposed to the world outside their mountain valleys and deprived of leadership." Relative peace has obtained since then, but there still remains a score or so of activists: "the miniscule remnant of Doukhobors who have not in some way been distracted from their millennial visions by the temptations of the Canadian world" (Woodcock and Avakumovic, 1977: xii-xiii). Recent press reports, however, indicate that the spark of resistance is still very much alive:

Police arrived Sunday to find a railway motor car, ties and other material burning while the 19 defendants stood by, many of them naked and singing Russian hymns ... The fire was out of control for some time but no one was injured ... Tension between the Sons of Freedom and the orthodox Doukhobors has been mounting ... (Ottawa *Citizen*, 2 October 1979)

RCMP in the Kootenays are continuing to investigate two bombings and the discovery of several undetonated bombs here [Grand Forks] in the past three weeks ... RCMP said there is no evidence to lay charges ... but they have not discounted the possibility of some association with Doukhobor factional disputes and the resumption of the [Bourne inquiry into the problems of arson and bombings among the Doukhobors]. (*The Globe and Mail*, 3 May 1984)

The total number of Doukhobor incidents is not known but Holt (1964: 8) gives a figure of over a thousand. Woodcock and Avakumovic (1977: 319, 350) offer some partial figures indicating a lower total: till the end of 1937, 153 "depredations"; the six war years, 44 incidents; 1946 and 1947, 118 incidents; 1961, 106 bombings and burnings; 1962, 274 "depredations." Yet in all these incidents only three people – all Doukhobors – lost their lives: a woman was killed in a fire in 1944, and two, one in 1958 and the other in 1962, were blown up by their own bombs. In addition, the first leader of the sect in Canada was killed with eight others when the railway coach he was riding exploded in October 1924. While the explosion seems to have been deliberate, no culprit was ever found nor any clues implicating the Sons of Freedom, who throughout their terrorist campaign have never used dynamite for the primary purpose of killing (Woodcock and Avakumovic, 1977: 257). Holt (1964: 54-60) suggests that the explosion was the work of a group from the main body of Doukhobors who were then engaged in a leadership struggle.

The other major anti-governmental campaign linked to an ethnically delimited group is that of the FLQ between 1963 and 1970. The main goal of the terrorists was the independence of the province of Quebec. They justified their violence by reference to the 200 years of "Anglo-Saxon" violence against the Quebec people. The FLQ believed that their acts would awaken French Canadians to their exploited and colonized position, demonstrate the weakness of the authorities, and provoke ill-judged governmental counter-attacks that would further undermine attachment to the existing regime. Marxism was another component in the FLQ ideology, present from the beginning but given varying emphasis by different cells.[8] The argument was that Quebec would not be truly independent until it had undergone a social as well as a political revolution. Latin American countries, nominally independent, were in reality no more than colonies of the United States. Fidel Castro, they believed, had shown what needed to be done.

Many among the first wave of terrorists had been active in the early separatist movement, the Rassemblement pour l'Indépendance Nationale (RIN). However, they came to the conclusion that the RIN was a dead end,

8 The tension between the Marxist and nationalist components of the FLQ's ideology was suppressed during the years of active campaigning, but emerged more clearly during the 1970s in the courses of action espoused by two former leaders. On the one hand, Pierre Vallières has called on Quebec separatists to rally behind the PQ, so that political independence may be achieved through the democratic process, to be followed afterwards by a transformation to a socialist state. On the other hand, Charles Gagnon, while maintaining the right of the Quebec people to determine their own future, has renounced separatism and the "petit bourgeois" PQ. Gagnon argues that Quebec workers are being repressed by the same forces as the workers in the rest of the country; the revolutionary class struggle accordingly must be fought from sea to sea. (On Vallières, see William Johnson in *The Globe and Mail*, 18 December 1971; on Gagnon, see the Canadian Press interview, printed in the Ottawa *Citizen*, 21 March 1978.)

unable to get its message across in the media or to defeat the old-line political parties. In October 1962, those who had lost faith in democratic means formed the Réseau de résistance. This split the following year, with its radical wing emerging as the FLQ. A number of cells with different names followed (for example, the Armée républicaine du Québec and the Armée de libération du Québec), although all groups used the name FLQ after August 1965. Clandestine papers, *La Cognée* and *Victoire*, were established. Training camps appeared in the Laurentians. Grandiose organizational plans were drawn up on paper of independent cells building up in a pyramid to a National Congress with an executive Central Committee at the top. In reality, there seems to have been little co-ordination in the campaign, with cells springing up and acting on the initiative of individual members.

The number of people involved in the FLQ is unknown. Marc Laurendeau (1974: 100) provides a list of 90 members who have been before the courts on various charges over the years, suggests that there were probably a few others who engaged in violent activities without being caught, and adds that there were "quelques centaines" actively assisting the FLQ in its propaganda activities and through the provision of financial support, transport, and concealment. Pelletier (1971: 51) believes that in 1970 there were (1) 40-50 (perhaps 100) violent activists;[9] (2) a smaller, non-violent "permanent cell" handling editorial and propaganda work; (3) 200-300 active sympathizers ready to offer concealment and financial aid; and (4) maybe 2,000-3,000 passive sympathizers who were not members of the FLQ but who supported its aims and methods – the "armchair cells." Thus, the total number of people who engaged in violent acts between 1963 and 1970 was quite small, probably not much more than 100.

Members of the FLQ came from diverse social backgrounds. The father of one was a judge, the father of another was a stevedore. They themselves had taken up various occupations, although many were students and at least six had had a military career. They tended to be above average in years of schooling. And they were young; on average they were only 24 when they became involved in terrorist activities. The leaders tended to be somewhat older, but in no case more than 33 years. Fourteen of the 90 members studied by M. Laurendeau (1974: 101) were united by family ties. Psychologically they have been pictured as impatient, with low tolerance of frustration. Many had chequered work and educational histories. Convicted members were unrepentant and expressed satisfaction in having done something concrete for French Canada and in acting in concert with others of like convictions. Only a very few seem to have been drawn in primarily in a search for thrills.

9 Gellner (1974: 93) places "no more than three dozen" in this category. Pelletier was writing to justify the imposition of the War Measures Act and may consequently have been open to accepting higher rather than lower estimates of FLQ participants.

Some 170 violent incidents have been attributed to the FLQ. 1963 was a year of heavy activity, as were 1968 and 1969. Lulls occurred when the police succeeded in rounding up a cell, or when the activists were diverted by events in the wider society, such as the provincial election campaigns of 1966 and 1970 and Expo in 1967. FLQ violence was overwhelmingly directed against property rather than people. Nevertheless eight persons died as a result of the violence, and many more were injured. Some incidents indicated a disregard for human life, such as the explosion in the Montreal Stock Exchange which left 27 wounded. Generally the FLQ telephoned to warn that a bomb had been planted, but by the late sixties so many false warnings had been received that the calls were often ignored. The only case of premeditated violence against an individual was the murder of Pierre Laporte by his captors.

Roughly half of the 170-odd incidents involved bombs. Sixty per cent of the bombs were placed in the two years 1968 and 1969. These tended to be larger, more sophisticated devices than those of the earlier period, and fewer of them were dismantled in time. The choice of targets also shifted during the campaign. Three-quarters of the earlier bombs, but only one in five in the post-Expo period, were attacks on transport and communications facilities (TV installations, roads, railways, and mail boxes) or on federal properties, particularly those of the armed forces. A quarter of the later bombs were directed against Quebec political figures and institutions, and nearly half involved economic targets. The latter fell into two groups: the larger involved attacks against strike-bound companies, while a smaller number of bombs were placed in institutions representing economic power, such as the Montreal Stock Exchange.

Just under a third of the FLQ's violent incidents took the form of violent demonstrations. According to Pelletier (1971: 81) "the FLQ was active in *le Mouvement de libération du taxi*; it was to be found again in *opération McGill français* and in the Saint-Jean-Baptiste riot, it was behind the agitation at certain CEGEPs, and so on." M. Laurendeau (1974: 80) adds to the list. Nearly all the kidnappers of Cross and Laporte were previously known to the police through their "open" activities. The fact that they were not immediately picked up indicates not police inefficiency so much as the great number of people, a minority FLQ members, who participated in radical, often violent movements at the time. In focusing on the FLQ we have to keep in mind that they were far from being the sole users of violence. "Manifestations" and "contestations" were common. Groups of workers, students, those wanting immigrant children to receive French-language schooling, those agitating for the release of the "political" prisoners, all these contributed to the 121 non-terrorist incidents of collective violence that Frank and Kelly (1977: 148) enumerated for Quebec during the years 1963-73. It is not known in how many of these incidents FLQ members participated or the extent to which they instigated the violence. That they did on occasion seek to turn discontent into violent channels is suggested by the details published in a 1964 edition of *La Cognée* on how to be an agitator and how to direct a riot (cited in Pelletier, 1971: 232-6).

The third major form of FLQ activity involved armed robbery to secure the wherewithal to carry on their terrorist campaign. Some 30 thefts were linked to the FLQ. Targets seem to have been selected mainly on practical rather than on ideological grounds. Money was taken from banks and credit unions around the province. Firearms came from gunstores and armouries. Explosives were removed from construction sites and quarries. The thefts accounted largely for the few occasions on which the FLQ strayed outside its geographically restricted base of operations in Montreal.[10]

The climactic FLQ incidents were the kidnappings of the British diplomat James Cross and the Quebec Minister of Labour Pierre Laporte in October 1970. Both men were taken at gunpoint from their homes and secluded in Montreal area houses while the authorities were presented with a list of demands to be filled in exchange for the lives of the hostages.[11] The kidnapping of a diplomat was an established tactic of urban guerrillas by 1970: Cross was the twelfth to be seized in the western hemisphere in little over a year. FLQ activists devoted considerable prior planning to this kidnapping; earlier in the year police had uncovered plots to seize the Israeli and then the American consul in Montreal. The Laporte kidnapping, by contrast, was a hastily improvised affair, carried out independently after Cross's kidnappers appeared to be weakening. The authorities established a dialogue with Cross's kidnappers and agreed to have the FLQ manifesto read over the radio. On 16 October the War Measures Act was unveiled, giving the police extraordinary powers for use in tracking down the kidnappers. The next day Pierre Laporte was killed. Weeks passed before the police located where Cross was being held, so it was not until 4 December that he was released in exchange for a safe conduct to Cuba for his captors. Laporte's abductors were captured in early 1971 and sentenced to lengthy prison sentences. As well, the FLQ members who left the country eventually returned to face the courts.

After 1970 the FLQ faded from the scene. There were a number of reasons for its disappearance. In the 1970 provincial elections, the separatist Parti

10 Only 25 per cent of the of the FLQ incidents took place outside Montreal. Other non-Montreal incidents included four explosions during the 1969 Union Nationale party conference in Quebec City and three explosions in or near federal buildings in Ottawa around the start of 1970. As related by Morf (1970: 10), an early FLQ group set out to destroy one of the Ottawa bridges linking Ontario and Quebec. This would have been a splendidly symbolic act. That no further attempts were made indicates the importance to FLQ activists of familiar territory with support networks in place to provide information, encouragement, and concealment.

11 The kidnappers' demands were the publication of FLQ statements; the release of "political prisoners"; their own passage to Cuba or Algeria; the reinstatement of the Lapalme postal workers; a ransom of $500,000 in gold; the release of the names of informers; and the cessation of police activity in connection with the kidnappings.

Québécois (PQ) gained 24 per cent of the popular vote. The democratic road to independence again seemed a possibility. At the same time the repression of the War Measures Act was a warning against providing an excuse for further intervention that could crush the PQ before it could gain power. Such was the reasoning of Pierre Vallières in his *Urgence de choisir*. Another element in the decision not to revive the terrorist campaign must have been the unsuccessful record of the FLQ. Cells of activists were repeatedly informed upon or infiltrated. Through undercover efforts, the police managed to round up most cells in a reasonably short time. Strategically the campaign was a failure. The object had been to capture headlines and mobilize public opinion against the existing regime. The FLQ certainly gained publicity, but it had to escalate its violence in order to remain in the limelight, especially in the post-Expo period when so many groups were expressing their discontents through violence. The violence of the FLQ then became counter-productive; the authorities retained legitimacy while opinion turned away from the FLQ. Public opinion polls in 1970 showed between 80 and 90 per cent of Quebeckers disapproving of the kidnappings and supporting the use of the War Measures Act. The end of 1970 thus saw the FLQ isolated and rejected, but with a promising new and non-violent channel for separatist activities in the PQ.

OTHER VIOLENCE

The incidents still to be considered are a mixed bunch, though some minor groupings can be discerned. First are the unorganized riots that erupt suddenly to protest a specific issue. One example is the vaccination riot in Montreal in 1885. Vaccination was then a poorly understood procedure and when it was made compulsory during a smallpox epidemic, a night of violence ensued that included an attack on the pharmacy distributing the vaccine. The militia was ultimately called out to restore order. Another case is the riot of 1955 which erupted in and around the Montreal Forum in protest against the suspension of the popular hockey player Maurice Richard. The ensuing rampage resulted in 37 injuries and 70 arrests.

A second group of incidents involves universities and students. While students took an active part in earlier incidents (for example, the riot against the Boer War in Montreal in 1900), student violence was at a peak during the late sixties and early seventies. In some cases the issues were internal university ones, as with the students at Sir George Williams in 1969 who, partly in protest against marks, occupied the computer centre and ultimately set fire to it. The resulting damage was estimated at two million dollars. In other cases, students acted on behalf of political issues external to the university, as in the various demonstrations against the Vietnam War.

A third group covers violent protest in Canada's prisons. During the

Depression era imprisoned Communists at Kingston were fired upon, but not hit, by guards. More recently there was the riot at Kingston Penitentiary in 1971 in protest against prison and parole conditions in which extensive property damage occurred and one prisoner was killed and 11 others injured at the hands of other inmates. The hostage-taking incidents at New Westminster in 1975 and Dorchester in 1980 each produced a death when hostages were killed during attempts to recapture the prisoners. In 1982, the Archambault Institute erupted in a riot that left five dead.

Prison violence is usually not public but private, such as the 15 murders and three attempted murders in the first ten years of the Archambault Institute, most of which involved drugs, informers, and settling old scores (*The Globe and Mail*, 26 January 1980). Similarly the interpersonal violence in Kingston Penitentiary in 1971 and the objectives of the hostage-takers may also be regarded as private. Nevertheless, particularly at Kingston, there was a public element in the sense that the violence was seen by some as a reaction to and a form of protest against the prison system as a whole. (Within the violent subculture of prison life, even what the wider society may regard as private murder may take on public connotations and be seen as a means of enforcing the accepted norms of the subculture.)

A final pair of incidents that should be mentioned are also partly private since the assailants' mental stability was in doubt. One was the attempt by Paul Joseph Chartier in May 1966 to set off a bomb in the federal parliament buildings. Chartier killed himself when the bomb exploded prematurely. He had intended to make a speech before the House of Commons demanding that MPs pay less attention to partisan interests and more to those of ordinary working people. In the other incident, Denis Lortie shot his way into the Quebec National Assembly in May 1984, killing three and injuring thirteen others. According to a garbled tape he left at a radio station, he was motivated by a desire to destroy the Parti Québécois government.

CONCLUSION

Many of the incidents cited here have been forgotten over the years. They are public in the sense that they captured attention at the time they occurred, though they may have since slipped into obscurity. Perhaps we need a category of "historic public events," those that are kept alive in the memory from one generation to the next. Clearly Canada would have very few in such a category. There is nothing here comparable to the Boston Tea Party or the Fall of the Bastille. Indeed, a content analysis of university-level history texts on the post-Confederation period reveals that the only events mentioned consistently and covered in more than a sentence or two are the two Riel risings (Torrance, 1975: 229, 252).

Tilly (1979: 85-6) has remarked on "how fast we forget" collective violence. He suggests that "the most important reason [for this historical forgetfulness] is probably that so long as historians concentrate on political history as seen from the top, the only protests which matter are those which produce some rearrangement of power." Plainly Canada has had no triumphant political or social revolutions, and there have been no great turning points in its history attended by violence. Hence Canadians should not be surprised by the obscurity shrouding their limited and inconclusive violent past. Even Louis Riel, the closest Canadian history comes to a violent hero, is a figure of pathos, remembered less for his life's achievements than for the manner of his death.

Yet historical obscurity need not imply triviality. Canadians have gone to the extreme of surrendering life and livelihood in defence of the causes they have espoused. Police and soldiers have obeyed orders to fire on their fellow citizens. We may be uncomfortable recalling the desperation, the blood, the fire, and the bereavement, so often expended for naught and perhaps on behalf of causes for which we can find little sympathy, but our discomfort should not lead us to belittle the sacrifices of men and women who have felt compelled to act violently.

Historical obscurity has helped Canadians to believe in their self-image as a peaceful people. The myth of the peaceable kingdom, which will be examined in chapter 5, may suggest that a book on Canadian public violence is unnecessary. Yet the numerous incidents we have been discussing show that the myth does not reflect the reality, at least in the absolute sense that there has been little or no violence in Canada. Whether it is true in a relative sense – Canada has little violence in comparison with other countries – we shall see in the next chapter. The following is none the less indisputable: 22 Orange-Green riots in Toronto between 1867 and 1892 (Kealey, 1976), 300 violent strikes between 1900 and 1974 (Jamieson, 1979), several hundred cases of Doukhobor violence, the 170-odd events attributed to the FLQ, and 246 acts of collective violence in Ontario and Quebec between 1963 and 1973 (Frank and Kelly, 1977), along with all the other separate incidents described, indicate that, despite the myth, we have cases enough to justify a detailed study of the phenomenon of violence in Canadian society.

CHAPTER THREE

Characteristics of Canadian Public Violence

This chapter seeks to establish for Canadian public violence those salient features and peculiarities that require explanation. We shall look at the ways by which incidents can be classified and, briefly, at how the Canadian experience compares with that of other nations. What we are trying to identify are the dependent variables that the theories discussed in the remaining chapters should be able to account for. We can then judge these theories according to how well they explain not just the patterns of violence that Canada shares with other nations but also the features of the Canadian experience that are exceptional.

TYPOLOGIES OF PUBLIC VIOLENCE

Violent incidents are complex affairs. There are many characteristics or attributes that we can use to distinguish one from another. To select among them is no easy task. We may start by seeing how scholars have used typologies of violence to bring order to their subject matter. Inductive typologists take a given collection of violent events and seek out patterns within it. Deductive typologists identify key characteristics before they attempt to classify their data.

Inductive typologies. There are a number of recurrent types of violence, what might be called the "classic" forms. The following are among the most important:

Riot: Unplanned and unorganized violence by a large body of people, usually motivated by a desire to protest some policy or action by the authorities, and directed mainly at inanimate objects.

Attack: Violence by one group against another, with little prior planning or organization.

Clash: Small-scale violence involving the authorities, with little prior planning or organization.

Terrorism: Violent acts by small, conspiratorial groups, usually against governmental targets.

Assassination: The murder of prominent individuals for political motives.

Mutiny: Violence by members of the armed forces in defiance of lawful orders.

Coup d'état: Violence accompanying the seizure of power by elite groups, often the armed forces.

Rebellion: Violence between the armed forces and the civilians of a particular locality who are defying governmental authority.

Civil war: Violence between the armed forces of different segments of a country, one of which may be trying to secede.

Guerrilla conflict: The violence of anti-governmental soldiers, small in number and conspiratorial, seeking to overthrow a regime.

Revolution: Large-scale violence with mass and elite participation accompanying the overthrow of a regime.

Obviously this list could be extended. Other types are wars of independence or against aboriginal inhabitants, violent strikes, jacqueries, police riots, executions, lynchings, sabotage, and so on. The desire to reduce the list to manageable proportions has led many authors to use statistical techniques, mainly factor analyses, to assemble the various classic forms into groups. Several studies, using different bodies of data, have yielded three principal dimensions. As defined by Gurr (1970: 11), these are:

Turmoil: Relatively spontaneous, unorganized political violence with substantial popular participation, including violent political strikes, riots, political clashes, and localized rebellions.

Conspiracy: Highly organized political violence with limited participation, including organized political assassinations, small-scale terrorism, small-scale guerrilla wars, coups d'état, and mutinies.

Internal war: Highly organized political violence with widespread popular participation, designed to overthrow the regime or dissolve the state and accompanied by extensive violence, including large-scale terrorism and guerrilla wars, civil wars, and revolutions.

The criticism raised against all inductive typologies is that they are "unavoidably ad hoc and consequently are only as good as the data or cases from which they are derived" (Bell, 1973: 58). That is, different typologies emerge depending on the number and range of cases analysed. A more particular criticism is that Turmoil, comprising events which, it is generally agreed, are the most irregularly reported of all violent events, is too general a category. Improved data collection would probably yield further clusters of events within it.

Deductive typologies. Many attributes of violence have been used to develop deductive typologies of violence. They fall into five major classes:

Context of the violence: Is the violence within or between states? What is the nature of the host society: its level of economic development, form of government, rate of social change, and so on? What kind of societal relationship is affected by the violence: political, economic, or communal?

Indicators of the scope and intensity of the violence: How many people, including governmental forces, are involved? What is the geographic extent of the violence? How long does it last? What are the casualty and damage figures?

Characteristics of the violent: What is the social class of the violent? Are they civilians or soldiers? Are they acquiring, maintaining, or losing their position in society (Tilly, 1979: 108)? Have they planned their violence? What sort of organization, if any, do they belong to? Are they motivated by a coherent ideology? What are their objectives?

Targets of the violence: Are the targets pre-selected or random? Is the violence directed primarily at people or property? Are the victims members of the government, civilians, or members of a minority group?

Impact of the violence: Is the violence carried out as planned? Are the objectives of the violent achieved? Does the incident lead to further violence?

Again this is not an exhaustive list, but it demonstrates how we could go about constructing a complex deductive typology. There is little agreement among scholars about which are the key differentiating attributes of violent behaviour. Generally those attributes are selected which *a priori* are expected to yield an insightful analysis of the subject at hand – a foreclosing procedure that may leave doubts in the reader's mind.

In practice, scholars seek to avoid the pitfalls of typology-formation by not sticking rigidly to the inductive or the deductive mode. They shift back and forth, trying out differentiating attributes against the data at hand and examining the data for further attributes until they have developed a typology that suits their purposes. However, Bell (1973: 58) cautions that this practice "combines the worst of both inductive and deductive approaches," as when attributes, after inspection of the data, are illogically combined or dropped without further explanation.

The fine points of typology-formation need not be pursued further. This discussion serves to show how work on typologies has yielded a rich store of attributes for classifying and analysing violence. Some are more valuable than others when applied to Canadian material.

CLASSIFICATION AND ANALYSIS

Types of violence. Only some of the classic forms of public violence listed at the start of the chapter are part of the history of violence in Canada. That list can be divided into three groups. The first comprises violent acts absent from Canadian history: coups, guerrilla conflicts, civil wars, and revolutions. That is to say, many of the more serious forms of violence. In a second group are the forms with which Canada has had limited experience. It includes rebellions (the Northwest Rebellion of 1885), assassinations (the death of D'Arcy McGee in 1868), mutinies (in the repatriation camps in England in 1919), and terrorism (both of the small-scale, quasi-public variety carried on by the Donnellys and the large, public sort conducted by the Sons of Freedom and the FLQ). The third group comprises the forms of public violence most frequently found in Canada: riots, clashes, and attacks.

Thus, if we use the inductively derived typology of Turmoil, Conspiracy, and Internal War, we find practically all Canadian public violence falling in the Turmoil category. The only case of Internal War would be the Northwest Rebellion. Examples of Conspiracy events would have to be drawn from the limited number of assassinations and terrorist events. (Mutinies are usually included in the Conspiracy category, but the Canadian events lack the element of extensive, covert planning that is the essential attribute of Conspiracy violence.) Turmoil is plainly a large category that indifferently groups together several quite distinctive varieties of violent behaviour. The characteristics used to derive deductive typologies can help us discriminate among them.

Context of the violence. Almost all Canadian public violence has been without international complications. Exceptions are the assassination of McGee by Fenians, some limited American involvement in the Red River incident, the repatriation camp disturbances which took place in England, and attacks on visiting foreigners or on embassies and their staffs by embittered immigrants. The exceptions, however, are few in number, and consequently the national/international dichotomy is of no real use to a Canadian study.

Rather more promising would seem to be the division of the incidents according to which contexts of society – communal, economic, or political – produce the tensions that give rise to the violence. Such a differentiating characteristic is interesting theoretically in the light of Johnson's (1964: 8-10) delineation of the revolutionary process as the spread of "dysfunctionality" (the failure of a system or a subsystem to maintain itself) into progressively wider sectors. Canadian Turmoil events with an economic base (such as violent strikes) are probably the most common, followed by those with a communal base (for example, Orange-Green attacks). Far less numerous are events with a narrowly political base, such as election or anti-conscription violence. (Frank and Kelly [1977: 148] show 45 per cent of their Ontario and Quebec collective violence incidents during 1963 to 1973 to have arisen over immediate economic issues, while 41 per cent involved social or political issues.) One major source of communal violence is notable for its infrequency: that between English and French Canadians.

Examining the context of incidents forces a recognition of a salient characteristic of Canadian public violence: the mixed nature of so many of the incidents. The most prolonged and serious Canadian incidents – the Northwest Rebellion, and the Sons of Freedom and FLQ campaigns – have clear elements from all three contexts. They also extend beyond the bounds of Turmoil, which gives weight to Johnson's hypothesis linking "multiple dysfunctionality" to the more extreme forms of violence. On the other hand, we noted in the last chapter the high number of job-related incidents with at least communal overtones. These were not even remotely close to being regime-shattering events. For Turmoil to develop into Conspiracy or Internal War, the addition of a political dimension, whereby discontent is focused on the government, appears to be crucial.

Scope and intensity of the violence. To place the scope of public violence in context, there are two important points to remember. First, public violence accounts for only a miniscule proportion of all the violence that takes place in most countries. And second, violence of any kind usually accounts for only a very small percentage of the total number of deaths that occur in a given year. Mortality statistics (Statistics Canada, Catalogue 84-203) give an indication of the proportions involved. In 1980, there were 171,473 deaths recorded in Canada. Ninety per cent of these were attributable to disease.[1] Most of the remaining 15,740 deaths attributed to "external" causes were the result of accidents. However, there were 3,358 deaths from suicide and self-inflicted injuries and 495 homicidal deaths, accounting respectively for 2.0 and 0.3 per cent of the total. Most of the homicides were clearly private in nature, arising primarily out of quarrels among family and friends or occurring during the course of a robbery or other crime. Only 22 people were killed in a fight or a brawl – 0.01 per cent of the total. Presumably many of these were killed in drunken arguments rather than in riots or other forms of public violence. The number of deaths that could be attributed to public violence thus finally shrinks almost to the vanishing point.

While mortality statistics help place public violence in a wider context, they are not sufficiently detailed to tell us much about public violence itself,

---

1 It is instructive to compare the number of deaths from specific diseases with those from suicide or homicide. Ischaemic heart disease, for example, accounted for 29 per cent of all deaths in 1980, malignant neoplasms for 23 per cent, and cerebrovascular disease for 9 per cent. Thus heart disease killed nearly a hundred times as many people as homicides.

which, in any case, seldom results in loss of life. In reality, there is no Canadian body of official statistics that is directly helpful. Gurr (1976) has used police and court statistics from other countries to trace the historical cycles of public order offences (for example, illegal assembly, rioting, treason, and assaulting a police officer). However, I have found comparable Canadian statistics to be so incomplete and inconsistent as to be of no use.

In gauging the scope and intensity of Canadian violence, duration of an event is of little discriminatory value since few incidents ever last more than a day. The major exception is the Northwest Rebellion. Similarly, geographic extent as a criterion adds little since most incidents take place within a single community. Ideally what is needed are facts and figures on the number of participants, casualties, and arrests, and the value of property destroyed. Yet such figures are either unreliable or unavailable, particularly for earlier periods. From a practical standpoint, analysis based on the number of deaths in a violent event is the best choice simply because it is the indicator most likely to be precisely reported.[2] The Canadian incidents of public violence that resulted in deaths are listed in the appendix. (It should be stressed that this is a preliminary compilation that will undoubtedly have to be amended and added to as further research is done.)

According to this compilation, 40 incidents resulted in the loss of around 275 lives in total. Most of the incidents involved one or two deaths. Only the Northwest Rebellion with some 200 dead was sufficiently lethal to indicate violence of high intensity. Since no count has yet been made of the total number of public incidents, we cannot establish the ratio of lethal to non-lethal events. Yet out of an estimated 300 violent strikes between 1900 and 1974, only 11 would appear to have produced fatalities. Frank and Kelly (1977: 149) record no deaths for their 246 incidents of collective violence in Ontario and Quebec, 1963-73. (The authors also collected data on the number of injuries; in only 10 per cent of the incidents were more than 20 people hurt, a figure they consider "pas très élevé.") Figures such as these suggest that the proportion of incidents sufficiently serious to produce deaths is well under 5 per cent. The proportion is probably higher among Conspiracy than among Turmoil events.

Some characteristics of the lethal incidents merit comment. Guns were used in 17 of the incidents and explosive devices in a further nine. The number involving bombs indicates a Canadian tradition, reflecting the widespread use and availability of explosives in wider society. The bombing figures also suggest another characteristic, that the Canadian lethal incidents were the

---

2 The death toll provides only a rough indicator of the intensity of violence. Deaths during public violence are often accidental, and comparisons over time are complicated by changes in medical services and in weapons technology.

work of amateurs. Five of the nine bombing deaths were those of bombers blowing themselves up with their own devices. In very few incidents can we discern a murderous intent in the sense of a prior determination to kill particular individuals. Generally the deaths occurred inadvertently, or indiscriminately in the heat of battle. The FLQ and Sons of Freedom terrorists accounted for nine of these incidents.

Geographically the incidents were spread from British Columbia to Newfoundland, with a concentration in Quebec (16 incidents). Ontario, in contrast, recorded only eight incidents (and four of these involved attacks on the federal government and its institutions located in the province). The most lethally violent decade since Confederation was 1957-66, in which ten of the 40 incidents fell. Other above-average decades were 1877-86 (six incidents) and 1917-26 and 1967-76 (five incidents). No deaths were noted for 1887-96, 1907-16, and 1947-56.

The distribution of violent strikes, both lethal and non-lethal, is somewhat different. Jamieson (1979: 143, 154) argues that, as might be expected, levels of violence in strikes and levels of industrial conflict have generally gone hand in hand. From the turn of the century to the late 1920s, there were four peaks in which strike activity and violence were concomitant. In order of seriousness, they were 1919, 1924, 1912, and 1903. The Depression years produced relatively few strikes – there was a minor peak in 1937 – but the period is an exception to the usual pattern in that there was a good deal of violence relative to the amount of strike activity. The next period, which extends from the war years down to the late 1950s, is also somewhat exceptional. There were strike peaks in 1943, 1950, 1958, and particularly in 1946, but they were accompanied by low levels of violence. From the late fifties the incidence of strikes increased sharply to reach an unprecedented level in 1966 and to remain at a high plateau through to 1974. Violence also moved abruptly upwards until 1966, but declined thereafter except in Quebec.

Jamieson's historical study (1968) for the Task Force on Labour Relations indicates that violent strikes have occurred across the country.[3] However, British Columbia before the Second World War and Quebec generally have had a disproportionate share; and small, remote centres such as Blubber Bay and Flin Flon have figured more prominently than their population size would warrant. The three industrial sectors that appear to have been most affected are mining, forestry, and fishing; transport and communications; and textiles and clothing.

For the incidence of other forms of public violence in more recent years, we can turn to two sources. First, the *World Handbook* (Taylor and Hudson, 1972) data covers the years 1948-67. They indicate a generally quiet post-war

3 This paragraph is based on an analysis of the violent strikes that Jamieson (1968) mentions in his text.

period lasting up to the late fifties. Violence was particularly prevalent in the years 1962-6: 62 per cent of the riots, 74 per cent of the attacks, and 75 per cent of the deaths recorded occurred within these five years. Second, we have Frank and Kelly's (1977: 150; Jackson, Kelly, and Mitchell, n.d.: 260) study of Turmoil incidents in Ontario and Quebec for the years 1963-75. Their data show the peak of violent incidents coming at the start of the seventies.

What can we make from all this? A preliminary and cautionary conclusion is that various kinds of violence may follow different cycles. For instance, the peak in job-related violence before the First World War was not accompanied by much violence of other kinds. The *World Handbook* figures reflect mainly the incidence of Sons of Freedom and FLQ terrorism, while a large proportion of Frank and Kelly's entries are violent strikes. The different peaks shown by these various sources may thus be a reflection of the different cycles in the types of violence they cover.

However, we need some overall indication of when and where Canadians have been particularly prone to violence. Combining the various sources we have discussed, the following picture emerges:

1 The decade 1877-86 seems to have been particularly violent. The Northwest Rebellion falls within it, as do many other incidents of communal and/or economic conflict (Orange-Green, French and Irish, anti-Chinese, and the Donnellys).
2 1900-14 saw many violent strikes, but only two incidents in the earlier years were lethal.
3 The decade 1917-26 produced 17 deaths, arising from political, communal, and economic grievances (for example, resistance to the war, the Doukhobors, and the Winnipeg General Strike).
4 The Depression years saw a number of economically motivated incidents.
5 From 1958 through to 1972, we have a period of extensive violence involving political, economic, and communal issues. In particular, there were a number of violent strikes and the activities of the Sons of Freedom and the FLQ. Fifteen incidents resulted in deaths.

Characteristics of the violent. The participants in Canadian public violence come from diverse backgrounds. Young men have tended to play a prominent part. While women participated in the Sons of Freedom and FLQ in various capacities, for the most part public violence has been a male preserve. Participants may have been previously known to the police through their earlier protest activities, but very few had a criminal record. The initial participants have often been civilians, with soldiers or police later being drawn in to enforce the law or quell the violence. There are, however, a number of exceptions to this general picture: the arrival on the scene of soldiers and police prior to any illegality or violence has sometimes served to precipitate incidents; on occasion, the authorities have even initiated or escalated the violence (for example, the disturbances at the repatriation camps in the U.K., and the violence of the police at Asbestos).

The participants have not been drawn from any one social class. The numerous job-related incidents have naturally involved members of the working class. The unions concerned have often been weaker ones – those at the stage of seeking recognition, or in competition with other established unions, or with especially few resources vis-à-vis the employer. Such unions may espouse radical political doctrines or voice large demands on behalf of their members, thereby alarming employers and governments into intransigence and violent repression.

However, violence that is not job-related has attracted participants of varying backgrounds. Certainly the most serious incidents have risen among relatively disadvantaged groups, but the individual participants in the Northwest Rebellion and the FLQ (though not the Sons of Freedom) have included the better-off from within the group. FLQ activists, for instance, had on average more years of schooling than the general population of French-speaking Quebec. As to the Turmoil events, while some have been the work of low-status crowds (for example, the Montreal vaccination riot), others have been composed of mixed status or middle-class groups. Thus, the Lucan vigilantes included a justice of the peace; the Orange-Green disturbances in rural Ontario, as described by Bull (1936), were carried on by the farming population; and much of the Turmoil of the 1960s, inside and outside the universities, was the work of students, *ex officio* of middle-class status. In their study of Ontario and Quebec violence, 1963-73, Frank and Kelly (1977: 153) indicate that 55 per cent of the incidents involved "blue-collar" workers only, and the remainder involved mixed groups.

Public violence, then, has not been the exclusive preserve of any one class, although there are some groups that have been poorly represented. Not surprisingly, few participants have come from the upper end of the social scale; for here we find those with the fewest grievances and the most power to secure their wants by non-violent means. More surprisingly perhaps in the light of popular assumptions that link violence to the "dregs" or "riff-raff" of society are the few participants who have come from the most deprived and powerless sections of the population. Such people are far from being strangers to violence; see, for example, the passages of Maria Campbell's *Halfbreed* cited by Dietz (1978). Yet their violence is rarely of a public nature, which seems to require a level of group consciousness and organization that is beyond the capacity of a demoralized population.

Incidents arising from a diffuse sense of rage have been notably infrequent. Instead, with a few exceptions, the participants' objectives have been well-defined and narrow: protests against specific policies, the defence of specific rights, and the pursuit of specific goals. Usually only one or two issues are involved, such as union recognition, the use of strike-breakers, work for the unemployed, the disruption of an opponent's election campaign, compulsory vaccination, and conscription. The exceptions that have multiple grievances are associated with the more serious incidents. The participants in these – the Métis in 1885, the Sons of Freedom, and the FLQ activists – have not been concerned with righting a minor wrong. Rather they have sought to secure large-scale social and political change. They have been the only groups to develop and act upon an extensive ideology justifying their rejection of the existing regime. For the most part, however, radical left-wing ideologies have proved incapable of inciting anti-regime violence amongst Canadians for any great length of time.

Organizational base. Canadians seem to be an organized people even in their public violence. This is partly a matter of definitions since violence is more likely to be considered public and less likely to be dismissed as private deviance when the violent are perceived to be acting on behalf of an organization. A prior organization also helps to formulate specific demands and mobilize sufficient numbers to endanger public order. However, public violence does not have to have an organizational base: individuals may act on their own, for example, Chartier's attempt to bomb Parliament. Also there are the cases of unorganized crowd violence: the Montreal vaccination riot, the Quebec City anti-conscription riots, the Halifax V-E day riot, the Forum riot, and the turmoil during the Montreal police strike. In each of these cases, large numbers of people, not previously joined in any organization, suddenly coalesced, usually in protest against some action by the authorities.

Yet individual and crowd violence only account for some of the incidents. Probably a good majority did have an organization behind them. The participants usually belonged to a permanent organization employing legal means in the pursuit of specific, non-violent objectives, such as a union, religious sect, or ethnic association. In a few cases the organization was a special purpose, temporary one, such as the On to Ottawa trek. A few other cases consist of conspiratorial organizations with avowedly violent objectives, for example, the Lucan vigilantes and the FLQ. The leaders of all these organizations, while being amongst the most renowned and dedicated to the cause, rely on elections, committees, general meetings, and other bureaucratic-rational means to maintain their position and co-ordinate the actions of the membership. The only example of a charismatic leader is Riel among the Métis in 1885.

That Canadian public violence typically has an organizational base fits with Tilly's (1979) contention that historically the predominant form of collective violence has shifted from a communal base involving small-scale, local, traditional groupings to an associational base involving large-scale organizations serving a well-defined interest. Tilly further classifies events according to the participants' relation to the structure of power: whether they are acquiring position, demanding rights so far denied; maintaining position; or losing position, defending rights that are under attack. Over the long run, according to Tilly, "primitive" varieties of collective violence (communal base-maintaining position, for example, feuds, brawls among members of rival guilds or communities, and the mutual attacks of hostile religious groups) gave way as the dominant form to "reactionary" varieties (communal base-losing position, for example, anti-taxation and anti-conscription revolts, food riots, and machine wrecking), which in turn gave way to "modern" varieties (associational base-acquiring position, for example, demonstrations, violent strikes, coups d'état, and guerrilla conflict). Modern varieties occur when industrialization and urbanization are well established and when the national state and the national economy have triumphed over the particularisms of the past. Where this victory is uncertain, as in Spain, the progress from primitive through to modern is not clear-cut.

How does the Canadian example fit in with Tilly's scheme, based as it is on a study of European collective violence? We can find Canadian incidents that illustrate all but one[4] of his categories:

ORGANIZATIONAL	RELATION TO STRUCTURE OF POWER BASE		
	Acquiring position	Maintaining position	Losing position
Communal	Red River Rising	Lucan vigilantes Orange-Green riots Guibord riot	Northwest Rebellion Conscription riot
Associational	Violent strikes	Election violence	

As might be expected, given the time period in question, strictly communal incidents are rare. Rather what predominate are associations organized to promote the interests of a particular ascriptive community, for example, the FLQ. Thus the "communal" incidents above are mainly mixed communal-associational ones. Furthermore the historical trend from primitive to modern varieties as discerned by Tilly is unclear in Canada. Certainly the primitive varieties (communal-maintaining) appear to belong to the earlier years. What seems to have happened is that violence against and between communities has come to be regarded as improper, which not only helps to prevent these occurrences but also makes such attacks as do occur nowadays appear to be private, criminal violence, the work of pathological or undersocialized thugs.

4 As an example of an associational organization losing position, Tilly cites the case of Poujadism. The Créditistes might be considered the nearest Canadian equivalent, but they have never resorted to violence.

While rarely expressed in widespread violence, tension between communities still exists because Canadians have not yet given up their communal, particularistic identities ("hyphenated Canadianism") in favour of a national one. This can be seen even more clearly when we look at the "reactionary" varieties of violence which Tilly sees as being characteristically a nineteenth-century phenomenon, linked to the rise of the nation-state and its ensuing conflicts with local loyalties. The Northwest Rebellion of 1885 clearly fits into this category, but so too does the campaign of the Sons of Freedom in the 1960s against assimilation to Canadian mores and acceptance of governmental requirements. "Modern" varieties (associational-acquiring), at least in the form of the violent strike, also occur throughout the post-Confederation period. Further, the other major expression of public violence in recent years, the FLQ, while looking to the future to acquire new rights, can also be seen as the rebellion of a particularistic community against the centralizing nation-state. Nevertheless, Tilly's main point that the dominant forms of violence change as the society evolves still stands. It is just that in the 100 or so years with which we are dealing, Canada has become an industrialized and urbanized nation while the national state and the national economy have not managed to displace older communal loyalties.

Targets. Canadian public violence has been directed at both people and property. As we noted earlier, there have been very few cases of murder of a pre-selected victim. The main violence of the Northwest Rebellion, for instance, involved soldiers and rebels impersonally firing guns at each other in an effort to gain the field of battle. Sons of Freedom and FLQ terrorists (the kidnappings of James Cross and Pierre Laporte aside) directed their conspiratorial violence against property. People were hurt as a result, but the deaths and injuries were inadvertent even if at times the terrorists appeared to be careless of human life.

Both government officials and civilians have been the victims of public violence. In the lethal incidents listed in the appendix, there are 11 incidents in which government officials were killed by civilians, 5 incidents in which civilians were killed by agents of the government, 20 in which civilians were killed by other civilians, and 4 mixed-type ones. Even though cases in which government officials are victimized are perhaps more likely to have been recorded, these figures strongly contradict any notion of a bloodthirsty state preying on its citizen body.

Damage to property in those events characterized as Turmoil has generally been inflicted on limited pre-selected targets. Examples include: the pharmacy distributing vaccine in the anti-vaccination riot; the hotel at which Green supporters gathered in Toronto; the building housing conscription records in Quebec City; on several occasions the offices of a newspaper advocating an unpopular policy; and damage by strikers to company property.

These are attacks on "public" property. Attacks on "private" property – the homes and possessions of individuals – have been rare and largely confined to the province of Quebec. The homes of executives of strike-bound companies have been attacked in Murdochville, in Sorel, and in Montreal during the 1960s, as has the personal property of political figures such as Léon Balcer and Jean Drapeau.

Property damage has most commonly taken such forms as window-smashing, tire-slashing, and furniture-wrecking. Looting during events of Turmoil has been rare, although it did occur during the demobilization camp riots, the Nova Scotia Besco strike of 1925, the Halifax V-E day riot, and the Montreal police strike of 1969. Explosive devices have occasionally been used, for example, in the Montreal longshoremen's strike of 1966. Arson has been used more frequently, though not as frequently as one might expect given that it is a relatively accessible and effective means of destroying property. It is also something of a British cultural tradition that one might expect immigrants to have brought with them across the Atlantic. (Perhaps it is not too fanciful to suggest that Canadians' long battle to keep warm in winter without burning down their own houses has bred an aversion to uncontrolled fires. The Canadian climate has also provided strikers with an unusual weapon: the threat to prevent maintenance men into a struck plant to guard against damage caused by a freeze-up. This tactic was employed during the Ford Windsor strike of 1945.)

Interpersonal violence seems to have been at least as common as property damage, and maybe more so, in Turmoil events. This conclusion reflects the large number of clashes and attacks within the category of Turmoil events in which violence has taken the form of physical collisions between contending groups or between a group and the police. It is supported by Frank and Kelly's (1977: 149) finding that 47 per cent of the Ontario and Quebec incidents they studied were directed against persons, as opposed to 23 per cent against property and 30 per cent against both. While guns were employed in two out of five of the lethal incidents (and were used with less than deadly effect in several others), they are more the exception than the rule in Turmoil incidents. Instead participants have relied on an assortment of weapons: fists and boots, cudgels, railings, work tools, picket signs, stones, fire hoses and, in two unique cases, boiling water and a bulldozer.

Impact. There are a number of ways of assessing the impact of public violence. From a broad perspective one may ask what effect violence has had on the development of the country as a whole, both substantively and in the popular imagination. This will be considered in the concluding chapter. A narrower perspective, which looks at the intentions of the participants, would have to conclude that most public violence in Canada has not gone as planned. Partly this reflects incidents that erupted out of tense situations and were scarcely planned at all. Yet even in situations where prior planning is evident, matters often went awry: the police uncovered plots before they could be enacted; conspirators blew themselves up with their own bombs; violence escalated out of control, resulting in more damage than intended, or failed when participants simply neglected to show up. Totally fortuitous circumstances, such as mistaken identity, faulty weapons, broken lines of communication, the unpredicted behaviour of individuals, have all played their part in disrupting even the best laid plans. This appears to bear out Arendt's (1969: 5) dictum concerning the "all-pervading unpredictability" of violence, but one should not ignore the amateurism and less than brilliant improvisation (bordering on slapstick comedy) that characterize many incidents of violence in Canada. Of course this does not apply to all of them. Many of them have been all too successful, such as the assassination of D'Arcy McGee.

An incident may be regarded as successful for the participants if, as a result of the violence, they gain their objectives. In these terms, the violence of Canada's soldiers and policemen has almost invariably been successful. (For some minor qualifications to this, see the section in chapter 9 on the effectiveness of governmental violence.) Illegal parades have been broken up, and rioters and rebels captured, if not immediately, at least once reinforcements have arrived on the scene. In the end, it was ordinary, largely non-violent police work that disrupted the campaigns of the Sons of Freedom and the FLQ.

The most successful civilian resistance in Canadian history was the Red River rising but this, as has been pointed out, was essentially a non-violent affair with a few counter-productive incidents of violence. In fact, there is not a single incident in which civilian violence brought complete success. As a general rule, the resort to violence has had the effect of hardening the stands of opposition groups, employers, and governments. Minor concessions may be made, such as settling the Métis land titles in 1885 or reading the FLQ manifesto over the radio in 1970, but they are tactical means of gaining time or support to defeat the wider objectives of the violent. Canadian governments have also typically responded by trying to make any future resort to violence more difficult (Torrance, 1977: 487).

There are, however, other criteria for success than the complete achievement of objectives. Participants may use violence to place issues in the public forum and to demonstrate their strength of feeling, commitment to their cause, and sense of outrage. On this criterion, Canadian public violence can still be considered only partly successful. Violence generally captures the headlines, it is true, but as Jackson, Kelly, and Mitchell (n.d.: 275) have shown, Canadian newspapers tend to focus on the details of the violence and not the issues behind it: what people did and not why they did it. Poor coverage of issues has the effect of devaluing acts of violence and pushing them towards the private sphere as instances of momentary, motiveless madness or deviancy. The exceptions are prolonged incidents (such as the Asbestos strike), during which participants are able to explain their position to the public through the media. The longer incidents also tend to have the most sophisticated organizational bases with prepared platforms and designated leaders and spokesmen.

Yet another criterion is the extent to which violence settles an issue, favourably or otherwise according to one's perspective. Incidents may leave things as before, without alleviating any of the conditions that led to the initial act of violence. Examples are the Sons of Freedom terrorism and Orange-Green rioting which dragged on for years. Gradually they faded out as circumstances changed and the violence lost its meaning. By contrast, an incident may be a climax of a series of previous incidents, the point at which the government steps in with overwhelming force or when public opinion turns against violence. While some of the larger strikes fit this pattern, the FLQ provides the most notable example: the kidnappings of Cross and Laporte marked the climax of its campaign. Most common in Canada, however, is a single incident of violence climaxing a period of tension and non-violent resistance. Examples are the Northwest Rebellion, the June 21st riot in the Winnipeg General Strike, and the Regina riot that marked the culmination of the On to Ottawa trek. In these cases, one side is so thoroughly trounced that it loses the spirit to carry the conflict any further. That so much of Canadian public violence has taken this form suggests that violence often occurs when the adversaries in a conflict are unequally matched: either the weaker party uses violence as a last desperate fling, or its very weakness encourages the other side to attack it. (Chapter 8 provides a further discussion of this question.)

Summary. For the most part Canadian public violence has taken the form of Turmoil, although some cases of Conspiracy and one of Internal War have occurred. It has arisen chiefly from economic and communal grievances. The scope and intensity of the incidents have almost always been limited. The participants have been drawn from different social classes, and they have belonged to special purpose associations with specific non-violent objectives. They fail to achieve these goals because their single outburst is crushed by government forces, although the outburst may succeed to the extent of having grievances aired. Their targets have been limited and pre-selected; both people and property have been chosen for attack, although people have been rarely subjected to murderous assaults.

Such is the general picture. The exceptions to it, noted in the preceding paragraphs, have usually occurred in the non-Turmoil incidents. Canada's infrequent conspirators and rebels have provided nearly all the cases of people acting on political grievances, of high intensity and prolonged violence, and of clandestine associations established for violent purposes with broad-ranging, ideologically defined goals.

In examining the characteristics of Canadian public violence, a number of apparent peculiarities have cropped up. Why has there been so little violent conflict between French and English Canadians, and between aboriginal inhabitants and later immigrants? Why are so many of the incidents based on mixed discontents and why have communal organizations remained prominent to the present day? Why have there been so few deaths and why do these show time and geographic concentrations? Why was violence so prevalent during the 1960s? Why have the areas outside the major population centres provided so many cases? Why have some industries been more affected than others by job-related violence? Why are firearms used relatively rarely? Why have radical ideologies failed to mobilize more people for violence? Why has civilian violence failed so consistently while governmental violence has succeeded? Such questions represent our "dependent variables": the issues which the various theories examined in the following chapters should be able to explain.

Yet how peculiar are these "peculiarities"? A proper assessment of the Canadian experience of public violence requires that it be compared to that of other countries. The available cross-national data are neither complete nor entirely convincing, but they do enable us to amend and extend parts of the portrait so far developed.

CROSS-NATIONAL COMPARISONS

It is important not to be blinded by the seeming precision of cross-national statistics on violence. A number of caveats are in order. First, there is no doubt that the various data sets underrepresent the actual number of incidents, particularly the less dramatic events (Jackson, Kelly, and Mitchell, n.d.: 292). There is at least a strong suspicion that this underrepresentation is not consistent across countries and times, despite the efforts of data collectors to overcome the problem.

A second caveat is that the data sets emphasize the quantitative and not the qualitative aspects of violence. They were constructed to enable researchers to pursue sophisticated statistical analyses. Consequently much emphasis is given to gathering precise figures preferably in interval form, which tell us little or nothing about the political significance or historical context of an incident (Manzer, 1974: 84, 102).

A third qualification concerns the multifarious problems associated with conceptualization. Researchers work from different concepts of violence on the basis of which they include or exclude material. Examples were given in chapter 1. The labelling of information can give the impression that different authors are addressing the same subject matter when this is not the case. Consider the varying kinds of events that have been subsumed under the rubric "Internal War":

Eckstein: riot, turmoil, terrorism, mutiny, assassination, coup d'état, guerrilla, civil war (1964: 3)

Bwy: terroristic act, continuing terrorism, guerrilla action, guerrilla warfare, anti-government demonstration, revolutionary invasion (1968: 207-9)

Hibbs: armed attack, assassination, deaths from intergroup violence (1973: 11)

Another point to be wary of is that many studies include non-violent conflict events within the subject matter. Among the comparisons we shall consider below is Gurr's two-fold classification of types of violence as Rebellion and Protest. Rebellion corresponds to his earlier (see the first section of this chapter for definitions) concepts of Conspiracy and Internal War combined, but Protest is an expansion of Turmoil to include non-violent events. "*Protest* arises from conflict over limited issues ... The typical forms of protest are political strikes, demonstrations, riots, and clashes" (1979: 50-1). Obviously those studies which do and those which do not include non-violent events are dealing with rather different topics.

Most of the cross-national compilations are limited in the number of years, the number of countries, or the types of violence for which they have collected data. There are, however, four broad-ranging data sets that we can use in comparing Canada to other nations:

1 *Eckstein* (1964: 12) defines "internal war" as "a kind of social force that is exerted in the process of political competition, deviating from previously shared norms, 'warlike' in character (that is, conducted practically without mutually observed normative rules), and involving the serious disruption of settled institutional patterns." Each country's score is derived from its total number of recorded events. The source is the *New York Times Index*. The years covered are 1946-59. The data, expanded to a larger group of countries (114) and with the distribution logarithmically normalized, are reproduced in Feierabends and Gurr (1972: 219-22).

2 The *Feierabend* data set covers some 8,000 events in 84 countries for the years 1948-65. Their dependent variable, political violence, includes Turmoil events (riots and demonstrations, boycotts against the government, political arrests, governmental actions against specific groups, and sabotage), Revolt events (martial law, coups d'état, and revolts), Guerrilla Warfare events (guerrilla warfare, assassinations), and Civil War events (civil war and executions). Sources are *Deadline Data on World Affairs* and *Encyclopaedia Britannica Yearbooks*. The events are weighted for intensity (the weights are derived from a Guttman scale) and then added together. The data are discussed in various publications; for example, Feierabends and Nesvold

(1969) and Feierabends and Gurr (1972). The Feierabends also report on political stability, a larger concept which includes such events as cabinet resignations in addition to political violence.

3 The original *Gurr* data set identifies some 1100 events in 114 countries for the years 1961-5. The dependent variable is civil strife which is defined as all collective, non-governmental attacks on persons or property occurring within national boundaries. "Non-governmental" includes attacks by regime agents if they stray beyond role norms (for example, mutinies and military coups). Symbolic attacks, such as political demonstrations and strikes, are also included. Turmoil events with less than 100 participants are excluded. Sources include the *New York Times*, *News Year*, and *Africa Digest*. Total magnitude of civil strife (TMCS) is calculated for each country, comprising logarithmically transformed measures of pervasiveness (participants per 100,000 population), intensity (casualties per 10 million population), and duration (total days of strife). The data have been extensively analysed and reported upon. See, for example, Gurr (1969); some of the data are reproduced in Feierabends and Gurr (1972: 213-15). Gurr later produced an enlarged data set covering 2200 events for the years 1961-70 in 87 nations (Gurr and Bishop, 1976; Gurr, 1979).

4 The Yale World Data Analysis Program has yielded the data sets on violence reported in the *World Handbook of Political and Social Indicators*. The first edition, edited by Russett et al. (1964), has a table on deaths from domestic group violence per 1,000,000 population, 1950-62, which covers 74 countries. The second edition, edited by Taylor and Hudson (1972), has a broadened time-frame (1948-67) and range of countries (136). It presents tables both on non-violent conflict events, including political strikes and anti-governmental demonstrations, and on violent ones: riots (violent demonstrations or disturbances "involving a large number of people and characterized by material damage or bloodshed"); armed attacks (acts of "violent political conflict carried out by an organized group with the object of weakening or destroying the power exercised by another organized group"); and number of deaths from domestic political violence. The basic source is the *New York Times Index*, supplemented by a number of more specialized sources. The Taylor and Hudson data have been extensively analysed by Hibbs (1973).

Users of cross-national data are well advised to keep the limitations of the data in mind and to read the fine print in the methodological appendixes. It is also important to select with care the nations with which Canada is to be compared. Naturally we want to know where Canada stands in relation to the total number of countries included in the data set, but it can be argued that it is not particularly meaningful to compare Canada with, say, Afghanistan, Bolivia, or Zaire.

To arrive at a subset of appropriate nations to compare with Canada, we need to look for countries similar in terms of level of economic development, form of government, and geocultural region. Typically, richer nations are among the least violent, no doubt partly because they have more resources with which to satisfy demands. Conversely, countries in the throes of development tend to be the most violent, perhaps because they have the widest gap between expectations and the ability to meet them (Feierabends and Nesvold, 1969: 653-9). Democracies also have low levels of violence, but not of conflict. Within them, the more deadly forms of violence are rendered otiose by the widespread acceptance of the basic social and political institutions, and the presence of peaceful means of protest. In contrast, autocracies successfully curtail the amount of protest, but when violence does break out it tends to be more deadly. Elitist nations are the most violent of all. Deadly conflict in democracies is generally associated with a heterogeneous population (Gurr, 1979: 59-61). Most advanced democracies are European or, like Canada, were settled by Europeans, and thus share a common geocultural region, but there are a few, such as Japan, in which the significance and pattern of violence have differed.

Seventeen nations are similar to Canada in level of economic development, form of government, and geocultural region. These will serve as our reference nations. In the following discussion, we shall keep a particular eye on those among them which, like Canada, have experienced ethnic or linguistic conflicts: Belgium, Israel, Switzerland, the United Kingdom, and the United States.

Table I presents the summary statistics that were devised to capture the overall incidence of public violence. Most of the western democracies fall below the median level of violence for the entire sample. Canada ranks neither among the most nor the least violent of the countries being compared. On all three data sets, five countries show themselves to be more violent than Canada (Belgium, France, Italy, the U.K., and the U.S.), while seven countries (Australia, Denmark, Netherlands, New Zealand, Norway, Sweden, and Switzerland) consistently show themselves to be less violent. Joining Canada in the middle ranks are Austria, Eire, Finland, Israel, and West Germany.

A perusal of table I suggests another factor that correlates with the incidence of violence: the size of a country's population. The small nations tend to cluster at the top and the larger ones (the U.S., West Germany, the U.K., Italy, and France) at the bottom of the table. Large countries not only have more incidents, their rates of violence (number of incidents per given unit of population) are higher. Plainly the larger countries embrace many more diverse and competing interest groups; their higher rates of violence may thus be a reflection of their complexity. It is significant that the smaller countries that do appear towards the bottom half of the table – Belgium, Israel, and Canada – all contain ethnically or linguistically divided populations.

TABLE 1
Levels of Public Violence in 18 Advanced Democracies

Data set	Eckstein		Feierabends		Gurr	
Years covered	1946-1959		1948-1965		1961-1965	
Nations in data set	114		84		114	
Concept measured	"Internal War"		"Political Violence"		"Total Magnitude of Civil Strife"	
	Australia	.00	Finland	0	Denmark	.0
	Sweden	.00	Denmark	1	Netherlands	.0
	Switzerland	.00	New Zealand	1	New Zealand	.0
	Denmark	.30	Netherlands	2	Norway	.0
	Netherlands	.48	Norway	3	Sweden	.0
	New Zealand	.48	Sweden	3	Switzerland	1.2
	Norway	.48	Australia	4	Finland	2.1
	CANADA	.60	Austria	7	Eire	2.3
	Austria	.70	Eire	7	Australia	2.6
	W. Germany	.70	Switzerland	7	Austria	3.1
	Finland	.85	Israel	8	W. Germany	4.6
	U.K.	1.11	CANADA	10	CANADA	4.9
	Belgium	1.20	U.K.	17	U.K.	5.4
	Eire	1.32	Italy	19	U.S.	10.2
	U.S.	1.61	W. Germany	20	Belgium	10.5
	Israel	1.77	Belgium	31	France	12.1
	France	1.80	France	95	Italy	12.3
	Italy	2.09	U.S.	97	Israel	14.0
Median for all nations in data set		1.34		41		7.7

Source: Feierabends and Gurr, 1972: 219-22; Graham and Gurr, 1969: 652; Graham and Gurr, 1969: 628-30.

Table 2 considers one measure of the intensity of violence, the number of people killed. At the top of the table again come the small, homogeneous nations where no deaths were recorded. Then there is a middle grouping, including Canada, where a low rate is observed. The final group – Italy, Israel, France, and the U.S. – has much higher rates, although the median for the entire sample shows these countries are still far from being the most lethal in the world. Once more we can see, in Gurr's data set, that all the smaller countries that did record some deaths (Belgium, Canada, and Israel) had heterogeneous populations.

Another dimension of violence is the form it takes. Assassination is one of the classic forms of violence for which there are extensive cross-national compilations. (The two main sets, the Feierabends' and Leiden's are described and discussed in Kirkham, Levy, and Crotty, 1970: ch. 3; the Leiden set covers the years 1918-68 but with a narrower range of events than

TABLE 2
Deaths from Public Violence in 18 Advanced Democracies

Data set	World Handbook		Gurr	
Years covered	1948-1967		1961-1970	
Nations in data set	136		87	
Concept measured	"Deaths from Domestic Violence"		"Conflict Deaths per 10 Million"	
	Australia	0	Australia	0.0
	Netherlands	0	Austria	0.0
	New Zealand	0	Denmark	0.0
	Norway	0	Eire	0.0
	Sweden	0	Finland	0.0
	Switzerland	0	Netherlands	0.0
	Eire	1	New Zealand	0.0
	Finland	4	Norway	0.0
	Austria	6	Sweden	0.0
	CANADA	8	Switzerland	0.0
	U.K.	9	Belgium	[some]
	W. Germany	10	W. Germany	0.3
	Belgium	10	U.K.	0.5
	Denmark	14	CANADA	1.5
	Israel	49	Italy	8.0
	Italy	109	Israel	11.8
	France	112	France	17.1
	U.S.	320	U.S.	18.3
Median for all nations in data set		131	21.0	

Source: Taylor and Hudson, 1972: 110–15; Gurr, 1979: 59–62.

the Feierabends' for 1948-67.) They show that, at least since the Second World War,[5] assassination is a relatively rare phenomenon in the 18 western democracies, with only France and the United States running counter to the trend. Canada's lone entry is the attempt by Chartier to bomb the House of Commons.

When considering the occurrence of great civil wars, rebellions, and revolutions, we find again that the western democracies have emerged more or less unscathed. Only France turns up with an entry under Gurr's 1961-5 "Internal War." Public violence has not recently torn our reference countries apart and claimed the lives of thousands as it has in Hungary, Algeria, Nigeria, Vietnam, Indonesia, and Cambodia.

Table 3 indicates that the violence that has characterized the 18 democracies has mainly been low-level Turmoil events. The World Handbook shows

5 But note that the period between the two world wars shows countries, such as the Netherlands, Norway, and Austria which emerged as remarkably peaceful in the data sets for the postwar years, having three or more assassinations.

TABLE 3
Forms of Public Violence in 18 Advanced Democracies

Data set	World Handbook		Gurr			Gurr	
Years covered	1948-1967		1961-1965			1961-1970	
Nations in data set	136		114			87	
Concept measured			Magnitude of:			Man-days per 100,000 of:	
	Riots	Armed attacks		(a) turmoil	(b) conspiracy	(a) protest	(b) rebellion
New Zealand	0	2	Denmark	.0	.0		
Norway	0	3	Netherlands	.0	.0		
Australia	3	8	New Zealand	.0	.0		
Switzerland	4	7	Norway	.0	.0		
Denmark	6	5	Sweden	.0	.0	950	0
Sweden	10	1	Switzerland	.0	1.2		
Finland	11	3	Finland	2.1	.0		
Netherlands	4	10	Australia	2.6	.0	500	0.1
Eire	7	42	Eire	2.3	1.2	100	70
Austria	36	25	W. Germany	4.6	.0	3,100	0
Belgium	58	34	Austria	2.5	2.3		
U.K.	82	45	CANADA	2.7	3.1	40	700
CANADA	29	113	U.K.	4.4	3.2	400	20
Israel	59	91	France	6.9	2.3	130,000	15,000
W. Germany	98	96	U.S.	10.2	2.3	5,400	250
Italy	310	249	Belgium	10.3	1.0		
France	127	550	Italy	7.3	1.8	22,100	1,300
U.S.	683	779	Israel	13.9	4.9	1,500	70
Median for all nations in data set	34	47		4.6	2.3	900	130

Source: Taylor and Hudson, 1972: 94-109; Feierabends and Gurr, 1972: 213-15; Gurr, 1979: 58-60.

these countries experiencing some 1500 spontaneous "riots" and some 2000 organized "armed attacks" between 1948 and 1967. But there are many deviations from this average ratio of three riots to four attacks. In particular, Canada recorded 29 riots and 113 attacks; by contrast, figures for the United States were 683 riots and 779 attacks. If we divide the American figures by ten to adjust roughly for population size, we find the Canadians with less than half as many riots as the Americans, but nearly double the attacks.

Canada's unusual position is equally apparent in the Gurr data. For 1961-70, the median in the 18 western democracies for man-days of participation per 100,000 population is 700 for "political protest" and 9 for "rebellion." For Canada, the figures are 40 for political protest and 700 for rebellion. This is a stunning anomaly. None of the other nine individual democracies for which Gurr gives figures has anything remotely similar to this pattern.

Looking at Gurr's earlier data set for 1961-5, we begin to understand the events that are contributing to Canada's unique configuration. Canada and Switzerland are the only democracies showing a higher score for "conspiracy" than for "turmoil." Again we can note the discrepancy between Canada's scores of 2.7 and 3.1 for Turmoil and Conspiracy respectively and those for the United States, 10.2 and 1.0. Presumably the activities of the Sons of Freedom and the FLQ are behind Canada's high Conspiracy score. The 200 Freedomites who engaged in "black work" and the 100 or so actively violent "felquistes" have given the country an atypical profile among the western democracies.

It is difficult to get much sense of the development over time of Canadian violence in relation to that of other countries. We concluded in the previous section that the 1960s were much more violent years in Canada than were the 1950s. Yet this was true for most countries. Some 60 per cent of all the deaths from political violence over 20 years recorded by Taylor and Hudson (1972: 110-11) fell in the five-year period of 1963-7. The issue, then, is whether the Canadian increase in the sixties was any sharper than that experienced elsewhere. That it may have been is faintly suggested by table 1 which shows Canada ranking in the eighth position on the Eckstein data set for the fifties, but falling to twelfth position on the other two data sets which concern the sixties. More direct confirmation comes from the Taylor and Hudson data. The 18 western democracies under consideration experienced 63 per cent of their riots, 68 per cent of their armed attacks, and 72 per cent of their deaths in the second half of the twenty-year period. For Canada the concentration in this later period is even more marked; the corresponding percentages are 79, 80, and 100 per cent. Evidently the rising incidence of Canadian violence during the sixties was a reflection of a world-wide trend, but in Canada the factors behind the trend seemed to have been experienced particularly acutely, or there were additional factors in play.

Once we get beyond incidence, intensity, and form to the other dimensions of violence, cross-national comparisons become harder to find. Gurr's comparative essay on political violence (1969; 1979) does present data on the class origins of the violent, their organizational base, issues, and targets, but gives no separate figures for Canada. If we compare Gurr's results with those from Frank and Kelly's (1977) study of collective violence in Ontario and Quebec or with our own findings – a methodologically dubious procedure – we could infer the following four conclusions.

First, the distribution of the violent by social class is much the same in Canada as in other European countries. Gurr (1979: 65) shows the middle classes participating in 75 per cent of his protest events, while Frank and Kelly (1977: 153) show them appearing in 77 per cent of demonstrations. Where Canada may differ from other European countries is in the loyalty to the regime of its police, soldiers, and officials. Gurr (1979: 66) indicates that over a quarter of European rebellions involved dissident political classes.

Second, the organizational base of dissidents in Canada is probably broadly similar to that in comparable countries. Gurr (1979: 67) finds protest and rebellion in advanced or democratic countries most frequently (around 30 per cent) mobilized by open political parties or interest groups, followed by clandestine political groups, communal or territorial groups, and economic groups (around 20 per cent each). During the 1960s Canada was evidently not the only country to have its politics enlivened by the violent activities of clandestine or communal groups.

Third, in Canada and the other advanced or democratic countries, issues tend most often to be limited and specific. However, Gurr (1979: 69-71) reports that motives in these countries are often mixed; between a quarter and a third of political dissidence involved social and economic issues as well. The latter he attributes to politically active trade unions and communal groups. My impression is that the proportion of mixed-context incidents is probably even higher in Canada.

And fourth, the distribution of targets in Canada may be somewhat different than in the other European nations. Gurr (1969: 592) finds that "political actors" formed the target in 83 per cent of his European turmoil incidents and property in 39 per cent of them. Frank and Kelly (1977: 149) also show people to be the preponderant target in their Ontario and Quebec collective violence – in 77 per cent of the incidents – but find violence directed more often against property – 53 per cent.

CONCLUSION

Most of the "peculiarities" of Canadian public violence are thus not peculiar to this country at all. In many respects Canada is typical of advanced democracies. It falls in the middle of listings by incidence and intensity. With some minor exceptions, it would seem to follow the general pattern for social class participation, organizational base, issues, and targets. The possible exceptions are the loyalty of its public servants, the prevalence of mixed-context incidents, and the more frequent attacks on property.

Yet Canada was not completely typical. No other advanced democracy showed such a sharp increase in violence during the 1960s. And no other advanced democracy experienced so much conspiratorial violence relative to the amount of turmoil. These are peculiarities that require exploration.

The myth of Canada as the peaceable kingdom may lead one to expect the country to be among the least violent nations of all. Such expectations are clearly not supported by the facts. However, they are unrealistic given both the size of the population (the sixth most populous nation of the 18), and its heterogeneity. No large or heterogeneous country was among the most peaceful. We also have to take into account the time period under discussion. Manzer (1974: 83-4) points out that public violence in Canada has been essentially episodic, so that there might be "a false sense of security if the period examined were 1950-60, or an unwarranted pessimism if the period were 1960-70."

Another point about the peaceable kingdom myth is that most Canadians do not justify it by some absolute standard or by comparing their country with the 17 reference nations we have used. Rather they compare their country to the United States. Although the two countries are similar in many respects, it seems clear that they have experienced different patterns of violence. If the United States is taken as the norm, then Canada by comparison does appear on the whole to be remarkably peaceful. Why ostensibly similar nations should have violence that differs in incidence, intensity, and form is a question we shall have to explore further.

In short, the myth of the peaceable kingdom receives both support and challenge from international comparisons. On the one hand, Canada cannot be regarded as atypically peaceful if it is compared to the other western democracies. Even so, the data sets cover only a limited number of years and usually include Canada's most violent years; thus they may leave a false impression of the amount of violence in the country's historical record. On the other hand, if Canada is compared to the United States or to all the nations of the world, it can be considered relatively peaceful. On balance, then, there is some justification for looking for factors that would account for the relative absence of violence in this country. Peacefulness does appear to be the rule and violence the exception, although the numerous incidents mentioned in this and the preceding chapter show that such a judgment is less clear-cut than the proponents of the peaceable kingdom myth might welcome.

CHAPTER FOUR

The Meaning of Violence

What goes on in the world of objective reality affects our mental state, and this subjective response leads to actions impinging on the world around us. The complex relationship of individual to society tends to be taken for granted or dismissed as uninteresting. Students of violence generally focus on the objective realm, examining such variables as the socio-economic status of the violent, the condition of the times, and the resources available to governments and dissidents. Even when using psychologically based theories, they tend to infer the existence of a sense of relative deprivation or frustration in people's minds from a study of objective conditions because this is the only way they can test their theories and because they assume the subjective-objective link is non-problematic. Other scholars deliberately play down the subjective realm because they regard it as wholly subordinate to the objective and consequently incapable of providing any independent contribution to our understanding of violence.

Nevertheless there are several features of the subjective realm that, I believe, do merit consideration. Society imposes certain meanings on our subject matter. Our own prejudices and the prejudices of the observers whose accounts we must rely upon combine to influence our interpretations. This is of course true of all subjects, but violence seems to be especially prone to divergent interpretations.

In this chapter I shall examine the social-psychological mechanisms individuals employ to make sense of the world around them. How people interpret an incident affects their reaction to it – whether they will join in the fray, call for its suppression, or dismiss it as irrelevant. In particular I shall be concerned with how people use the word violence and how they determine whether an incident is an issue of public importance or a case of private deviance.

CONSTRUCTING THE SOCIAL REALITY OF VIOLENCE

The first chapter looked at attempts academics have made to define violence, and the criteria employed were those of academics: Could a particular definition be easily used in a study? Could it be applied to different cultures? Did it distinguish related concepts? The chapter concluded that the basic, unelaborated definition of violence (behaviour that results in physical injury to people and damage to property) would best serve our purposes. However one criterion the basic definition failed to meet was its approximation to everyday usage. This is because everyday usage is itself inconsistent. On some occasions actions are said to be violent when no injuries or damage result. On other occasions, acts that do produce injuries or damage are not called violent.

While such variations may be confusing, they are not arbitrary. Rather we find that people do not call acts violent if they sympathize with the actor and his aims and if they consider his acts to be legitimate ones. For example, many people value the maintenance of law and order. They therefore avoid labelling the physical injuries inflicted by police as violence and use in its place more positive or neutral terms such as "force" or "law enforcement."

Conversely, when there is no sympathy for the actor and his acts are considered illegitimate, his actions are commonly labelled violent even when no physical injury is involved. An example of Canadians seeing those they distrust as violent is the description of the mainly peaceful Winnipeg General Strike that was carried in the *Toronto Star* of 7 June 1919: "Lawlessness and disorder are rampant throughout the city all day and every day. Men and women are wantonly assaulted upon the streets. Men, women and children are attacked and threatened while going about their lawful avocations" (cited in Hopkins, 1920: 471).

Often enough the question of what is or is not violence arises in mutual recriminations between contending parties. The standard belief is that our friends are acting in pure self-defence. Establishing in what ways the other side is the aggressor can so extend the meaning of the word violence that it becomes virtually synonymous with all that is wrong with the world. Consider the following taken from an exchange between Conor Cruise O'Brien and Paul O'Dwyer, in which the latter writes (*New York Review of Books*, 2 December 1971: 34-5):

It is obvious that your definition of causative violence and mine have come to differ of late. Violence is the treatment of your fellow man with derision and contempt. Violence is claiming him to be inferior. Violence is denying him a job because of his affiliations – political or religious. Violence is depriving his child of food or shelter. Violence is a political and social system which poisons the mind of a child against his fellow man. Violence is the segregation of a child in school or at play and sowing the seeds of bigotry and the consequent debilitating cancer of hate. Violence is a hell of a lot more than an IRA man on the roof of a building under Derry's walls while the Anglicans' protectors move in their armor to teach the natives another lesson.

Direct evidence of the impact of sympathies on usage of the word violence emerges from the study of Blumenthal et al. (1972). In it they asked an all-male sample which actions from a list of nine items were examples of violent behaviour. As the authors (1972: 74) remark on some of their findings, "in view of the dictionary meaning of the word, it is curious that only 35 percent of American men defined 'police shooting looters' as violence, and only 56 percent defined 'police beating students' in this manner." A semantic differential test reveals that all the respondents are working with much the same definition of violence. It is just that they apply it variantly, depending on their sympathy for the group at issue. For example, those who take a generally dim view of students, in contrast to more sympathetic respondents, would tend to define as violence activities like draft-card burning but not the actions taken by police against students.

Blumenthal et al. (1972: 77-80) also note their respondents' general tendency to classify items involving the police in the opposite direction to the protest items. Either the police actions or the protest ones are called violent, but not both. The authors suggest that the issue of legitimacy lies behind this pattern. Thus the respondents who regard the state as illegitimate call the actions of the state's agents violent, but not the actions of the protesters who would change the state. Conversely, the respondents for whom the state is legitimate assume that police actions are also legitimate and hence non-violent, while dissent is illegitimate and labelled violent.

There is another reason for the variable use of the word violence besides its normative connotations. Behaviour that is nowadays defined as violence is almost automatically subsumed under the category of political violence in the sense that a government is expected to be concerned with it. If we regard the behaviour as a social problem we tend to label it violent; if we do not regard it as socially problematic and so requiring the government's attention, we tend to avoid classifying it as violence. The point is brought out by Currie (1971: 457-8) in his critique of the Eisenhower Commission's final report:

What is astonishing about this chapter [on violent crime] is its implication that the routine use of violence to deal with problems is confined to the urban lower class and particularly lower-class youth. This is a matter of conventional political definitions being transformed into misleading sociological generalizations. The government uses violence on a massive scale to deal with its Asian difficulties; the police use it routinely at home; but only when ghetto kids ... use it does violence become a "social problem" requiring the establishment of presidential commissions.

In short, we tend to call an act violent if we have no sympathy for the perpetrator, if we regard the act as illegitimate, and if we believe something should be done about it. These tendencies need to be recognized because a number of consequences flow from our choice of definition. There is the obvious one of bestowing a pejorative label on acts we disapprove of. There are also some more subtle consequences: labelling an act violent is a call to action to eradicate it, an attempt to persuade the world that the act can no longer be tolerated. Labelling two or more acts violent tells us that they are similar in kind and should be judged by the same standards. The FLQ, for instance, justified its terrorism by demanding that "Anglo-Saxon violence" (referring to the socio-economic structure that left Francophones disadvantaged relative to Anglophones) be weighed in the same balance as its own acts. Finally, the way we define violence determines what we can say about the characteristics of violent behaviour, when violence is justifiable, who is violent, and why. An alternative set of definitions could give us a whole new subject matter.⟩

So far we have talked about isolated individuals constructing their own meaning of violence. But individuals do not operate in isolation. They are influenced by others, and by some people in particular since the capacity to influence behaviour and perceptions is unequally distributed in every society. As Skolnick (1969: 4) explains:

The kinds of acts that become classified as "violent," and, equally important, those which do not become so classified, vary according to who provides the definition and who has superior resources for disseminating and enforcing his definitions. The most obvious example of this is the way, in a war, each side typically labels the other side as the aggressor and calls many of the latter's violent acts atrocities. The definition of the winner usually prevails.

Governments especially play a key role in providing public definitions. By their actions and pronouncements they can lend authority to a particular interpretation against which other groups can compete only with great difficulty, providing of course the government still commands respect (Turner, 1969: 827; Edelman, 1971: 7; the perceptions of governments are discussed further in chapter 9).

⟨Pronouncements by influential people reflect the definitions that prevail in a given society. These conventional definitions provide the shared meanings people need to understand each other and carry on a social life. The conventional definition of violence comprises that subset from the many kinds of injurious behaviours which most people in a society consider to be illegitimate, deviant, and a problem about which something needs to be done. Such definitions are part and parcel of people's values; and just as values may be self-interested, contested, and variant over time and place, so too may conventional definitions.⟩

Conventional definitions are never totally self-interested or arbitrarily imposed by a ruling-class conspiracy. Rather they are shared meanings which necessarily involve a measure of consensus, although self-interest undoubtedly does play a part. How big a part will vary from one society to another, although we can generally anticipate that the people with the greatest capacity to influence opinion – high-status groups and governments – will use their capacity to exclude their own injurious acts from the conventional definition. Students of violence who unthinkingly accept a conventional definition risk studying only the actions of lower-class or marginal groups.

In open societies, especially, one can expect to find challenges to the conventional definition. Challenging groups call into question the legitimacy of existing practices and make one reconsider words and ways of thinking that always have been taken for granted. In Canada today, for example, some argue that the criminal justice system is no longer legitimate and that the injurious acts of police, judges, and jailers should be labelled as public violence. Others would consider violent those acts of manufacturers that injure people and damage property – acts such as creating unsafe working conditions, polluting the atmosphere, casually disposing of toxic wastes, and putting unsafe products on the market.

A group challenging traditional perceptions seeks to sway public opinion to its interpretation. It is trying to set the agenda for political action by defining areas of social life that are illegitimate and that can and should be tolerated no longer. A government confronted by an increasingly powerful group of this sort is in a particularly awkward situation when the group takes its stand by challenging the conventional definition of violence. A government is expected to protect people and their property from violence. If it does not constrain the irresponsible manufacturer to mend his ways, the challenging group can argue that the government itself is no longer legitimate since it is apparently incapable of performing the most elementary of its functions.

Conventional definitions may appear discouragingly immovable to a challenging group and while there is no doubt that, once established, they are resistant to change, it is also true that they are not carved in stone. As we shall see in the next chapter, definitions of what is illegitimate violence evolve over long periods and vary from one culture to another. Thus the student of violence who relies on a conventional definition should also be aware that it expresses the values prevailing in one specific society.

"Conventional definition" and "challenging definition" are only terms to describe patterns of usage and, as such, we cannot say one definition is better than another. Ultimately, however, we have to decide whose definition to use in delimiting our subject matter. Whatever the choice, it will have far-reaching effects on what, in fact, will be studied. My choice has been to stick to the conventional Canadian definition of violence. It is the dominant one in society, reflecting what the elite and a majority of Canadians mean when they speak of violence. The choice needs to be a made explicit, however, so that we can be sensitive to the limitations of whatever definition is selected.

One reason Canadians can talk about their peaceable kingdom with an air of conviction is that they exclude many injurious forms of behaviour from their reckoning. The irresponsible manufacturer; unethical and incompetent doctors, lawyers, and engineers; transport companies and building contractors who disregard safety regulations; witnesses who perjure themselves; judges who sentence certain classes of offenders to particular institutions; policemen who use "force" to do their job; politicians who vote for capital punishment or cutbacks in programs for the desperately needy – all are performing acts that result in physical injuries and damage to property. Yet they are not conventionally defined as violent people. If they were, not only would we be studying a broader and rather different range of human behaviour, but also the notion of Canada as a peaceable kingdom would be utterly untenable.

CONFLICTING PERCEPTIONS OF VIOLENCE

Besides attaching different meanings to violence, people also arrive at different perceptions of what is going on in the incidents they do recognize to be violent. They do this by manipulating the information available to them to bring it into line with their preconceptions. In some cases available information may be rejected as irrelevant ("I don't need to know what slogans the rioters are chanting; my past experience tells me that all rioters are just out to make trouble"); in other cases preconceptions may be so powerful that they twist information beyond recognition ("I can see that the rioters are half-starved, but I know that they are really the willing agents of a foreign power"); and in yet other cases the information itself may be so sketchy that the individual is forced to fall back on his own resources to make sense of it ("I heard there was a riot last night; I suppose that agitators have been at work again"). The subject of violence seems to be a good breeding ground for divergent perceptions. There are a number of reasons why this should be so.

In the first place, there is the tendency to place a favourable interpretation on the actions of participants with whom sympathies lie. They are seen in the best possible light, while the other side to the conflict is assessed harshly. The possibility of "neutral" perception is further impeded by the very nature of violence. Violence represents conflict at its starkest, when issues have been brought to a head, and opposing parties are already clearly delineated. Such elemental conflict acts as an invitation to all the world to take sides.

Divergent perceptions may also arise from imperfect and contradictory information. Governments may impose news blackouts for one reason or another. Even if the flow of information is not artificially curtailed, chaotic events are a poor environment for information-gathering. Rumours fly, sources cannot be located for checking, witnesses are hysterical, free movement is impeded, and it is difficult to collate information so as to provide an overall picture.

Another reason for varying perceptions of violence lies in the emotional condition of the observer of violence. An incident will all too often foster a sense of anxiety and insecurity in an observer. According to Allport (1964: 303):

Anxious people are distrustful, apprehensive and insecure in handling even simple percepts. Postman and Bruner have discovered a kind of "perceptual recklessness" among persons under stress: such persons seem to jump at premature hypotheses and demand a definiteness in the outer world that it may not in fact possess.

People feel threatened by violence not only because they fear for their lives and property, but also because, as Jervis (1968: 475) puts it, "actors tend to see the behavior of others as more centralized, disciplined, and coordinated than it is." That violent behaviour is very often the unintentional product of chance occurrences, and that the violent may be internally divided and command few resources, are factors apparently difficult to grasp. People tend to assume instead that the violence is an intended element of a sinister plot.

Finally, violence of crisis proportions may lead to conflicting perceptions if some observers opt to suspend their individual judgments in favour of a blind acceptance of official interpretations of an incident. Edelman (1971: 97) points out that, "where people are baffled by complex and threatening events they cannot control, they need to believe that the highest official of the state is both benevolent and able to cope." As well, Coser (1956: 87-95) notes the demand for social cohesion in the face of external threat. In such an atmosphere the critical evaluation of available information will be subordinated to the need to close ranks to meet the menace.

There are several features of violent incidents that can attract conflicting perceptions. One is the type of violence that is occurring. Despite the best efforts of typologically minded social scientists, words like "riot" and "disorder," "rebellion" and "revolution," are used in everyday life with an exasperating disregard for the niceties of definition. The 1830 Swing riots in England were variously labelled by contemporaries as, among other things, insurrections, a Jacquerie, a vile conspiracy, riots, mobbing, outrages and outrageous proceedings, commotions, disorder and disorderly acts, disturbance, turbulence, excesses, illegal/tumultuous/riotous assemblies, breaches of the peace, pillage, and "the Horrid Attempts of some Diabolical Miscreants to injure Property and produce Confusion in this Country" (Hobsbawm and Rudé, 1969) – all of which together provide a fine illustration of the fecundity of the English language in this area.

Yet if the numerous choices available to the would-be classifier contribute to the looseness with which the terms are used, the confusion is further

---

1 Numerous foreign words for violent events have also been incorporated into the English language, for example, putsch, coup d'état, jacquerie, and guerrilla warfare.

compounded by the varying degree of undesirability attached to particular words by different groups. Grimshaw (1968) has analysed the various labels given the American ghetto riots of the 1960s. One set of labels, which he identifies as neutral and conciliatory, comprises words like "disorder" and "disturbance." Another set emphasizes the legal aspects of the situation: "lawlessness" and "insurrection." And a third set stresses the seriousness of events: "revolt," "rebellion," or "warfare." A desire to play down the riots produces words from the first set; a desire to stress their criminal aspects produces words from the second set; and a desire to see the riots as significant public events produces words from the last. Thus, black respondents who regarded the Watts riot with favour preferred to call it "a 'rebellion' or used some other word denoting a planned movement toward a social goal and disliked the connotations of the word 'riot'" (Edelman, 1971: 30). Sympathy with the rioters also led commentators in the radical *Monthly Review* to enlarge on the significance of the violence: the riots were termed "colonial rebellions," "risings of the oppressed," and "revolution," which interpretation according to Fogelson (1968: 32) is "as much a vision as a definition."

People also fail to see the events that occur within a given incident in the same way. There does appear to be a systematic bias in eyewitness accounts towards exaggerating the amount and seriousness of the violence that is taking place. An example is provided by the wild overestimates of sniper fire in the American violence of the sixties that later investigations have shown to be largely groundless. In the Swing riots, "a desperate gang amounting to upwards of 200 persons" turned out afterwards to have comprised 20, and with later recruits, 50 men (Hobsbawm and Rudé, 1969: 99). This phenomenon is no surprise to psychologists who have found that "numbers, time estimations, and any form of quantification represent a major kind of 'unstable item', highly susceptible to omission or distortion" (McKellar, 1968: 147).

Over and above this general bias, it seems that those who are fearful of the violence and unsympathetic towards the violent will be the most likely to exaggerate the degree of disruption. In doing so, they justify their own fear and any harsh countermeasures against the violent. More surprisingly perhaps, observers are also prone to exaggeration when they sympathize unreservedly with the cause of the violent. In this way they seek to stress the political importance of what the violent are doing. Clearly if one believes that grievous injustice stalks the land, a minor demonstration will not serve as a sufficient expression of protest against it. To take a Canadian example, the anti-conscriptionist *Le Devoir* estimated the numbers involved in a 1915 recruiting meeting that broke up in violence at 12,000, while the pro-government *Gazette* reported there were no more than 1,500 (Armstrong, 1967: 111).

Who is involved in an incident of violence might be expected to be an easily verifiable matter of fact; nevertheless, this too seems to be particularly susceptible to conflicting perceptions. Four types of people tend to turn up more frequently in accounts of violence than the available evidence warrants. First are criminals, the assumption being that decent law-regarding folk would not engage in violence. Second are fools, since reasonable men are believed incapable of engaging in such desperate business. Included in this category are the ignorant, the drunk, the mob hysterics, and those easily led astray such as youths. Third are agitators. Dangerous conspirators and demagogues are considered necessary to rouse normally peaceful people. Fourth are strangers or foreigners, on the assumption that the local population would not engage in such activities. For an illustration, we can take the assessment of the Quebec City riots of 1918 by one of the members elected from the area, Sir Wilfrid Laurier (House of Commons, *Debates*, 5 April 1918: 392):

[The incident] was caused by a secret association of some kind ... The origin of that association is not in the city of Quebec. The instigators of the trouble are not Quebec men ... That the movement was organized is undoubted. Who were behind it? ... the same gang which attempted to terrorize the city of Montreal last summer. This gang was composed of the scum of the city of Montreal[,] such scum as is to be found in every large city and is ready to create disturbance in every civil commotion. The leadership of it were penitentiary birds, convicts ...

An equally extravagant example comes from the Court of Inquiry into the Kinmel Park demobilization camp riot of 1919 which found "a few men of bad character ... deliberately took advantage of the discontent and unrest ..." The group included "a number of 'jail birds' recruited by the British Mission in the Western States. These were soon joined by a number of Russians, other foreigners and some French Canadians, men more easily excited than the average Canadian" (cited in D. Morton, 1980: 353, 352).

If the facts of the violence are subject to varying perceptions, so too are the causes found for it. The identification of who is involved is generally associated with some idea of how the violence was caused. Thus the presumed presence of criminals, agitators, and strangers in the American riots of the 1960s gave rise to the celebrated "riff-raff theory" of riot causation (Fogelson and Hill, 1968). In particular the identification of conspirators working among the violent offers an immediate explanation of why the violence occurred. According to Edelman (1971: 96), "perhaps the fundamental tendency in political perception is to attribute unwelcome developments to the deliberate planning of particular people." Edelman and Simon's (1969) study of the impact of President Kennedy's assassination provides a fine illustration of the potential for conspiracy to crop up in the search for causes and goals. The Russian press blamed the FBI or "ultra-right-wing fascist and racist circles" and saw the murder as an attempt to stir up anti-Soviet and anti-Cuban "hysteria." An African leader also linked the assassination to American racism. "The Arab press identified Jack Ruby as Jewish and reasoned from this fact that Zionists were behind the assassination." A Cuban exile blamed the machinations of Castro. As the authors conclude (1969: 218), "what is impressive is the unlikely variety of groups on the world political scene which were able to interpret the event so as to pin responsibility on their classic enemies."

Clearly, if violence is regarded as evil, it will be all too easy to attribute it to a group mistrusted on other grounds. For example, in 1918 a Canadian official associated a political group with violence and two of the classic enemies of the time: "[the Social Democratic Party is] the party of the Red Revolution, advocating submission to German might, subversion of all constitutional government, robbery of personal property, and the accomplishment of its avowed aims of sabotage and the general strike" (cited in Robin, 1968: 166).

By contrast, those who accept violence tend not to stress the enmity or the distance between the perceiver and the violent. It is no longer "they," but "we" who are involved (Grimshaw, 1959: 314). Thus Brinton (1965: 79-86) notes that the supporters of a revolution maintain that it involves the rising of the entire nation against oppression; thus they deny any division between themselves and the violent. By contrast opponents of the revolution attribute it to "a series of interlocking plots initiated by small but determined groups of malcontents."

Observers may also arrive at different conclusions on whether the violence is justifiable. Not surprisingly, one group that is particularly apt to allow violence comprises the violent themselves, and in this case justification becomes self-justification. According to Edelman (1971: 107-8):

Once a group of people have committed violent or aggressive acts they develop shared perceptions of a kind that justify their actions. Blacks who have rioted or supported violence become all the more highly sensitive to past aggressions and injustices and very likely exaggerate these at times ... More readily documented are the *post hoc* exaggerations of law enforcement officials who come to perceive their violent actions as justified by aggressions of restive minorities ... Police on a riot scene invariably perceive sniping after they have fired their own guns.

We can expect not only the participants but those who identify with the participants to justify the violence. Because violence is generally regarded as improper, the violence of our allies must be excused. Either they were provoked into attack by injustice, or they were acting out of self-defence, or they were employing an appropriate means of securing legitimate goals. Thus, newspaper accounts of an attack on Anglophone executives by a Francophone employee varied according to the papers' viewpoint. French-language papers reported the assailant to be "a nice, quiet guy," a victim of discrimination, goaded by oppressive bosses who had fired him. English-language papers, on the other hand, found no justification for the assault; they noted instead that the assailant was an ex-convict and encouraged sympathy for the victims by providing details of their home life (McKenzie, 1971: 20).

A final potential area of disagreement arises with the assessment of an incident's significance. One event can be all but ignored or treated as a case of private deviancy, while another captures the attention of the nation. The actual scope and intensity of the violence is not necessarily related to the amount of attention it attracts. Indeed, Jackson, Kelly, and Mitchell (n.d.: 263) conclude "categorically" from their content analysis of newspaper coverage of Ontario collective violence between 1965 and 1975 that "there is no relation between the magnitude of the incidents and how the press chooses to handle them." On average, incidents involving university-related issues each received 289 square inches of total coverage, compared to 265 for those with domestic political isses and 194 for those with foreign political issues. Considerably less space (98 square inches) was devoted to economic incidents, where the violence was often the most intense, while "issueless" ones (vandalism, motorcycle-gang rampages, brawls) received the least attention (54 square inches).

The status of the violent would appear to be one factor affecting significance. The more middle-class and the fewer working-class participants there are in an incident, the more attention the middle-class media devote to it. More generally, perceptions of significance seem to turn on a judgment of how avoidable and exceptional the violence is. If we expect motorcycle gangs to rampage or picketlines to degenerate into scuffles, such behaviour is dismissed as unremarkable. Extraordinary public events are those which upset our comfortable expectations of predictable behaviour from others.

Breton (1972: 50) points out that undefined situations "provide an opportunity for interested groups to structure them to their advantage." An incident may become significant if numerous and powerful groups, even if not directly involved in the violence, nevertheless feel that their interests are affected and that they can "win" or "lose" by it. Thus he attributes the high degree of significance accorded the FLQ kidnappings, not simply to the status of the victims, but also to the opportunities they gave to varied groups on the federal, provincial, and municipal scene to try their hand at shaping events. Sons of Freedom incidents, by comparison, have never been seen to be in the same league, even though the Freedomites have carried on a much longer and eventful campaign and attracted far more heroic measures of governmental coercion than did the FLQ. Few Canadians apparently have felt their interests to be at stake or figured out how to turn Freedomite violence to their advantage.

SOCIAL BASES OF CONFLICTING
PERCEPTIONS

As the preceding sections have shown, two observers of the same incident can come to quite different conclusions on whether violence is occurring, who is involved, what kind of violence is at issue, how extensive the destruction is, what caused the violence, whether there is any justification for it, and how significant it is. These conflicting perceptions originate with the different values held by observers, by which they arrange the available information into patterns that are meaningful to them. Since these values are socially learned, we should expect to find systematic perceptual biases stemming from the observers' social position. The illustrations used have suggested how this comes about.

The crucial factor in shaping perceptions appears to be the extent to which the observer identifies with the violent. The previous section provided repeated examples of people manipulating the information they have so as to excuse the behaviour of those with whom they sympathize and to condemn the behaviour of those whom they dislike. Thus, an observer who identifies with the violent is apt to justify their actions by seeing them as everyday people provoked into violence by unredressed grievances or by the violence of others; an observer without empathetic ties to the violent is apt to perceive them as monsters of destruction, acting without justifiable cause. The former will stress the public aspects of the violence; the latter will tend to define it as private in nature.

But who is going to sympathize with whom? People's attitudes to others are obviously highly variable, since prejudices are partly formed by each person's unique experiences. Also, for various psychological reasons, some individuals view groups outside their own through a screen of prejudice while others are more open to people of different backgrounds. None the less, despite such individual variations, attitudes can be linked to objective social conditions. To the extent that these can be determined, we can make some generalizations about which groups of people are likely to view with sympathy or hostility the violence of other groups.

In the first place, sympathetic identification with the violent is more probable when the observer and the violent share membership in a common group. Thus, when the violent can be characterized in terms of some such associative principle as ethnicity or occupation, the members of the same group may well take a benign view of their actions. Contrariwise, when the violent are characterized as belonging to a different group than the observer's, or as not belonging to any particular group, such as a "faceless" mob, or when the observer shares common ties with the victims rather than with the violent, then the probability of sympathetic identification with the violent is reduced.

Second, sympathetic identification also seems unlikely the more the behaviour of the violent is seen as a threat to the observer. An anxious observer will interpret an incident so as to justify the immediate restraint of the violent. Anxiety may be occasioned by such factors as geographic proximity to the violence, physical vulnerability (for example, the fears of the elderly), membership in a traditional scapegoat group, or in one that is currently under attack. As well, some acts of violence arouse more alarm than others. The assassination of a head of state, for example, will seem more alarming than the assassination of a municipal official.

Third, the chances of sympathetic identification with the violent probably diminish as the personal cost of accommodating them is seen to increase. Personal costs may take the form of higher taxes to pay for social reforms, changes in the workplace to create employment for the violent, other adjustments in, for example, schools and housing to improve the social condition of the violent, and changes in values, behaviour, political power, and relative social status. Such costs are not borne evenly. Generally those closest to the violent in social standing are called upon to make the largest adjustments. Those finding the cost of accommodating the violent unacceptably high will probably fail to see remediable grievances behind the violence, relying instead on an interpretation that stresses the deviant or inherently violent characteristics of the group involved. Those who are not called upon to bear the brunt of the called-for social adjustments may be more willing to accept that the violent are reacting to genuine grievances. Sometimes it is the victim who is seen as trying to impose unacceptable costs, such as a government collecting new taxes or an employer in the throes of an efficiency drive. In these cases, sympathy will tend to go to the violent.

While these three propositions are analytically distinct, in practice they often run together. Thus a person may have a distorted perception of an incident because he shares membership in the same group as the victims, is fearful that he too will soon be a victim, and sees appeasement of the violent in terms of costs to himself. However, working singly or in combination, propositions like these can be used to understand the distinctive reactions to violence of various groups in society. Their use is illustrated in the following, brief examples.

One group whose reactions to violence have been frequently commented upon are the "hard hats": the white union members in the United States who came out strongly against the black and student activism of the sixties. Their unsympathetic perceptions of incidents involving blacks and students are readily understandable; their job security and neighbourhoods were most affected by integration plans and their wage packets hardest hit, proportionately, by increased taxes for social reforms. Costs can be psychic as well as material. Many of the "values expressed by student protesters are directly destructive of the beliefs by which the hard hats maintain their self-esteem in the face of limiting economic and social realities" (Blumenthal et al., 1972:

12). Further, as Turner (1969: 819-20) points out, sympathetic identification with students is unlikely to come from those who are by and large of lower social status and who therefore have difficulty empathizing with the professed troubles of people apparently better off than themselves.

In contrast to the "hard hat" is the "liberal reformer" who, secure in a middle-class environment, is more ready to interpret violence in terms of justifiable protest against grievances. Such a perception costs the liberal reformer little in psychic, social, political, or economic terms. (Indeed, its acceptance by government along with a program of social reform could be a gain as research and administrative jobs are opened up; moreover the liberal's self-esteem may be enhanced by a feeling of his or her own benevolence and enlightenment.) The protest interpretation also serves to reassure the liberal reformer that only a few social adjustments are required to stop the violence, that apart from some institutional malfunctions the society is basically sound, and that there is no need for any real shifts of power that might damage his or her own position (Kopkind, 1971: 384). As well, by defining violence as an expression of protest, the liberal reformer explains an incident without actually legitimizing the resort to violence. This fits well with the reformer's probable distaste for violent means since, as Silver (1968: 152) observes, "no group has been more unconditionally committed to this development [in standards of public order], its maintenance, and its enhancement, than the professional, upper, and middle classes concerned with liberal democracy and social meliorism."

Policemen – and soldiers as well to the extent they are called upon to play a role in civil disorders – are an occupational group whose attitudes are particularly important in a study of violence. Police officers have little sympathy for those who directly threaten their lives. From the nature of their work, policemen are often socially isolated from the local community, and this, along with an *esprit de corps*, fosters their sense of identity as a group. Thus they may identify strongly with the victim when that victim is a fellow policeman who has been assaulted or killed, but not with a victim who has been subjected to police violence. Police can justify their own resort to violence in a number of ways. Among the most important justifications is the fact that society entrusts them with violent means to carry out their tasks; their own violence is thereby legitimated, and there is a tendency for it to be taken as the most efficacious means of handling problematic situations (Westley, 1953: 35).

Women make up another important group. Because women are often physically weaker than men, they might be expected to see violence as an inappropriate and ineffective means of resolving conflict. Further devaluing

2 For instance, the advocacy by Canadian police chiefs and police unions for a return to capital punishment as the only effective means of deterring certain violent crimes.

violence for them may be norms regarding "womanly" behaviour that stress gentleness, forebearance, conciliation, and the provision of a loving and peaceful home environment for husband and children. However, we have little research on women's perceptions of violence to guide us. One of the few studies to report male and female responses separately (Campbell and Schuman, 1968) shows women having somewhat less "hawkish" perceptions than men. Otherwise there is little difference between the sexes on most questions – a reflection perhaps of women simply accepting the dominant male interpretation of violence.

Women on the receiving end of violence, such as rape victims and battered wives, have traditionally experienced difficulties, stemming from their own socially induced inhibitions and from deficiencies in the judicial system, in securing public redress for the violence inflicted upon them. The blind eye that is so often turned to their condition is justified by definitional contortions obscuring the reality of their injuries[3] and by attitudes denying their status as true victims – the common assumption is that they have invited the violence they receive by violating the social canons of "proper" behaviour or by masochistically acquiescing to it. A similar assumption comes into play in reports of police assaults on those regarded as trouble-makers. The underlying attitude is that such victims have only themselves to blame if they get roughed up by the police.[4]

Similar analyses can be performed for particular incidents of violence. We can ask how social roles have influenced the attitudes and perceptions of participants and observers. The way participants see each other and the degree of sympathy for them among observers can profoundly affect the nature and outcome of an incident.

Rather less obvious is that an outbreak of violence in itself will have an effect on attitudes and perceptions. First, it reinforces attitudes. We have already seen that violence tends to be associated with those previously mistrusted. That these previously mistrusted people should actually resort to violence gives us further evidence of their unworthiness. Second, violence polarizes attitudes. When conflict has become intense enough to produce open violence, the opposing camps become clearly demarcated into "us" versus "them." The moderates who typically carried on prior intergroup

3 An article in *The Globe and Mail* (7 December 1978) cites the sociologist Susan Small's observation that the violence of wife-beating incidents is played down by the police who call them "domestic disputes" and by social scientists who prefer terms like "interspousal conflict." Similar obfuscations have traditionally surrounded rape as well, but they may now be on the decline. Recent changes in the Criminal Code removing rape as a separate offence and bringing it within the general category of assault recognizes the violence that is its essential attribute.

4 See also the social psychology experiments showing that observers who punish a "victim" justify their actions morally by arriving at the conclusion that the victims deserve their punishment (Goode, 1972: 516-17).

communications are forced off stage. Gone then are the personal contacts that would have encouraged the contending parties to deal flexibly with the issues between them and to see each other as individuals rather than stereotypes. Third, public violence mobilizes opinion throughout society. The starkness and urgency of the conflict, and as well the appeals and actions of the participants, gradually force the uncommitted to take sides.⟩

The classic theory of guerrilla warfare shows a profound understanding of the effects of violence on attitudes. As developed by Guevara (1969) and Debray (1967), the theory maintains it is unnecessary to wait for the objective social conditions normally required as a prelude to revolution by Marxist doctrine. Revolution can be initiated by a small band of mobile and dedicated men who use pinprick attacks on the regime. This violence serves to place the issues before the people. The government is provoked into indiscriminate acts of violence in order to put down the elusive guerrillas, thereby breaking ties of sympathy for the regime and shifting support to the insurgents. Men, supplies, and public support flow into the insurgents' camp, enabling them to escalate the conflict steadily until the regime's armed forces can be ultimately defeated in open battle.

The theory purportedly depicts the process by which Castro wrested power from Batista in Cuba. However, Gude (1969) points out that not all governments faced with insurgency proceed through their own ill-planned violence to exasperate public opinion. The process of acquiring public support through attacks on the regime may backfire or never get off the ground, as indicated by the fate of Guevara himself who lost his life while trying to put the theory into practice in Bolivia.

CONCLUSION

It should be stressed that what have been described in this chapter are psychological tendencies. There is a tendency, no more and no less, (1) for people to attach different meanings to the word "violence" depending on their reliance upon conventional definitions, their sympathies for the participants, their notions of legitimacy, and their beliefs about what can and should be changed; (2) for people to let their sympathies influence their perceptions of events and the characterization of incidents as public or private; (3) for people's sympathies to be determined by their relationship to the violent, so that social groups are liable to have distinctive perceptions according to how they identify with the participants, feel anxiety, and reckon costs; and (4) for violence to reinforce, polarize, and mobilize sympathies.

Nevertheless, tendencies are not inescapable. Some people do achieve a less distorted and biased perception of violence than others. But we need to be aware of the force and prevalence of these predispositions. Awareness makes it easier for analysts to recognize their own prejudices. It should induce them to approach their data warily; an account of an incident is a "socially constructed" document. Most importantly, it should make them sensitive to the fact that both people generally and theorists of violence in particular can mean different things when they speak of violence. Definitions affect the conclusions we can reach. Specifically they affect our estimates of the amount of violence in a given society. Canada can only be described as a peaceable kingdom if we stick within the fairly narrow limits of the conventional definition of violence.

The process of perception helps us to understand how we arrive at the distinction between public and private violence. Not all perceptions carry equal weight. It seems very likely that those whose perceptions are aberrant – those who are unable to convince others to achieve similar perceptions – are going to have their violence deemed private. These are the individuals whom we dismiss as psychopaths, cranks, and criminals. We have already noted that the ability to convince others depends on status and power. Consequently those who can disseminate and enforce their interpretation of events are the people whose violence will tend to be considered public in nature (if they allow it to be considered violence at all). The powerless are seen to engage in private violence; the powerful in public violence.

As an explanatory theory, the social-psychology of perceptions accounts for the incidence of violence in only a limited way. Perceptions are part of an explanation of how some incidents start and how they are carried on. Blumenthal et al. (1972: 100) explain:

The objective observer sees only a series of violent acts by A and B, a process without an identifiable beginning or imminent end. But A insists that the initial act of violence was done by B, and that the episodes of violent provocation and justifiable retaliation form a sequence properly described as B-A, A-B; B-A, A-B; etc. His antagonist agrees to the description of the process but not to its origin; that he assigns to a violent act by A, which initiated a sequence A-B, B-A; A-B, B-A; etc. ... [The chances of seeing the other side as initiating the violence are] increased by the wide discrepancies among American men in respect to what acts are defined as violent ... Such discrepancies make it possible for the cycles of perceived violent provocation and justified violent response to be set in motion unintentionally. An initiating act may be nonviolent in the actor's terms, but violent in the eyes of some others.

In the next chapter, we shall be looking at justifications for violence more extensively.

Sometimes it seems the two sides in a dispute inhabit different worlds. They work from such disparate assumptions about the nature and goals of society that they can only talk at cross-purposes to each other. What the government thought would satisfy the Métis in 1885 was quite different from Riel's grand designs (Flanagan, 1983: 90-100). For many years the government was baffled by the Sons of Freedom. And the 1935 interview between the On to Ottawa trekker delegation and the federal cabinet showed a remarkable mutual incomprehension in the exhange of insults ("liar," "your record in the penitentiary," "foreigners," "propaganda," or more imaginatively, "not fit to be premier of a Hottentot village"; Liversedge, 1973: 194-216). Where contending parties are so far apart in their values that they cannot even talk to each other, the chances of settling the dispute by non-violent means are remote.

The study of perceptions also reveals the significance of misunderstanding in the creation and playing out of incidents. Participants often misinterpret the intentions of the other side. A good example is the Estevan riot of 1931. The municipal authorities did not anticipate trouble, believing that the striking miners had received and agreed to their directive against parading in town. Only a small reserve of police were left in the town itself, with the majority posted out at the mines. The miners, however, thought that the police would allow a motor procession and so brought their wives and children along with them for the ride. Three men died in the ensuing clash between strikers and police as a result of this "tragedy of errors" (Hanson, 1974: 51).

The most tragic errors seem to be associated with the common perception that the other side is stronger and has more sinister intentions than is in fact the case. Reactions then become overreactions. In retrospect, it appears that the various governments overreacted to the anti-conscription riots in Quebec City, to the Winnipeg General Strike, to the On to Ottawa trek, and possibly to the October crisis. At the time, though, the governments were unsure of the magnitude of the challenge facing them. In all these instances, some government members perceived a conspiracy behind the violence and worried that the incident heralded the onset of a revolutionary struggle for power.

Ill-founded rumours of malevolent designs circulate among the general public as well. They serve to raise the level of excitement and prompt a more violent response than is appropriate. For example, whites attacked the Chinese in Calgary in 1892 because they believed that the Chinese were deliberately trying to spread smallpox among the white population; Montrealers rioted against governmental vaccination requirements in 1885 because they thought the government was putting them at risk of catching the disease.

Theories of violence inevitably simplify the events they purport to explain, often by ignoring how people perceive their own society. Yet this chapter has shown that biases, misperceptions, and misunderstandings are inherent in violent incidents. It thus serves as a caution against theories that glibly depict people reacting mechanically to a given stimulus; reactions, in truth, depend on how people interpret stimuli. As we shall see, they can interpret them in ways unanticipated by the theorist.

CHAPTER FIVE

Culture and Ideology

The culture of a country or an ideology may contain ideas that justify or condemn the use of violence. Justificatory ideas take two forms (Gurr, 1970: 155-6). There are the normative ideas that claim violence to be the morally right response, and there are the utilitarian ideas that urge violence to be the expedient response. Justificatory ideas may specify the targets against which the violence is to be directed – those whose property or person may be rightfully or expediently attacked. Condemnatory ideas also come in a normative and utilitarian form. The former express moral repugnance for violence, while the latter stress its inutility. To illustrate:

Normative condemnatory: Thou shalt not kill; turn the other cheek.
Normative justificatory: An eye for an eye, a tooth for a tooth.
Utilitarian condemnatory: Violence only begets more violence.
Utilitarian justificatory: The squeaky wheel gets the grease.

Justificatory or condemnatory ideas may be acquired in the process of socialization. They then inhere in the norms and knowledge of historical precedents that we unwittingly absorb as we grow up. These are "cultural" ideas. In contrast are what I shall call "ideological" ideas that are consciously formulated and usually embraced in the adult years.[1] "Subcultural" justifica-

---

1 "Ideology" is notorious as a word of many meanings. It is sometimes used to denote the set of values derived from and supportive of one's relations to the means of production. Such class-based values are unconsciously absorbed, and as such I assign them to "culture." Generally the mainstream culture contains (but is not limited to) ideas consistent with the interests of the dominant economic class. Other segments of the population may develop subcultures that run contrary to part of the mainstream culture. That is, a society's cultural ideas are not necessarily homogeneous. A useful distinction is maintained if "ideology" is reserved to refer to consciously formulated programs and doctrines. In this sense they are, in Johnson's (1966: 83) words, "incipient value structures" that challenge those in place. Ideologists want to convince us to substitute the values they are propounding for those we learned at our parents' knees.

tions arise when a segment of the population develops norms partly at odds with those prevailing in the wider society (Wolfgang and Ferracuti, 1967: 100). Cultural, subcultural, and ideological justifications exist long before violence breaks out. In contrast are the more evanescent "emergent norms" that develop in the process of collective activity. They will be discussed in the next chapter.>

In what follows I first look at the historical decline in the cultural legitimacy of violence in industrial countries. Then I consider some countries and subcultures where violence still retains its legitimacy. Next I suggest that in Canada the prevalence of the peaceable kingdom myth has rendered violence particularly illegitimate. Finally I examine the impact of ideologies and try to assess the causal status of ideas in relation to violence.

THE DECLINING LEGITIMACY OF VIOLENCE

In Canada today most violence used by citizens is both illegitimate and illegal. Canadians tend to think that violence is undesirable and they expect the state to protect them from its manifestations. Yet these are modern notions which would puzzle previous generations. A brief historical analysis of the evolution of notions regarding violence, especially the concept of the "Queen's Peace," is essential to an understanding of our modern ideas about violence.[2]

In feudal England the significance of the royal peace was that breaches of it would be punished by the king, his courts of law, and his officials. Victims were not left without redress or with recourse only to the less efficient or potent justice of the barons or manorial courts. A person subject to the king's peace could therefore feel more secure than one without it. The residents of Anglo-Saxon or early Norman England, however, spoke more properly of "a" peace rather than "the" peace. The king's peace was not universally available, but applied only in a number of specific situations. There was a peace, for example, to protect traffic on the four great highways, and another one for the king's coronation day and the week thereafter. The establishment of a peace was a matter of royal policy designed to encourage or discourage particular practices. Thus William the Conqueror sought to prevent ethnic strife between his Norman men and the Anglo-Saxons by decreeing that "all the men whom I brought with me or who have come after me shall be in my peace and quiet" (Allen, 1953: 23-4). Over time, as the Norman kings grew more powerful and were able to extend the mantle of their justice, the local and temporary character of this justice faded. Eventually any wrongdoing committed *vi et armis* was, at least in theory, automatically taken to be a

2 Another historical background, making much the same point but using different data, is provided by Wolin (1963).

breach of the king's peace and therefore to be tried in the royal courts.

In practice whether a person could rely on the law of the land to guard his security depended very much on his position in society. In the eighteenth century, the great landholders had erected a wall of savage legal penalties to protect their property. Poachers could face the gallows or transportation for life. Compare with this the position of the small farmer:

The poorer population of London and any large town every Sunday, and many weekdays, would pour out into the country with bags in their hands and strip the [farmers'] lands... For protection, a farmer had to rely on the strong arms of himself and his sons: there were no police in the country and the town police were uncon-cerned. (Cole and Postgate, 1961: 95)

All this sounds very remote from our lives today. Since the Industrial Revolution, the sphere of violence that is prohibited and that the state takes responsibility for punishing has grown steadily. A number of forces have been at work.

Social and technical changes facilitating increased control. Urbanization has concentrated the population and made it more accessible to control. A scattered population in outlying areas cannot be intensively policed because the cost would be too great. In the 1830s, for instance, the Ottawa Valley was strife-torn as the lumbermen, particularly the Shiners, pitted themselves against each other and the citizens of Bytown. Complaints to distant Toronto yielded only the answer that the authorities could do nothing (Cross, 1970: 81-2).

Bureaucratization has permitted the growth of large, complex law enforcement agencies whose reach extends across the land. It has also permitted the taxation of the population to support these agencies. In striking contrast to this is the financial and jurisdictional confusion obtaining in the years after Confederation. To quell a riot then, a municipality had to turn to the militia and bear the full cost of doing so. It was the personal responsibility of the officer commanding the militia to sue the municipality if payment was refused, as could happen when mayor, municipal council, and magistrates were at loggerheads. After 1885 a militia officer might apply to Ottawa for an advance covering immediate expenses. However, this required a special order-in-council that might not be readily obtainable, and the officer still had to recover the money from the municipality. One veteran concluded in 1900 that, faced with an incident, the wise officer "will do as little as possible, and will do nothing without a positive order from a justice of the peace" (D. Morton, 1970: 408-9, 419).

The development of transport and communications has played a key role. When news of violence reaches the authorities only after long delays, and when troops or police can be moved to the scene of an incident only with great difficulty, much violence will be ignored as not worth the bother and expense. In this respect it is interesting to note the increasing ease with which Canadian governments have been able to respond to unrest in western Canada. At the time of the first Riel rising in 1869-70, there were no telegraphic links between Ottawa and Fort Garry. Dispatches between the two took up to six weeks to arrive. An expeditionary force, dependent on canoes for much of the distance, and which therefore could not be sent during the winter months eventually struggled into Fort Garry some three months after its June departure. Fifteen years later the situation had changed dramatically. With the second Riel rebellion in 1885 the telegraph lines were in place, and troops were transported over the nearly completed CPR track in three weeks. In 1919, a RNWMP unit from the east reached Winnipeg, then at the start of its general strike, in three days. Today airplanes could deliver reinforcements in a matter of hours.

The growing role of the state. When the doctrine of laissez-faire prevailed, a good deal of violence was overlooked because the state was considered to have no business regulating the situation out of which this violence arose. Thus the violence inflicted upon apprentices could be ignored because it was not held proper for the state to interfere in the relations between masters and men. However, governments now routinely act in far-ranging economic and social policy areas, so that the impact of the government can be felt in nearly all aspects of our lives. An example is the protection offered children from abuse: parents must face teachers who are public servants, doctors who are required to report suspicious cases to the authorities, nurses who are public health officials, and various child welfare agencies which have the power to monitor behaviour in the home and to make application to have the child removed from it, all in addition to regular police forces, many of which have developed special units to deal with "domestic" violence. Child abuse certainly continues, but with the growth of government the chances of it passing undetected and being ignored have considerably diminished.

The belief that more violence can and should be controlled. Over the last two hundred years there has been what might be called a humanitarian revolution in values that has raised the importance attached to individual human life and the quality of it. Before the nineteenth century, life for a good section of the population was "poor, nasty, brutish, and short," and there seemed little that could be done to alleviate it. Low life expectancy bred an attitude of passive acquiescence: dirt, disease, and dietary inadequacies decimated the infant population and could strike adults down in their prime. As well, perhaps, in a more religious age, the promise of an afterlife and resignation to God's will helped people to accept the ephemerality and unpleasantness of their existence. And much more so than today, violence was regarded as normal and inevitable. There was the belief that mankind (especially the lower orders when gathered together) was naturally vicious and violent. As a French official put it, "qui assemble le peuple, l'émeut" (Cobb, 1970: 267): the mob would always be with us, just as surely as boys would always torment animals and parents would beat their children.

Such fatalism is with us no more. With the decline in religious faith and the development of medical science we no longer resign ourselves to suffering. The scope of violence regarded as inevitable, necessary, or about which nothing can or should be done has been progressively narrowed. This narrowing is still perceptible: since the Second World War Canadians have seen the abolition of capital punishment, the passing of the strap from most schools, and the rise of child-care practices calling on parents to shun the physical "disciplining" of their offspring. Recently there have been expressions of concern for violence in the media, in the hockey rink, against women, and against laboratory animals and seal pups.

Values reflect our socio-economic arrangements. They change as our institutions change. If they do not support a predominant social system, they wither and die. Yet it is a difficult problem to relate the humanitarian revolution to changes in social forces. As the example of the landholders versus the small farmers cited above shows, the state has always sought to protect the dominant classes in society from the violence of their inferiors. But what we have seen over the last two hundred years is a general decline in the acceptability of violence, including that inflicted on the poor and powerless. This might be seen as simply reflecting the modern state's rejection of the doctrine of laissez-faire. Just as the Norman kings extended their peace as they gathered more power into their hands, so have governments become increasingly interventionist as they have acquired the technological and organizational means to control the population. Nevertheless, we can trace our modern concern over violence to other changes in the social system as well.

It can be argued that changes in the nature of society since the start of the Industrial Revolution make violence appear a more threatening phenomenon. Our social networks are much denser so that we regularly come in contact with a far broader range of people who are strangers to us. We encounter them in the workplace, in stores, on the bus, at the baseball game, and so on. As a result we face many more unfamiliar and potentially violent situations than did the eighteenth-century villager. As well, the concentration of population in the cities, our easy mobility, and the widespread accessibility of the mass media make us much more aware of the extent of the violence occurring beyond our immediate neighbourhood. Furthermore, while urbanization and mobility have made us better informed, they have also disrupted our sense of community and the related social controls against violence provided by a closely-knit village society. Our neighbours may be no more than vaguely familiar faces for whom we feel no personal responsibility to protect or to supervise; that is what policemen are paid to do. Consequently we wonder if anyone will come to our assistance should we be attacked on the street. Further heightening our sense of alarm is the fact that almost all the violence we hear so much about takes place outside the narrow circle of our acquaintances. We do not know personally the character and circumstances of those involved. Our unfamiliarity makes violence an anonymous and hence threatening force; like lightning, we never know when or where it will strike next.

Second, we live in an unprecedentedly complex and productive society in which a high level of effective collective action is dependent on predictably patterned behaviour. A sophisticated society cannot flourish when the fundamental questions of social organization are in violent dispute (Johnson, 1966: 28-30). Hobbes pointed out long ago in his *Leviathan* (I, 13) that where violence prevails

there is no place for industry; because the fruit thereof is uncertain: and consequently no culture of the earth; no navigation, nor use of the commodities that may be imported by sea; no commodious building; no instruments of moving, and removing, such things as require much force; no knowledge of the face of the earth; no account of time; no arts; no letters; no society ...

The preservation of our complex civilization thus requires that the use of disruptive violence be discouraged as much as possible.

A third element is the nature of work in an advanced or post-industrial society. At the upper end of the occupational spectrum, we have seen the elimination of an aristocratic, warrior class. Our "gentlemen" no longer carry swords or engage in duels; they carry briefcases, stethoscopes, and calculators. At the lower end, physical feats of strength are less important; machines now clear the land, excavate the ground, and mine the coal. Brain and technique have replaced brawn as criteria of prestige. The decline of physical prowess as a means of gaining prestige, both at the upper and lower ends of the occupational scale, has rendered us squeamish about overt displays of physical aggression, except in the acceptable rituals of sport. This applies particularly to the upper and middle classes in society who have everything to lose and nothing to gain in eruptions of violence. Not surprisingly, these classes have used their dominant social position to propound norms and laws that discountenance the use of violence.

Yet if violence is generally frowned upon, it is still a subject of considerable concern to dominant class interests which attempt to shape our reactions to particular kinds of violence. First, throughout history dominant groups manipulate the law and its practice to protect themselves from violence.

Violence inflicted among members of more marginal groups or against them continues to arouse less public concern. For example, the middle class can rely on better police protection than can members of the lower class (Shearing, 1981: 287). Police in the southern United States of the early 1960s turned a blind eye to white violence against blacks and civil rights workers. And women, victimized by their husbands or rapists, have had difficulty in gaining legal recourse.

Second, the arousal of public concern for a given type of violence can sometimes be directly traced to special interests. One of the best examples of this is abortion in the United States; it was nowhere forbidden in 1800 but had been proscribed by virtually every jurisdiction by 1900. During this period the concept of abortion as a form of murder was propounded, most notably by the increasingly powerful medical profession who were in competition with the abortionists for professional prestige and patients. The doctors won out. Abortionists became disreputable and the exercise of their profession classed as an illegal form of violence (Gordon, 1978: 37-8).

What we have in Canada today, then, is a situation whereby most acts of violence are considered illegitimate and illegal. The most notable exceptions involve police and military forces, the agents of the state empowered to employ violence in the service of social control. Even so, as we shall see in chapter 9, these forces do not have a blanket dispensation to use violence. When, where, and how much they can use are subject to close regulation. Those acting in excess of their orders may be prosecuted or subject to internal discipline. But there is a distinction here between illegality and illegitimacy. According to the dominant view in Canadian society, policemen are by and large honest men trying to perform a difficult job. Some overzealousness in the pursuit of disreputable or elusive elements such as members of organized crime, motorcycle gangs, or terrorist groups may be overlooked or quietly condoned as a necessary evil.

The use of violence by one country against another in warfare may also be regarded as legitimate. Pacifism is rarely taken to be a virtue when the call goes out to defend the interests of one's country. A hawkish stance in international relations, support for the military-industrial complex, and a celebration of the martial virtues may go hand-in-hand with the discouragement of violence within society. Indeed, while we have noted upper- and middle-class disapproval of violence, these same classes have not been backward in lauding its use in warfare or for the purposes of social control.

Civilians too are permitted some use of violence. The law recognizes the right of individuals to use a reasonable amount of violence to defend themselves or their property. Another more interesting if less clear-cut case is the use of violence to rebel against injustice. Political philosophers through the ages have tried to spell out when citizens may legitimately use admittedly illegal violence to overthrow an oppressive government or change an unjust policy (Bell, 1973: ch. 2). Generally they concede some right of rebellion, but it is invariably conditional: for example, all legal means of recourse must be exhausted and the injustice in question must be a grave, general, and long-standing one. Popular concepts of rebellion are more nebulous, especially in a country like Canada with no revolution or war of independence in its history to provide a precedent (but see Turner's [1969] "folk concept of social protest" discussed in chapter 9). However, there is no doubt that the right of rebellion does exist within our cultural tradition. The concept is available for disgruntled elements of our society to call upon and make a case for their actions in terms comprehensible to us all. Of course, we may not accept that the conditions for rebellion have been met and so regard their violence as completely illegitimate.

CULTURES OF VIOLENCE

Elsewhere in the world we can find different perspectives on the legitimacy of violence. In some societies, violence is considered to be a legitimate political means. For instance, Payne (1965) argues that in Peruvian politics it is impossible to treat violence as an aberration. It is normal and accepted as essential to the functioning of the system, in much the same way as Canadians accept elections.

There are as well what Wolfgang and Ferracuti (1967) call subcultures of violence in which it is shameful *not* to respond violently to a specified provocation. Typical of such communities is the Mexican village of Acan with its inordinately high political homicide rate. As described by Friedrich (1972: 270), "the culture to which both killer and victim belong often justifies or enjoins political homicide." If they are not to be ostracized, the villagers must conform to a code of honour that requires the murder of a father, son, or brother be avenged.

In addition to general legitimations of violence, cultural norms prescribe when, where, and how violence may be used. In the village of Acan, for instance, it is considered improper to dispatch a victim sadistically, or while he is at work, or in a situation where women and children may get hurt. Another culturally influenced decision is the choice of weapons. This choice has significant consequences for the type and degree of violence expended: flying fists cause bruises, flaming brands produce arson, a gun kills. In some societies particular weapons are ostentatiously worn: the sgian dubh in the highlander's stocking, the kirpan of the Sikh, the trusty six-shooter at the cowboy's side. So flaunted, they symbolize a readiness to put them to use. In these and other societies weapons often assume a ritualistic value as a sign of either manhood or status. Wolfgang and Ferracuti (1967: 281) point out that in one vendetta subculture "a gun is a common gift of the godfather to the child at the time he is baptized." Similarly, the gentleman's sword marked his class position; he would no more carry a cudgel than engage in physical toil.

Acceptable targets of violence and its form are also shaped by popular tradition. According to Edwards (1970: 99):

A crowd is open to suggestions that are in line with its previous experiences ... Ancient Jewish mobs always stoned their victims to death, Alexandrian mobs nearly always threw theirs from the tops of high buildings – Hypatia is almost the only exception. She was cut to pieces with oyster shells. Medieval mobs regularly decapitated those they killed. Except in unusual circumstances American mobs use the noose. A Belfast mob could no more be brought to lynch negroes than a Chicago mob could be brought to lynch Catholics. An Odessa mob will lynch Jews, not negroes or Catholics.

In his study of pre-industrial crowds, Rudé (1964: 241-2, 253-5) also notes the recurrent forms of popular protest in which conventions governed the violence. It was almost without exception directed against property rather than people, and only the property of the specific villains of the day was liable to be attacked. Typical forms of violence were arson (especially in England), machine wrecking, and the "pulling down" of houses (see also Tilly's [1978: 151-6] discussion of the "repertoire of collective actions available to a population").

Several theories have emerged to explain the development of cultures of violence. Four factors are commonly mentioned: (1) the presence of violent models; (2) extrapunitiveness (the turning of aggressive impulses against external objects rather than the self); (3) "machismo" values; and (4) a view of the world as a cold and menacing place. These factors have been related to varying levels of explanation (and the analysis often slips confusingly among them without spelling out the necessary linkages). Some accounts examine differences among national cultures. Others look at the subcultures of groups or regions. A good deal of effort has gone into detailing supposed class-based norms regarding violence. Still others focus on the development of psychological differences among individuals.

The presence of violent models. It is argued that we learn to use violent behaviour just as we learn to use any other. Thus the more familiar we are with violent behaviour in our childhood and later years, the more likely we are to use it ourselves. According to Allport (1964: 332), we come to accept violence as a legitimate problem-solving mechanism, and once this is so it becomes "pretty much of a habit." Other problem-solving mechanisms, such as adaptation or retreat, are poorly developed or atrophy. The *violencia* of Colombia, for example, was transmitted from one generation to the next in part "by the constant presentation of violent stimuli and values to the children," including "the ever-present feeling of menace, fear, and death, the actual visual presentation of mangled bodies and of other sadistic manifestations," and the "indoctrination of children about methods of killing" (Wolfgang and Ferracuti, 1967: 278-9).

The prevalence of violent models is also supposed to vary along social class lines. This proposition has a certain amount of surface plausibility when we remember middle-class concern about exposing children to examples of violence. The research purporting to establish the proposition has nevertheless run into criticism. Differences in child-rearing practices are a case in point. Many studies have argued that lower-class children are given more violent models than middle-class children because they are subjected to more physical forms of punishment (the cuff on the ear versus the child being sent to bed). Yet even here the evidence is contradictory; Kohn (1977: 95), for example, finds that "middle-class mothers punish children physically as often as do working-class mothers." Nor is it self-evident that a child will extend what he has learned about violent parent-child relations to other kinds of relationships once he is an adult. As Hackney (1969: 518) points out, "restrictive child-rearing practices in Europe evidently do not lead to the physical violence that such practices among the lower classes in America are supposed to produce."

Another case in point is the presentation of violent models in the media. Lower-class families tend to watch more television than middle-class ones. Since television programs are saturated with violence – according to one estimate, eight out of ten programs contain violence (Goranson, n.d.: 3) – children of poorer families will be presented with more violence than children from better-off families. There is a good deal of controversy over the effects, if any, on perceptions and behaviour of a steady diet of "fantasy" violence. Goranson (n.d.: 6), however, cites two British studies that "have shown that working-class boys are particularly vulnerable to the effects of observed aggression in comparison with middle-class boys." Yet the fact that aggressive imitation is found more often among boys than girls shows that many factors can intervene between the stimulus and response, in this case cultural norms governing the behaviour considered appropriate to the two sexes.

In short, the evidence is too contradictory to confirm the existence and effect of class differences in the prevalence of violent models. The case for regional or national differences seems to be better founded. Gurr (1970: 168-77) has shown that past levels of violence correlate with present levels. Part of the suggested mechanism linking the two time periods is that a previous successful experience can embed a model in the popular tradition that, first, provides knowledge on the specifics of conducting a violent event, second, turns people's minds to the possibility of again resorting to violence, and third, justifies and legitimates a further outbreak by an appeal to traditional practices.

The "contagion" theory might also be mentioned here, although it does not strictly fall within the current subject of cultural legitimations of violence. According to this theory, violence against grievances in one place provides a model for others suffering similar grievances elsewhere, so that violence spreads as news of it is disseminated.[3] Thus there develop vogues for particular types of violence. One example was the spate of skyjackings in the early seventies. The guerrilla, followed by the urban guerrilla, was another popular model of about the same time.

Extrapunitiveness. Different world-views and socialization practices are thought to create individuals who tend to be either intrapunitive (frustration turned against the self) or extrapunitive (frustration legitimately turned against external targets). In extreme cases, the intrapunitive individual turns to depression and suicide, while the extrapunitive one turns to acts of violence against others. The argument has been generalized to countries and status groups. Norwegian children are permitted to express more outward aggression than Danish or Swedish children, and this is used to explain the higher rates of suicide in Denmark and Sweden as compared to Norway. Middle-class families are more likely than working-class ones to be concerned by their children's loss of self-control (Kohn, 1977: 106). Their more negative attitude to their children's displays of aggression are brought into the explanation of the class differences in suicide-homicide ratios, which show suicide to be more of a middle-class phenomenon and homicide of a working-class phenomenon (Gurr, 1970: 165-8). Sex differences might also be noted here; for if girls are given less leeway than boys to express aggression, this might help account for the fact that women turn their violence more often against themselves and less often against others than do men.

The construction of suicide-homicide ratios posits an underlying common dimension for suicide and homicide. In many cases, it seems justifiable to treat them as the two possible alternative responses to a common stimulus, since countries, regions, and groups scoring high on one frequently rank low on the other: where there is much homicide, there is little suicide (it was virtually unknown in Acan), and conversely (Sweden has a high suicide but a low homicide rate). But not all cases neatly fit the pattern, and Canada, which scores relatively low on both the homicide and the suicide scales, is one of the exceptions (Kirkham, Levy, and Crotty, 1970: 197). This would imply that Canadians are taught not to act out their aggression either against themselves or against others. Whether this is the case is hard to say, at least simply from

3 The contagion theory is nicely illustrated by Rudé's (1964) maps charting the spread of French and English popular disturbances, 1730-1848. The theory has fallen into disrepute because too much was claimed for it. An incident is not explained simply by the observation that the violent are copying others. Nevertheless, police have learned from experience that they need to step up security for a victim and others similarly placed after one spectacular attempt against the victim has been made.

an inspection of suicide-homicide ratios. Many non-cultural factors have been identified as contributing to suicide and homicide respectively. Thus, to infer norms concerning the legitimation of violence from only the ratio between the two sorts of behaviour seems dubious at best.

Machismo values. Machismo values equate masculinity with toughness and physical strength. Tolerance, loving kindness, and gentleness are dismissed as effeminate irrelevancies. Prestige in groups holding machismo values depends on the ability to fight and win, either by using one's own strength or by marshalling the strength of others. Any backing away from violence is deemed cowardly and leads to loss of face in the peer group. Weapons, such as knives and guns, are often carried as symbols of manhood.

The vandal, whose story is told in figure 2, wanted to be a "hero" to his group, to "feel good." In order not to lose face, his situation required him to respond violently to his teachers. Along the same lines, a study of violence in Canadian hockey (Smith, 1975) emphasizes the importance of peer pressures. While much of hockey violence is illegal in terms of the law of the land and officially discouraged by spokesmen for the NHL, television provides youngsters with repeated exposure to violence on the ice. The professional hockey player has a glamorous image of toughness, of being able to walk tall precisely because "he can beat 'em in the alley as well as on the ice." Hockey players and spectators form a subculture, according to Smith, in which violence is expected and rewarded. The players in the school teams he interviewed felt that their non-playing peers came to the games just to see the violence, and two-thirds of them considered that their peers approved the starting of fights.

There have been attempts to associate machismo values with lower-class culture. (For a discussion, see Hagan, 1977: 104-15.) But again it is difficult to accept that such cultural differences are neatly and universally coterminous with class lines. Indeed, Smith (1975: 75) finds that socio-economic status is not a relevant variable in explaining the legitimation of hockey violence. And another Canadian study (Vaz, 1965) shows both that vandalism is not confined to lower-class youths, and that machismo values are found among middle-class adolescents.

A menacing world. The perception of the environment as insecure and threatening is also considered to contribute to the legitimation of violence. In such situations, human life is devalued in a fatalistic acceptance of insecurity. Furthermore, threats requiring a violent response are perceived to be ubiquitous. In his study of criminal homicide in Philadelphia, Wolfgang (cited in Wolfgang and Ferracuti, 1967: 153) notes that "the significance of a jostle, a slightly derogatory remark, or the appearance of a weapon in the hands of an adversary are stimuli differentially perceived and interpreted by

Negroes and whites, males and females." Lower-class males of both races are quick to define a situation as a threatening one requiring a combative response; middle-class men regard the provocation as trivial. Wolfgang's account of class, race, and sex differences, however, leaves us wondering to what extent we are dealing with culturally based perceptions of the world as opposed to actually experienced differences in levels of security.

Another relevant study is Hackney's examination of the high levels of violence in the American South, in which the author (1969: 519) contends there is "a style of life that is handed down from father to son along with the old hunting rifle and the family Bible." After reviewing various socio-economic and psycho-cultural variables, he suggests that the most promising line of explanation lies in "a Southern world view that defines the social, political and physical environment as hostile and casts the white Southerner in the role of the passive victim of malevolent forces" (1969: 524). Hackney combines the notions of an environment perceived as full of menace and of extrapunitiveness by arguing that anger is only turned outwards when the self is not blamed or with the refusal to take responsibility for one's own condition. Yet his historical account of how this world-view developed seems to apply equally as well to Canada vis-à-vis the United States as to the South vis-à-vis the North.[4] If this world-view makes for high levels of violence in the South, it does not seem to do so in Canada as a whole, though possibly the relatively high levels of violence in Quebec are related to a world-view that casts the Quebecker "in the role of the passive victim of malevolent forces."

The four factors said to lead to the cultural legitimation of violence (the presence of violent models, extrapunitiveness, machismo values, and a menacing world) have been subjected to various criticisms. Chief among them are the presence of awkward exceptions, the weakness of the indicators used, confusion among levels of explanation, and, in particular, generalizations about class-based differences. Nevertheless the concept of a culture of violence need not be dismissed. There is much here that is suggestive and valuable. The idea of subcultures of violence helps to explain the behaviour of particular groups in society, such as hockey players and spectators. The discussion of violent models stresses that violence is learned behaviour. Even

4 In Hackney's (1969: 524-5) account of the southern world-view, the correspondence between the South and Canada is striking. "Canada" can be appositely substituted for "the South" in the following quotation: "The South was created by the need to protect a peculiar institution from threats originating outside the region. Consequently, the Southern identity has been linked from the first to a siege mentality. Though Southerners have many other identities, they are likely to be most conscious of being Southerners when they are defending their region against attack from outside forces ... This has made for an extreme sensitivity to criticism from outsiders and a tendency to excuse local faults as the products of forces beyond human control or beyond local control ... Added to this experience with perceived threats has been the fact that almost every significant change in the life of the South has been initiated by external powers. This is even true of industrialization ... [in which] absentee ownership has been characteristic."

FIGURE 2

Portrait of a Vandal: He was Known as a Nasty Kid and Felt He Never Got a Break

By Mary Kate Rowan

He doesn't look like a violent kid. He's small and slight for his 15 years. He wears thick glasses and has, at first meeting, a deceptively gentle manner.

His name is David (a pseudonym). He's been out of a regular classroom for two years, ever since the day he rushed home in a rage, grabbed a hockey stick and ran back to his junior high school. He started breaking windows and when he saw the principal inside, dared him to come out and fight. The principal called the police instead. David was charged, sent to juvenile court and suspended from school for six months. For the past year and a half, he's been back at school in a special class for problem students. He expects to be back in a regular class next September.

David is a student in North York. The North York local of the Ontario Secondary School Teachers Federation has said repeatedly that violence is increasing in the schools. Lawrence Crackower, chairman of the North York board, said in a recent interview that school violence – teachers being assaulted and verbally harassed, vandalism – is a "big problem." But, when asked why they feel students are becoming more difficult to handle, neither the teachers nor the board can give concrete answers.

Almost anxious to talk

David is quite willing, almost anxious, to talk. He realizes now that he shouldn't have broken the windows. He did overreact, he admits, but still, he thinks he had a reason. He says a lot of kids have reasons for exploding in class.

David has never been a good student. "I've gotten mostly Cs and Ds." He was thrown out of several North York elementary schools for unruly conduct. By the time he got to junior high school, his reputation was established. He was known as one nasty kid.

He says he was treated as a nasty kid, too. "If there was a fight, I was the instigator. If something went wrong, I got blamed." Sometimes it was his fault but as often as not it wasn't, he says. "They wouldn't let me explain."

David didn't think that was fair. He's black and thinks the teachers picked on him unnecessarily because of his color. There was the time in one class he forgot his book. "The teacher said about eight times that the class was okay except for the stupid kid who forgot his book. I was just getting smaller and smaller. Teachers don't understand that you can get your feelings hurt."

Teachers also don't understand what kind of peer pressure a child comes under when a teacher belittles him, David says. Every time a teacher blamed him for something he didn't do or mocked him, the other students would crowd around him the moment the class ended. "They'd say, 'You stupid idiot. How can you let the teacher talk to you like that?'" Then if David went back to the teacher and yelled or threw something, "I'd be a hero. The kids would say 'All right.' That would make me feel good, especially after being put down so much."

FIGURE 2 (*concluded*)

It became an endless cycle. David would feel he'd been slighted by a teacher, the other students would egg him on, the teachers would react with more discipline and the students would continue their taunting. It all continued until the day David, who says he has a short fuse at the best of times, blew.

He doesn't remember all the details now. He met the teacher, the one who had made the comments the day he forgot his book, in the hall. He doesn't remember why but he ended up throwing his books all over the place. Then he started kicking doors and lockers. The principal tried to stop him and at one point, David says, the principal pushed him and he hit the wall. That's when David went home and got the hockey stick. After it was all over the school authorities said that David should never be allowed in a regular classroom again.

He was sent to the North York Centre for Youth Services, a counselling service, for help. His youth worker says that there is no way of proving whether the teachers were too harsh on David but that he believes that David honestly felt he was being treated unfairly. "I think that if teachers had sat down and talked to him about why he was angry things would have been different."

Eric King, clinical director for the centre, says there are two types of problem students in the schools. There are those who are disturbed and don't have a sense of wrongdoing. Then there are children like David who get in situations "where a kid has to lose face in front of his classmates. A violent reaction is their way of having some control. It gets to be a power struggle. The teacher doesn't want to lose face, either."

Susceptible to peer pressure

Mr. King says teachers should learn how to handle children like David, "kids with a low self-image who are susceptible to peer pressure."

David lives in an Ontario Housing project. His father deserted the family when he was 4. His mother works as a cleaning lady. He has two older sisters. The area he lives in has a reputation for being rough. "To me it doesn't seem so rough," he says. Still, he admits he's developed survival skills. He steers around fights and he's very careful "not to badmouth anybody I don't know. If you do, they'll come after you."

He's made new friends in the past two years, "people who don't think it's so great to talk back to a teacher." He thinks the counselling helped. He especially enjoyed events like camping trips and discussion groups. He still has a short fuse and, he said, probably always will. He thinks he has things more under control now.

"There is still a long way to go, but I'm a normal student now." He wants to go to university so he can get a job in an advertising agency. "I don't want to work in a factory. I want a nice house and a car. My family has never had that."

His youth worker thinks he's worked it out, too. When you're dealing with people you can never be 100 per cent certain, he says. Both he and David will find out next year when David goes back into a regular classroom.

(*The Globe and Mail*, 15 June 1979. By permission.)

if there is a genetic predisposition towards aggression or a psychological affinity between frustration and aggression, people still have to learn from others that violence is the appropriate response to a challenge. The differences between what is considered acceptable conduct in men and women, in a subculture and the dominant culture, and in the cultures of different nations all stress the importance of coming to an understanding of the ideas people hold about the proper role of violence.

Where does Canada fit into this? There are few studies to indicate what Canadian cultural norms regarding violence might be, and even less on how they compare with the norms of other nations. However, the meagre evidence and scholarly consensus imply a low level of toleration for violence in the dominant Canadian culture. Canada is identified as the peaceable kingdom. A brief examination of this idea illustrates how norms discountenancing the use of violence can evolve and become functional to the society they serve.

CANADA: THE PEACEABLE KINGDOM

The kernel of the idea of a peaceable kingdom[5] is that Canada can be distinguished from other countries by its unusually low levels of violence. Commentators remark on the absence or infrequency of various types of violence, particularly those popularly associated with the United States: revolution, civil war, disorderly frontier, lynchings, mobs, and the violence of the cities. Several reasons are advanced to explain this happy state of affairs.

First is the absence of positively valued violent models. In other countries, violence has contributed to the foundation of the nation-state, to the removal of those whom the victors have defined as tyrants or imperialist oppressors, or to the expansion of national territory. Canada, by contrast, failed to christen its national existence with a revolutionary celebration, and virtually all of Canada's major violent events have been failures. The expansion of settle-

---

5 In its origins, "peaceable kingdom" is a reference to the biblical prophecy of Isaiah: "They shall beat their swords into plowshares, and their spears into pruninghooks ..." (2:4); "The wolf also shall dwell with the lamb, and the leopard shall lie down with the kid ..." (11:6). The prophecy was depicted by the American painter Edmund Hicks in 1830 who showed Indians and settlers concluding a treaty, while in the foreground domestic and wild animals mix together in harmony. Northrop Frye turned to this work when seeking to sum up an essential element of the Canadian literary tradition. Referring to Hicks's "haunting vision of a serenity that is both human and natural," Frye argues that "if we had to characterize a distinctive emphasis in that tradition, we might call it a quest for the peaceable kingdom" (1971: 249). The characterization was also adopted by William Kilbourn who subtitled his collection of essays on Canadian topics "A Guide to the Peaceable Kingdom." For Kilbourn, many of "the subtle but profound ways in which Canada differs from the United States," such as the greater Canadian respect for the law and the tolerance of other groups, can be grouped around the idea of Canada as the peaceable kingdom (1970: xiii).

ment into the Canadian frontier regions was preceded or accompanied by the institutions of government so that no hiatus of lawlessness enabled folk heroes like Billy the Kid to emerge. Instead, the definitive image is of a scarlet-coated Mountie resolutely tracking down his man.

Second, Canadians have not only lacked their own violent models; the nation grew on the active rejection of other societies' violent models. By 1800 the French Revolution had been anathematized in French Canada, while the founders of English Canada – the Loyalists – had voted with their feet against the American Revolution. Accordingly Canadians defined themselves as the people who stuck by their established institutions. They were not afraid of what governments could do to them; they did fear what would happen when government collapsed.[6]

Third, from this historical experience has emerged a culture at odds with machismo and related values. Canadians are said to be notoriously law-abiding and respectful of authority. Evolution, compromise, and pragmatism are supposedly their watchwords in accomplishing political and social change. Toleration is celebrated as the key national virtue; the society is characterized as a mosaic, not a melting pot.

Fourth, Canadians are credited with a pessimistic view of human nature. There is little of the liberal-individualist's faith in the capacity of mankind to grapple with destiny and wrench it into a desired course. Rather, the prevailing philosophy is a more conservative one that emphasizes restraint (both social and self-imposed) and a very pragmatic acceptance of the limited scope for improving one's condition.[7] Canadians do not resort to violence because they see little point in the exercise and because they acquiesce in the restraints believed necessary to curb the selfish instincts of fallen man. The concepts of intra- and extrapunitiveness simply do not apply: Canadian pessimism means that hopes are seldom raised and hence seldom dashed, while attaching blame – whether directed against oneself or others – is seen to be futile.

6 On the formation of the Canadian political culture, see Bell and Tepperman (1979), especially chapters 2 and 3. Bell develops his idea of Canadian "cratophilia" (love of government) in his article on the Loyalists in Canada (1970: 27-9).

7 The ferocity of the "unrestrained" Canadian (that is, in situations where the sanctions against violence are lifted) has been noted by various observers. Besides what Europeans have come to regard as the neanderthal tactics of our hockey players and seal hunters, there is the record of Canadian soldiers on the battlefield and off it. Canadians seem to be an unmilitary people when it comes to taking an interest in military affairs or a readiness to bear military expenses, but not when someone encourages them to go out and fight (Preston, 1964: 90). Compare also W.L. Morton's (1965: 5) argument that the "alternate penetration of the wilderness and return to civilization is the basic rhythm of Canadian life, and forms the basic elements of Canadian character whether French or English, the violence necessary to contend with the wilderness, the restraint necessary to preserve civilization from the wilderness violence, and the puritanism which is the offspring of the wedding of violence to restraint."

The fifth reason put forward is the all-pervading insecurity of Canadian life. The elements and the land are hostile. To the south is the menacing presence of the United States. The national existence is constantly in peril; economic and geographic conditions daily call the country into question, and sectionalism, especially the French-English split, conditions Canadians to expect their country to fly apart at any moment. In the previous section, it was noted that a menacing environment was considered conducive to the legitimation of violence. In Canada it is said to have the opposite effect. Precariousness has produced the notion that Canada cannot afford turbulent excesses. National survival sternly dictates the pursuit of peace, both in foreign and domestic policy.

This national portrait has been drawn by a number of distinguished observers. Figure 3 gathers together some illustrative quotations. How well the portrait relates to the actual behaviour of Canadians is not the present issue. What we are dealing with is a myth, that is, "a belief held in common by a large group of people that gives events and action a particular meaning ... [which is] not susceptible to empirical check or revision ... What is mythical and unobservable is publicly affirmed and believed, for it evokes social support" (Edelman, 1971: 14-16). Sentiments about Canada as a peaceable kingdom have been voiced for nearly two centuries by a diverse array of Canadians, both Conservatives and Liberals, French and English, of elite and less exalted status (Torrance, 1975: ch. 7).

The widespread social support for the myth is a function of the useful purposes it has served. First it has provided a focus for nationalist sentiment. It is commonplace for a nation to describe itself as "peace-loving," but the claim in Canada's case cannot be dismissed as a limp platitude. This is partly due to the paucity of agreed-upon definitions of Canadian national attributes. In the absence of believable alternatives, an idea as widely expressed and as durable as that of the peaceable kingdom grows in stature. Partly it is due to the idea's broad thematic scope. In the effort to explain Canadian peaceful-ness, the argument reaches out to embrace – and draw strength from – the few other identified national attributes such as elitism and tolerance. Most importantly, the exalted stature of the idea in Canada has to do with its focusing on the differences between Canadians and Americans. For many Canadians the idea has provided a convincing argument that they are in fact distinct from Americans and that they should remain so.

A second function of the idea of the peaceable kingdom is its legitimation of a strong interventionist government. The idea calls on Canadians to respect and defer to government as the provider of the restraints necessary for a social existence. For those able to use governmental powers to their own ends, deference is an attribute to be encouraged. Many commentators have drawn attention to the streak of Toryism in Canadian values (see, for example, Horowitz, 1966). In the United States the emphasis is on the right of the individual, untrammelled by government dictation, to pursue his own self-advancement. In Canada the emphasis is more on the creation of the collective, governmental authority deemed necessary to push forward the development of a less favoured and more backward economy than that existing to the south and also to protect individuals and minority groups from the selfish and bigoted depredations of others. In place of the "life, liberty, and the pursuit of happiness" found in the Declaration of Independence, the phrase in the Canada Act is "peace, order and good government."

The idea of the peaceable kingdom thus provides Canadians with a nationalist credo and legitimation for a strong government. The consequences of living with such a self-image are several. In the first place, it has affected the conception of Canadian history. McNaught (1970: 68) has spoken of the lack of attention given to violent conflicts in Canada's past.[8] Instead Canadian historians have assumed "that our history has been largely free from the violence and extremism in action that have scarred American history" and that "on the whole resort to violence was pretty clearly an aberration from the norm in the Canadian experience." Conciliation, not conflict, is emphasized in Canadian historical writing. As a result, it can be argued, knowledge of Canadian violence has been limited and the overall picture of the country's development unbalanced.

The historians' neglect of violence serves to belittle the efforts of those Canadians who have resorted to arms. The violent have also tended to be disparaged by their contemporaries as well, but on the grounds that they were foreigners, or under the influence of foreign ideas or leaders, as if no true son of the peaceable kingdom would engage in such desperate business. Governments at the time have found it convenient to draw on this proclivity to blame the violence on outsiders – Yankee wire-pullers, German agents, international conspiracies, and other nations' radicals and terrorists – rather than their own shortcomings.

Another consequence of the idea of the peaceable kingdom, a consequence which has been noted by a long line of distinguished observers of the Canadian scene from André Siegfried to John Porter, is the dulling of politics to uncreative mediocrity as politicians assiduously work to defuse potential confrontation. In the Canadian political tradition, conciliation, moderation, and quiet diplomacy have been the guiding themes. As a result, it is said that political life in Canada is dull, that Canadians are frightened of ideas, and that they refuse to polarize the country on a left-right axis. It might be added that this desire to settle disputes quietly behind closed doors has encouraged governments to clothe themselves in excessive secrecy.

Canadians have been keenly interested in American violence, every

---

8 Jamieson (1968: 7) and Abella (1974: xi) have also referred to Canadian historians' lack of interest in violence.

FIGURE 3
The Peaceable Kingdom

S.D. Clark (1962: 198)

Canada has no revolutionary tradition. At no time in their history have the people turned their back on the past and placed their whole faith in the future. The lack of such an emotional experience has affected the development of all aspects of Canadian society. It is this which accounts for what is most distinctive in the national character.

Sir Wilfrid Laurier (Skelton, 1965: I, 126; II, 142)

I am not ignorant of the fact that there can be no nation without a national pride, nor am I unaware that in almost all cases national pride is inspired by those tragic events which bring suffering and tears in their train ... Our history under Confederation presents none of the dramatic events which make us so attached to the past; it has been calm and consequently happy. But peace has also its glories and its heroes.
... a policy of true Canadianism, of moderation, of conciliation.

Pierre Elliott Trudeau (1972)

The Mounties represented law and order, and they rode into the west in advance of the settler. That fact has influenced all of Canada. The Mounted Police ensured that the relationship between the settler and the Indian did not involve the excesses which occurred south of the border. The Battle of the Little Big Horn, the lore of a Billy the Kid, and the exploits of Jesse James may be more dramatic in the telling than is the orderly development of the Canadian west, but a vigilante sense of justice is not a good model for a modern state. Nowhere in this country do Canadians now carry guns for their own protection. Nowhere do Canadians believe that confrontation and violence are superior to moderation and the orderly settlement of disputes.

André Siegfried (1966: 113-14)

Canada, we know, is a country of violent oppositions ... Let a question of race or religion be raised, and ... elections will become struggles of political principle, sincere and passionate. Now this is exactly what is feared by the prudent and far-sighted men who have been given the responsibility of maintaining the national equilibrium ... That is why they persistently apply themselves to prevent the formation of homogeneous parties, divided according to race, religion or class ... The clarity of political life suffers from this, but perhaps the existence of the federation can be preserved only at this price.

Frank Underhill (1960: 228, 5, 12)

[U.S. liberalism essentially depends on a] faith in the rationality of man ... [a] belief in progress, in the indefinite perfectibility of man and his institutions. Liberalism is in essence a Utopian faith with a confidence in the possibilities of human nature.

   Our Confederation was achieved at the very time in the nineteenth century when a reaction was beginning to set in against the liberal and democratic principles ...

   The intellectual life of our politics has not been periodically revived by fresh drafts from the invigorating fountain of eighteenth-century Enlightenment ... In Canada we

FIGURE 3 (*concluded*)

---

have no revolutionary tradition; and our historians, political scientists, and philosophers have assiduously tried to educate us to be proud of this fact.

George Grant (1965: 4, 71)
To be a Canadian was to build, along with the French, a more ordered and stable society than the liberal experiment in the United States.

The early leaders of British North America indentified lack of public and personal restraint with the democratic Republic. Their conservatism was essentially the social doctrine that public order and tradition, in contrast to freedom and experiment, were central to the good life.

Northrop Frye (1971: 14, 218-19)
Historically, a Canadian is an American who rejects the Revolution ... There is in Canada, too, a traditional opposition to the two defects to which a revolutionary tradition is liable, a contempt for history and an impatience with law.

The United States, being founded on a revolution and a written constitution, has introduced a deductive or *a priori* pattern into its cultural life that tends to define an American way of life and mark it off from anti-American heresies. Canada, having a seat on the sidelines of the American Revolution, adheres more to the inductive and the expedient. The Canadian genius for compromise is reflected in the existence of Canada itself.

Kaspar D. Naegele (1961: 27)
There is *less* emphasis in Canada on equality ... In Canada there seems to be a greater acceptance of *limitation*, of hierarchical patterns. There seems to be less optimism, less faith in the future, less willingness to risk capital or reputation. In contrast to America, Canada is a country of greater caution, reserve, and restraint.

Hugh MacLennan (1970: 10)
It was out of the Canadian's capacity ... to function in an environment full of unavoidable frustrations, that most of us came to the conclusion that the most important problems of life can never be solved, but merely lived with.

---

manifestation of which could be taken as proof of the superiority of the peaceable kingdom. This preoccupation with American violence and American troubles has tended to deflect Canadians' interest in their own problems. Canadians are often so excited by the conflagration in their neighbour's backyard that they overlook the incendiary material lying about their own.[9]

9 Stewart (1976: 283-4) makes much the same point: "The myth that we, of all peoples under the sun, have been magically endowed with qualities refused all others, especially those bastard Americans ... [has a crippling effect] because it prevents us from making the changes in our laws and institutions that must be made if we are to become the kind of nation we already think we are."

Thus, during the sixties, Canadians avidly followed southern white violence, ghetto riots, student revolts, and assassinations below the border, while congratulating themselves on having no Ku Klux Klan, ghettoes, or draft cards; and turned their backs on their own problems such as the demoralization of the native population in places like Kenora and the growing racial tension in certain communities.

Another key effect of the idea of the peaceable kingdom has been to condemn sternly most expressions of violence, and particularly those used for the purpose of social change, as unequivocally illegitimate. Violence is perceived to endanger national unity, as an expression of the unrestrained passions of fallen man, and as an affront to the national identity. The violent are disparaged as traitors, selfish anarchs, or foreigners. This does not mean that violence is ignored by contemporaries as opposed to historians. As McNaught (1970: 84) points out, Canadian governments have been quick to deal with violence. There has been no dithering around waiting to see how the situation develops. Other countries, with positive models in their past or that are less alarmed by turbulence, may hesitate to quash an incident. In Canada there is no uncertainty over the moral status of the violent or over the serious threat they constitute. Moreover, Canadian governments have been able to move quickly to repress an outbreak, confident of being backed up by a large measure of public support, at least until the incident is concluded. Strong government actions against the violent, such as the War Measures Act, are popularly endorsed.[10]

In short, the myth of the peaceable kingdom attaches a particular poignancy to violence in Canada. The illegitimacy of violence is tangled up with notions of national identity and survival. The violent are doubly damned; their acts are not only morally wrong, they are an affront to the nation. Canadians subject to the myth, then, are rarely sympathetic observers of the violence used by their fellow citizens.

IDEOLOGIES

In his turn-of-the-century analysis of Canadian life, André Siegfried was struck by "the absence of ideas or doctrines to divide the voters." In an election, "the question is not whether [a policy] ... shall be carried out but who shall carry it out. In such circumstances what can the names Conservative or Liberal mean? They mean nothing but government and opposition." Canadian leaders prudently reckon that "an explicit attitude towards burning questions"

---

10 See J. Armstrong's (1972) analysis of letters to the editor during the October crisis of 1970. The majority of letters contained a call to stand firm behind the government. (See also McNaught, 1975a: 154.) The reactions of Canadian governments are considered further in chapter 9.

would serve to drive away more supporters than it would attract (1966: 113-14). Eighty years later, this characterization of Canadian political life remains as telling as ever. Successful political parties and movements usually avoid ideological commitments. Nevertheless, an examination of ideologies is called for because they have played an important role in the violence of other countries and because they have surfaced in some of Canada's unsuccessful, violent movements. A key question is the role an ideology plays in determining the fate of a movement.

Ideologies are wonderfully diverse: they may harken back to a golden age or look forward to a new order; they may be secular or religious; anarchic, democratic, fascist, nationalist, or Marxist; extol violence or utterly condemn it; and so on. There are however a number of recurring themes.

In the first place, ideologies usually provide a sense of group coherence and solidarity. They answer the questions: Who are "we"? In what respects are we all alike? Why should we all pull together? Often there is a moral re-evaluation of the group. No longer is the group dismissed as marginal, impotent, or responsible for its own problems; rather it is a worthy bearer of a proud historical tradition or the potent servant of divine will, destiny, or historical necessity (for example, Riel's conception of the Métis as a chosen people; Flanagan, 1979: 185).

Second, ideologies analyse what is currently wrong. Discontents are specified. There is an explanation of why the world is not as it should be, sometimes based on a new set of moral ideas, and responsibility is ascribed.

Third, goals are specified: ideas about what the world can and should be like, the utopias whose achievement justifies present sacrifices. An intervening period of struggle is generally postulated, but the movement's goals are regarded as achievable in the not too distant future. The inevitability of ultimate success is often stressed: God or history is on "our" side, right will triumph in the end.

Finally, ideologies may spell out the means a movement should adopt to achieve its goals. Details may be provided on the tactics to be employed, the resources to be accumulated, and the appropriate organizational mode to be followed.

Ideologies obviously vary in the extent to which they develop a sophisticated treatment of these four themes. More importantly, however, within any movement some members will be more informed of the subtleties of its ideology than others. Gurr (1970: 195-6) suggests that:

Most participants ... do not carry complex ideologies around in their heads. The subtleties of justification articulated by revolutionary leaders penetrate to many of their followers in a congeries of phrases, vague ideas, and symbols ... The slogans ... may be derived from complex ideologies, but their operative force lies not in the ideology itself but in the relevance of the slogans to the actors' perceptions of their situation and the cues the slogans provide for violent action [or, it should be added, for non-violent action].

However, the examples Gurr gives – among them, "workers of the world unite" and "burn, baby, burn" – indicate that such slogans are not interchangeable. Each movement has its own slogans, and these slogans alone are meaningful to its adherents. They are meaningful because they encapsulate an ideology, whether sophisticated or crude, that has united the group, specified its discontents, provided it with goals, and justified its means. The slogans may be simplifications and the fine points of the ideology may be grasped only by the movement's leaders or intellectual cadre, but without the ideology the words are meaningless to even the most humble participant.

There appear to be periods of ideological effervescence when several ideologies circulate and compete for adherents. Gurr (1970: 199-200) suggests that these are times when anxiety, uncertainty, and discontent are widespread. Johnson (1966: 84-6) characterizes them as periods of disequilibrium and sees the heightened ideological activity as an attempt "to overcome the deficiencies of the existing culture." (When society is in equilibrium, ideologies are isolated and contained; they "will circulate only among occupants of marginal statuses or will remain unknown to any group within the system.") One ideology may eventually come to dominate all the others, and when this happens the stage is set for turmoil to give way to revolutionary violence. It is thus important to see whether there are any characteristics that differentiate successful ideologies from those that fall by the wayside.

The very prevalence of ideological constructs has led some authors to dismiss ideology as an unimportant variable. They argue that there are so many available alternatives that an aggrieved group can always find one suited to its purpose and that the choice has little effect on either the group's chances of success or the means it will adopt. Success turns on the resources the group can muster, and tactical decisions depend on what the group has to work with and the reactions of others, particularly the government, to it (Oberschall, 1973: 194-5). Yet, irrespective of the extent of disequilibrium, discontent, resources, or the reaction of others, there do appear to be some characteristics of ideologies in themselves that affect their chances of gaining adherents.

First is the ideology's degree of generality and insight. As will be illustrated in chapter 7, protest movements try to put forward broad platforms in order to attract as large a following as possible. Coalitions across groups cannot be built with an ideology relevant only to a narrow segment. In Johnson's (1966: 83) words, "some ideologies will be very simple intellectual constructs which serve as psychological scape-goats, such as anti-Semitism ... These simple, tension-managing ideologies will rarely become sufficiently generalized to absorb more than a few groups of status protesters."

Second is the appropriateness of the ideology. People may simply be unable to see how a particular ideology relates to them, in which case it will be dismissed as irrelevant. The course of syndicalism in Canada serves as an example. It achieved limited success in western Canada towards the end of the First World War, culminating in the founding of the One Big Union in 1919. Robin (1969: 274-5) shows how "social and political conditions peculiar to British Columbia favoured the propagation of syndicalist ideas" at that time, notably the workers' previous experience with direct action and large industrial unions, and their disillusionment with "parliamentarism." Syndicalism made sense to these workers. But to the differently situated workers in the rest of the country, it did not; it was inappropriate to them and they failed to support it. Even the western workers quickly dropped the idea. According to Bercuson (1975: 245-6), it

was initially successful precisely because western workers did not fully realize what ... had [been] created; when they did begin to find out ... they left the One Big Union almost as fast as they had joined it. The One Big Union may have been one manifestation of western labour radicalism but it did not suit the needs of western workers and shortchanged them organizationally, industrially and ideologically.

Third is the compatibility of the ideology with the society's culture. This appears paradoxical, given the definition of ideology as an alternative value structure competing with the established culture. An ideological movement nevertheless has to make converts of those who grew up in an established culture. An ideology is consequently more likely to be attractive if it challenges only some of the established values; if the alternative values it is offering do not challenge values that still receive widespread support; if the alternative values are voiced by spokesmen who are endowed with prestige in the existing culture; and if there is some historical precedent supportive of the new values. The point is that the ideology must contain sufficiently novel values to be able to promise a new and better order, but not so different that they appear unacceptably alien to potential converts. Thus Gurr (1970: 204-5) attributes the failure of Marxism in Latin America in part to its irreconcilability with some of the region's pervasive cultural themes. Robin (1968: 276-7) also interprets the failure of Marxist socialism and the modest success of democratic socialism in Canada in terms of the two ideologies' relation to the country's culture. The Marxists remained isolated, but democratic socialism, drawing on Christian socialism and British ideas, was "culturally acceptable."

Canadian socialism could claim to be an indigenous rather than "alien" ideology. The political radicalism of the new ideology was offset by its cultural conservatism. The category of "alien" in Canada was reserved almost exclusively for the Communist Party, supported by low status ethnic groups who derived their socialism from Eastern

Europe ... [In contrast] socialism in America was foreign in both ideology and personnel and the Socialist Party was an alien subversive organization. The Socialist Party of America suffered its greatest defeat during and following the first world war when it could not escape the alien stigma. In Canada it was the [Marxist] S.D.P. and minority ethnic groups who suffered. Neither the I.L.P. nor the S.P.C. were declared illegal and both flourished in the late phases of the war period. Socialism in Canada therefore escaped the stigma of being "alien" through association with a highly valued British cultural tradition. The different position of the ideologies in the value systems of the two countries at least partly explains both the relative success of Canadian socialism after 1930 and the more tolerant attitude of organized labour towards socialism.

These factors of generality, appropriateness, and cultural compatibility indicate that a movement's choice of ideology will affect its chances of success.

Another question is what contribution, if any, does ideology make to the outbreak of violence. Oberschall (1973: 195) dismisses ideology as all but irrelevant here, arguing that "the means used grow out of the confrontation itself ... [and] depend not on the goals, but what reception the goals and the demands of the protesters get in the society." Yet Gurr (1970: 156) argues that the potential for political violence "varies strongly" with the extent to which justifications for this means have been developed. He adds (1970: 205) that "since the discontented have a fundamental disposition to aggression, *ceteris paribus*, doctrines justifying violence are likely to seem more appropriate and hence to gain wider currency." ("Fundamental disposition" refers to the psychological link between frustration and aggression.)

There are many possible justifications for violence. Normative justifications often take the form of: "Others have been violent to us and, if we are violent now, it is only in self-defence or retaliation." This reasoning was used frequently in FLQ documents that argued that French Canadians had long been on the receiving end of the "violence" of political and economic structures. An alternative is an appeal to a higher law or tradition: "If it was right and proper for our founding fathers to rise up in rebellion, so too is it right and proper for us to rebel now." This justification has not been used in Canada for obvious reasons. Another and rarer form treats violence as a healing or purifying force (as in Sartre [1968] and Fanon). A variant in Canada has been espoused by the Sons of Freedom who see the destruction of worldly goods as enabling the victim to live more in accordance with the divine will.

Alternatively the effectiveness of violence may be stressed. It may be seen as an efficient way: (1) to bring down regimes, as in the guerrilla theory of Guevara and Debray, which was adopted in part by the FLQ; (2) to coerce governments into acceding to one's demands, as in Riel's 1885 tactic of capturing hostages in the belief that the government would then have to bargain with him; (3) to redress grievances by drawing public and governmental attention, as in protest violence; or (4) to secure dominance over other people, as in the terrorist campaigns of the Donnellys and Hal Banks's SIU, or in the election violence designed to keep an opponent's supporters away from the polls. Utilitarian justifications also encompass references to different movements that have apparently succeeded through the use of violence at others times or places.

Given this range of possible justifications for violence, it might well be assumed that the question of ideological justification is essentially a trivial one since some kind of justification can be readily found. This holds for the great majority of movements that carry on their work through electoral politics, lobbying, and other legitimate means and whose formal ideological documents contain no reference to violence. If and when these "neutral" groups are drawn into a violent incident, they will extemporaneously justify their actions. But Oberschall's observations cited above apply. Their justifications are unimportant; what counts in the causation of the incident is how society has reacted to their demands.

However, there are a small number of groups with ideologies that either enjoin adherents to engage in special, non-violent tactics such as passive resistance or civil disobedience ("anti-violence groups"), or actively urge violent tactics ("pro-violence groups"). Here ideology does seem to be important. Anti-violence ideologies will restrain their adherents from resorting to violence. Pro-violence ideologies may incite their adherents to initiating violence, although we have to exclude the armchair revolutionaries who advocate violence but do not act. Further, both anti-violence and pro-violence groups may be challenging the traditional, legitimate tactics of political protest. To the extent that their ideologies call on their adherents to go outside the accepted channels, we can expect a repressive and often violent response from other groups, including the government, towards them. For example, among the 53 American protest groups in his study, Gamson (1975) finds seven that ideologically espoused violent tactics. These groups were twice as likely as the ideologically neutral groups to use violence (29 per cent versus 13 per cent), but the really striking figures are that 71 per cent of the pro-violence groups were on the receiving end of violent attacks or subjected to arrests in comparison with only 22 per cent of the ideologically neutral groups.[11] In short, both pro- and anti-violence ideologies have some effect on the violence of campaigns, both in restraining or encouraging its use by the group and in prompting others to violently suppress the group.

Another way in which ideologies affect violence lies in their choice of targets, that is, in their specification of who or what is to blame for the source

11 Percentages are calculated from the figures Gamson gives in his appendix d.

of discontentment. The choice of targets is linked to justifications for violence in that once an individual or institution is identified as meriting or vulnerable to attack, an implicit justification for carrying out the attack has been created. On the one hand, we find, once again, researchers for whom the issue is non-problematic. Piven and Cloward (1977: 20-1), for example, suggest that people automatically turn their anger against the individual or institutions that frustrate them in their daily lives – the assembly line, the foreman, the slumlord. On the other hand, there is evidence that some movements are more effective than others because they have ideologically selected more appropriate targets and that violent campaigns can be cut short by unwisely chosen targets. For instance, Wedge compares student political violence in Brazil and the Dominican Republic in the mid-sixties. The former was ineffectual, the latter effective. One of the reasons Wedge (1972: 308-9) finds for the difference is that the Brazilian students went after vague ("U.S. imperialism") and inaccessible targets (it was always people overseas or in the distant capital city who were to blame), while the Dominican students directed their energies against precise targets that were near at hand, such as local police stations.

Targets may also be inappropriate if they are too insignificant for others to worry about their destruction, or too well protected so that the attackers are discouraged; if they raise ambivalent feelings among the attackers; or if they alienate public sympathy by involving innocent victims or those not seen as properly subject to attack, such as children. The ideal target, in short, is accessible, significant, vulnerable, and acceptable to both the attacking group and the wider public. Piven and Cloward notwithstanding, these conditions are not always readily met with. One example of poor target selection in Canada is Riel in 1885 who declined to follow Dumont's advice to attack the railway line and harry the oncoming soldiers with guerrilla tactics. By keeping his men close to Batoche, Riel had no option but to face the overpowering strength of the military. Another example is the Sons of Freedom campaign in the late fifties and early sixties. Their indiscriminate bombings not only further alienated public sympathy but displayed a confusion of goals. The sect sometimes seemed to be courting persecution and martyrdom, sometimes to be fighting a materialist society, and sometimes to be asking the world to go away and leave it in peace. The stealthy dynamiting of the power lines across Kootenay Lake may have served the second goal, but hardly the first or third.

Coser's (1956: 156) distinction between realistic and nonrealistic conflict (alternatively called instrumental or expressive conflict) is relevant here. Realistic conflicts "arise from frustrations of specific demands within a relationship and from estimates of gains of the participants, and ... are directed at the presumed frustrating [target] ... Nonrealistic conflicts, on the other hand, are not occasioned by the rival ends of the antagonists, but by the need for tension release of one or both of them." The importance of the distinction is that alternative means can be found for carrying on realistic conflicts (for example, from the FLQ to the PQ), but in nonrealistic conflicts the only alternatives are to be found in the choice of targets – to release tension, "the chosen antagonist can be substituted for by any other 'suitable' target." The confusion in the Sons of Freedom targets suggests that at least part of the group's violence can be considered as a means of releasing the tension created by their fanatical and chaotic lives. Coser (1956: 47) also makes the point that the satisfaction obtained in the release of tension is momentary; further release will be sought as long as the tension remains. Again this fits the Freedomites, and accounts both for the persistence of the violence and for its decline after the sect came in contact with the wider world and could no longer dominate the lives of its members.

CONCLUSION

Justificatory ideas appear to be a necessary but not a sufficient condition for violence. Whether they are drawn from the culture, a subculture, or an ideology, they do indeed seem to accompany outbreaks of violence. Justifications are so readily available that they might easily be dismissed as trivial in the causation of violence. Still there is a marketplace of ideas, and some are more successful than others in attracting adherents. A successful ideology may direct its adherents to use violence or non-violent tactics, legitimate or illegitimate ones, and in doing so it obviously influences the course of the ensuing campaign. Its choice of targets also has an effect. Thus if we want to explain the relatively low levels of violence in Canada, one reason is that pro-violence ideologies have been insufficiently general, appropriate, or compatible with the culture to attract many followers. And where violence has been justified, the selection of targets has often been astray so that the ensuing violence has gained few successes.

Another reason for low levels of Canadian violence is the strength of condemnatory ideas in the culture. Canada, like other industrial nations, has seen the sphere of acceptable violence steadily circumscribed, but I have argued that the myth of the peaceable kingdom has lent a particular force to violence-condemning ideas here. Although there are subcultural pockets in which violence is enjoined – among the prison population and hockey spectators, for instance – the use of violence to achieve social change has been widely regarded as un-Canadian behaviour.

The Canadian political culture sternly enjoins protest groups to work for limited objectives within established channels. There is a conservative cast to the culture that emphasizes restraint, acceptance of a less than perfect existence, the rejection of sweeping ideological changes in favour of incremental, evolutionary development within the traditional framework, indeed a general suspicion of novel ideas as potentially too disruptive in a fragile society. Equally evident is the expectation that authority is to be respected. Governments deserve support, particularly on those rare occasions when they are violently challenged by citizens unmindful of their heritage and of the constraining realities of Canadian life. These notions all find expression in the myth of the peaceable kingdom.

We cannot say to what extent Canadians have shunned violence because they think it is improper. Still there is evidence from a number of incidents of movement leaders seeking to avert an outbreak because they believe it will alienate popular support and attract the wrath of the authorities. Some examples are given in chapter 8. The myth has also apparently affected the behaviour of Canadian governments, both in restraining their own use of violence and in their expectations of popular support, as will be further examined in chapter 9.

In brief, ideas do play a role in hindering or hastening the outbreak of violence. They are, however, only one factor in the chain of causation. Ideas have to be implemented. When and how they are put into practice is the subject of the remaining chapters.

CHAPTER SIX

The Breakdown
of Restraints
against Violence

In the previous chapter it was noted that violence was widely regarded as an illegitimate tactic in the Canadian culture. For the most part Canadians apparently either learn to live with their problems or seek to remedy them by peaceful means. There have nevertheless been many incidents of violence in the country's history. Thus if we accept the idea of cultural restraints, we also have to explain how these have been overcome.

There are competing schools of thought on how individuals come to make the decision to resort to violence. The Tillys (1975: 4-8) have labelled them "breakdown" and "solidarity" theories. The former emphasize the processes by which the cultural restraints against violence become weakened; the latter concentrate on the building up of solidarities with accompanying norms justifying the use of violence. The present chapter examines the breakdown theories; chapter 8 examines the solidarity theories.

Cultural restraints against violence have been identified as weak in three different situations. In the first there is only a temporary suspension of restraints. This occurs in *crowds* when an excited group of people behaves abnormally. In the second situation, the cultural norms themselves are crumbling often as a result of strains experienced by a society in flux. Individuals lose their sense of integration with society and are hence reduced to a state of *anomie* or normlessness in which barriers against violence and other anti-social behaviour are dropped. Thirdly, the society may be so structured as to preclude the integration of certain *marginal* groups. While the mainstream social groupings maintain their normative integration, marginal groups receive at best an attenuated version of these norms. Marginal populations are in a limbo where no firm guides to conduct exist, although they may be in the process of forming a subculture of their own. In this weakness of cultural norms they resemble anomic populations, and I shall consequently discuss the two together.

THE VIOLENT CROWD

Whether a crowd turns to violence depends on the presence of vulnerable antagonists and on the actions of the authorities. In addition to these factors, however, conventional wisdom buttressed by a long line of theoretical writing holds that there is something in the very nature of the crowd experience that facilitates the outbreak of violence.

Initially people may gather calmly to form an audience or parade, but speeches or unanticipated events or even just the excitement of gathering together will raise the emotional atmosphere. Or people may arrive on the scene already in an excited state, attracted by news of an unusual or inflammatory event, usually called the precipitating incident. High levels of interaction occur in the assembled throng; strangers talk to each other, rumours are passed around, and attempts are made to define the situation and establish an appropriate course of action. Symbols emerge that simplify the situation, remove ambivalent feelings, and direct and legitimate action against specific targets. Slogans, songs, and speeches firm up the symbols. Violence erupts.

Turner and Killian (1972: 80) argue that "the attitudes that are expressed in the crowd are those which, while being sanctioned in the culture of the crowd members, are ordinarily limited in their expression ... Thus it may be said that the basic condition out of which crowd behavior arises is one of cultural conflict, or a breakdown of normative integration." The point is that hostility and discontent exist prior to the gathering of the violent crowd. The crowd situation merely serves to facilitate their expression by removing inhibitions against violent behaviour. How and why this happens has been variously explained.

First, it has been suggested that the very size of a crowd is a factor. Sheer numbers give a sense of power, so that targets appear vulnerable to attack. Furthermore, they confer a feeling of immunity from responsibility or reprisal since crowd members believe that they cannot be singled out from all the other anonymous individuals.

Second, the emotional frame of mind of the crowd has been implicated. Anxious or excited individuals often jump to wild conclusions and do not weigh the consequences of their acts. They tend also to be suggestible and permissive in allowing themselves normally inhibited behaviour.

Third, the cohesiveness of crowds is sometimes stressed. Norms emerge for the occasion, and outside reference groups are forgotten, so that individuals caught up in the crowd feel intense pressures to conform to the definitions and expectations of the group. Dissenters and would-be peace-makers are silenced. Those taking the lead in the violence (providing they remain in line with the norms of the crowd) are egged on and receive enthusiastic approbation.

Psychological experiments have shown that aggression is more readily expressed by groups than by individuals, and that the more cohesive the group the greater is the likelihood of aggression being expressed (Gurr, 1970: 287-8). The explanation is that individuals on their own hesitate to ventilate their feelings because they lack confirmation from others that aggression is called for. They may feel like striking out but are unsure whether such a response is appropriate. Yet when these individuals sense that others feel the same way, they deem their individual assessment to have been confirmed. The more cohesive the group, the more quickly does the interaction take place that confirms the "correctness" of an aggressive response.

The working of such mechanisms can be seen in a couple of Canadian examples. A case of minor election violence is given in figure 4. A large number of people have assembled to hear a political speaker and cheer him on; a small number of hecklers have come to jeer. Despite the presence of external restraints (police officers and party organizers), the crowd becomes "testier" at the continued interruptions, and some present begin to behave in ways that would shock them "in normal circumstances." Verbal abuse leads to physical assault.

The riot against Japanese and Chinese that occurred in 1907 in Vancouver provides another example. According to Ormsby (1971: 351):

On September 8, the [Asiatic Exclusion] League organized a parade to the City Hall, located, as it happened, near "Chinatown". There, after the playing of "Rule Britannia", an effigy of the Lieutenant-Governor was burned, and then followed speeches, including an inflammatory one by the Secretary of the Seattle Exclusion League. Suddenly the crowd turned into a mob, invaded "Chinatown", and swept on to the Japanese quarter.

The ensuing battle resulted in $36,000 worth of damage to Chinese and Japanese property. The sequence of events in this incident is typical of many others: the initially peaceful gathering, an intervening stage of affirming the crowd's norms and lowering inhibitions against violence through the use of symbolic violence and "inflammatory" rhetoric, and finally the sudden eruption of violence.

As was mentioned in chapter 1, studies of the crowd in the tradition of collective behaviour research have been strongly criticized, particularly for their elitism, neglect of the role of the authorities, and stress on the irrationality of the crowd's behaviour (Skolnick, 1969: 330-9). It is not good enough, the critics say, simply to point to such factors as emotional contagion or irresponsibility; for that is to serve an ideological purpose in dismissing as irrelevant the political aspirations and experienced injustices of those assembled. These strictures, however, certainly do not apply to all theorists who have studied crowds. The work, for example, of Turner and Killian

FIGURE 4
Violence in a Crowd Situation
The Winter Campaign: No One Immune When Politics Shows Ugly Side
By Paul Palango

Political rallies are, by their nature, passionate affairs. Politicians usually can handle the heat, but sometimes their supporters can't. Things can get ugly, as was the case at the Conservative rally at the Etobicoke Olympium on Thursday night.

Three female hecklers worked overtime trying to throw Prime Minister Joe Clark off his course. At times they were successful, but, in the end, Mr. Clark prevailed and the women paid for their efforts with physical, as well as verbal, abuse.

The three women, two sisters in their mid-20s and their mother, waved placards and wore red, form-fitting "I Love Pierre" T-shirts. Their persistence and energy quickly enraged some of the Clark supporters.

A Tory placard came crashing down on one of the daughter's heads. Undaunted, she moved forward. People blocked her. Two women, who appeared to be in their 70s, grabbed the oldest heckler, Felicia Hardy, and pulled down the front of her T-shirt. Mrs. Hardy's daughter, Lisa, tried to get closer to the stage. Two men blocked her. A teen-ager taunted her. Lisa's sister, Alana Hardy Smith, tried another avenue to the stage. She too was stopped.

Some of the women in the crowd began swearing at them. Curses were hurled that might have shocked their sources, in normal circumstances.

"Commies," one man yelled. "Look at those red shirts. They're commies."

Many others chimed in.

The crowd was becoming testier by the minute.

Tory worker Janus Raudkivi moved in.

"Leave them alone. The more you bother them, the louder they'll get. Don't touch them. The press would love to get their hands on that."

Another placard dinged Lisa on the head, but she continued in her attempt to upset the Prime Minister.

She sang a Liberal version of the opening lines of the song Jambalaya: "Come on, Joe, you gotta go . . . ." Every time Mr. Clark criticized Liberal Leader Pierre Trudeau, she took a shot at Mr. Clark. He used many of his standard putdowns to counter – "There's another lonely Liberal out there."

When Mr. Clark spoke of foreign relations, she called him a warmonger.

A long-haired teen-ager took issue with her assessment.

"Do you want to go to war?" she asked.

"I'm a patriot," he said, sneering at her.

"Well, my father was a veteran," she replied.

Three Mounties assigned to the force's VIP section made their way into the crowd. One burly man who was being particularly aggressive toward the women suddenly felt a hand on his shoulder.

FIGURE 4 (*concluded*)

Sgt. Jim Mairs told him he was "getting close to the line and he'd better calm down." The Mounties positioned themselves around the hecklers to protect them.

"Kick them out," a group yelled out.

Sgt. Mairs answered: "This is a democratic country. They have every right to be here. They have every right to protest. So leave them alone."

Minutes later, a man threw a punch over a Mountie's shoulders and hit Lisa in the side. She began to cry. The crowd jeered her.

Another man, standing with his son, yelled out: "There are three good reasons for birth control."

The same man pulled his son close to him and told him loudly: "Some day, son, I'll let you read Das Kapital."

As the rally ended, the same man fell to the floor when Lisa passed. He immediately jumped up and told Sgt. Mairs he wanted to charge her with assault. He said she had ripped the rear end out of his pants.

Lisa and Alana offered to give the man their names. Sgt. Mairs appeared not to believe the man's story.

The crowd filed out of the auditorium and the policemen left the three women. Then, as they went out a side door, joyous with their performance, a middle-aged man lunged out of the crowd, grabbed Lisa around the throat and carried her 10 feet. She lost control when he let go.

She chased the man. She called for the police but there were none in sight.

The man and his wife hurried away.

After Lisa calmed down, the three women went home convinced they had successfully done what they had come to do.

(*The Globe and Mail*, 16 February 1980. By permission.)

(1972) and Oberschall (1973: ch. 9) on the dynamics of the crowd experience contribute substantially to an understanding of this kind of incident.

ANOMIC AND MARGINAL POPULATIONS

Explanations of violence in terms of the lack of internal restraints in anomic populations have tended to fall into disrepute because on occasion they have been seized upon and used crudely by those patently hostile to the violence of oppressed groups. In Canadian official circles, the more simple-minded of such explanations have generally been avoided. Governments and royal commissions have typically seen violence as the product of several factors. One is the presence of discontent, often seen to be in the form of unjustifiable expectations. To explain the conversion of this discontent into violence, attention is usually drawn to the presence of agitators working in the crowds and the existence of an exceptional period of crumbling normative restraints.

Thus Sir John A. Macdonald, in considering the Red River resistance of 1869-70, blamed the rising in part on the collapse of the Hudson's Bay Company authority prior to the takeover of the territory by Canada. The inhabitants were in the grip of uncertainty, not knowing what the future held for them. However, "they would have preferred their present wild and semi-barbarous life to the restraints of civilization that will be forced upon them by the Canadian government and the new settlers." A transitional period was in prospect. Until the residents were "altogether swamped by the influx of strangers who will go in with the idea of becoming industrious and peaceable settlers," trouble could be expected.[1]

Macdonald again linked the agitation in the West prior to the 1885 rebellion to a poorly integrated society. A series of bad harvests had created discontent. The feverish activities of land jobbers and speculators had raised unrealistic expectations. The "stable" element in the population was weak; as he wrote to the Lieutenant-Governor of Manitoba, "you, however, will not have much peace until there is a public opinion – a real opinion formed by a body of well-to-do settlers." The Indian and half-breed population were still basically "savages," and consequently there was always a danger of an outbreak. Riel's agitation was another factor; his influence in the Northwest was great where he was considered "a sort of half-breed Mahdi." Macdonald's Minister of Justice went so far as to state that "there has never been a rebellion more completely dependent upon one man ... Had he been removed a day before the outbreak, it would, in all probability, never have occurred."[2]

In considering the Winnipeg General Strike, government members also saw agitators at work in a weakened society. The First World War had created strains, and in its aftermath strange new ideas and demands were being raised. As one minister confided to his diary: "But what a seething time it is in the world! ... Certainly the foundations of things are being uprooted in a thousand ways ... How much this war has to answer for."[3] The Prime Minister, Sir Robert Borden, made a similar analysis in his memoirs (1969: 214): "In Canada, as elsewhere, the conditions of business and employment were abnormal. Equally abnormal was the state of mind of the people in

1 Quotations in this paragraph are from: Pope (n.d.: 134), Macdonald to the Earl of Carnarvon, 14 April 1870; PAC (Public Archives of Canada), Macdonald Papers, vol. 516, Macdonald to Bown, 14 October 1869.

2 Quotations in this paragraph are from: Pope (n.d.: 314), Macdonald to Aikens, 28 July 1884; House of Commons, Debates (6 July 1885), 3119 and (26 March 1885), 745; PAC, Macdonald Papers, vol. 109, In the Case of Louis Riel ..., Report of Sir Alexander Campbell (1885: 6).

3 PAC, Foster Papers, vol. 8, Diary, 2 and 25 May 1919.

general, or at least of the great majority of them. There was a distinctive lack of the usual balance; the agitator ... found quick response to insidious propaganda."

The royal commissions appointed to report on the incidents also heavily favoured similar theories. The Robson Commission (Manitoba, 1919: 11, 22) that examined the Winnipeg General Strike saw it as "a protest against conditions and a demand for general relief." But the "relaxation of war tensions" and "the difficult conditions of the times" had so unsettled opinion that "a matter which would not in ordinary times be thought to justify a sympathetic strike was quite sufficient on the occasion in question." Violence occurred because Winnipeg was "a receptive ground for seed of disturbance, and it brought forth the restless element that would be attracted by street demonstrations." The Regina Riot Inquiry Commission (Saskatchewan, 1936: 269) attributed the On to Ottawa trek to a combination of unrealistic expectations and agitators. According to the Commission, the relief camp strike was "partly due to a lack of appreciation ... of the difficulty of finding a method of really solving the unemployment problem as a whole and partly due to outside and disruptive influences that are and have been constantly sowing the seeds of discontent."

Blaming the abnormal conditions of the times as a source of violence has a definite ideological bias. As in some collective behaviour theories of crowds, attention is diverted from governmental ineptitude and coercion, and also from the political dignity of the violent and their sense of injustice. Even so, the theories relating to anomic and marginal populations remain interesting as they suggest a number of hypotheses that are accessible to empirical investigation. Furthermore, the theories do appear plausible. Surely the people who should most readily turn to violence are those whose norms against violence are being eroded or were only poorly acquired in the first place, and not those fully integrated into a society with a strong normative structure upholding peaceful relations.

In evaluating the theories, the first task is to establish where and when conditions of anomie and marginality have obtained. With anomie, we can look for the conditions that are theorized to produce crumbling norms (for example, rapid socio-economic change) and for indicators that such a crumbling has taken place.

INDICATORS OF ANOMIE

Suicide and homicide. Durkheim distinguished various forms of suicide, including the egoistic and anomic. Both are caused by "society's insufficient presence in individuals" (1951: 258), but differ in several other respects. Egoistic suicide "varies inversely with the degree of integration of the social groups of which the individual forms a part ... The more weakened the groups to which he belongs, the less he depends on them, the more he consequently depends only on himself and recognizes no other rules of conduct than what are founded on his private interests" (209). As life loses its collective objectives and meaning, an exaggerated individualism results, "characterized by a state of depression and apathy" (356). There is no passion for life, so that while the number of suicides climbs, the homicide rate falls since the latter, according to Durkheim, is dependent on passion. In contrast are "great social disturbances and great popular wars [that] rouse collective sentiments, stimulate partisan spirit and patriotism, political and national faith, alike, and concentrating activity toward a single end, at least temporarily cause a stronger integration of society" (208). Suicides then go down, but, with the greater release of emotions, homicides go up.

Anomic suicides relate to how individuals are regulated by society, rather than the extent to which they are attached to it. According to Durkheim, "every disturbance of [societal] equilibrium, even though it achieves greater comfort and a heightening of general vitality, is an impulse to voluntary death" (246). This is because "when society is disturbed by some painful crisis or by beneficent but abrupt transitions" (252), the social restraints on aspirations and ambitions are weakened. A condition of anomie is produced that "begets a state of exasperation and irritated weariness which may turn against the person himself or another according to circumstances" (357). The rates for both homicide and suicide increase.

Durkheim's theory, then, covers the following situations:

1 Collectivity orientations: low suicide, high homicide
2 Individual orientations: high suicide, low homicide
3 High social restraints: low suicide, low homicide
4 Low social restraints: high suicide, high homicide.

While he does not specifically deal with public violence, the logic of his argument is such that we could expect it to follow the incidence of homicide. Thus when people withdraw into an exaggerated individualism and apathy (situation 2 above), public violence should be low, but it should rise when people become passionately involved in furthering the interests of their group (situation 1). Similarly, when social restraints on ambitions and aspirations are strong (situation 3), there should be little public violence; when they are weak (situation 4), public violence should increase.

Some support for Durkheim's theory comes from international statistics on suicide, homicide, and public violence. As predicted, countries with low rates of both homicide and suicide or with low rates of homicide coupled with high rates of suicide (situations 3 and 2 respectively) tend to be stable and have few assassinations. Also as predicted, countries with low suicide but high homicide rates (situation 1) are preponderantly unstable and have many assassinations. However, the high suicide, high homicide countries (situation 4) run counter to the theory in that two-thirds of them exhibit low levels of instability (Kirkham, Levy, and Crotty, 1970: 197-8).

If we turn to comparisons over time, again we can find some support for Durkheim's theory. Table 4 gives the rates of Canadian homicides and suicides over the last sixty years. A brief study of the table shows that Canadian homicide and suicide rates tend to move in tandem. At no time do we find the two rates diverging over a period of years. Evidently, Durkheim's theory on collectivity versus individual orientations, which was designed to explain divergent rates, does not apply to Canada. However, his concept of high restraint versus anomic periods is more instructive.

We find an early anomic period peaking around 1930. Thereafter suicide and homicide rates declined to reach a period of high restraint during the years of the Second World War. There was a minor upsurge of anomie immediately after the war, but the 1950s were restraint years. From the late fifties both rates started to move upwards. By 1970 each had surpassed their previous highpoints in 1930. After 1975 the homicide rate started to fall, likewise suicides. Although it is too early to confirm these recent trends, we seem to be passing into a restraint period.

Can we predict the incidence of collective violence from the waxing and waning of the homicide and suicide rates? The restraint periods of the war years and the fifties were indeed relatively peaceful ones. We can link the turmoil of the Depression years, the industrial conflict after the war, and the turbulent sixties to anomic periods. Yet the match is not precise. Anomie would seem to have peaked somewhat earlier than public violence in the thirties, but later than public violence in the early seventies. It may be that suicide and homicide rates only roughly capture the concept Durkheim was interested in. To see if this is so, we can turn to other indicators of restraint versus anomie, in particular to crime rates.

Crime. Durkheim (1951: 358) characterized anomic periods as times of increasing "moral instability." During them, we should consequently expect to find all forms of conduct regarded as deviant, not just homicide and suicide, to be on the rise. Contrariwise, during periods of restraint, we should expect them to be declining together.

There is some evidence that the levels of various forms of deviancy do tend to go hand in hand. For example, Manzer (1974: 91-3) has assembled a table ranking Canada's provinces by their rates of crimes of violence, suicide, divorce, and "percentage of drinking population consuming hazardous amounts of alcohol." The violent crime rate, 1962-1970, was highest in British Columbia and then declined fairly steadily from west to east. The suicide, divorce, and alcoholism rates showed a similar west to east decline. This would suggest the existence of deviancy-related anomie, especially in

TABLE 4

Homicides and Suicides, Canada, 1921-1980

	Homicides			Suicides		
Year	Number	Rate per 100,000	Average rate	Number	Rate per 100,000	Average rate
1921				496	5.7	
1922				548	6.2	
1923		(Not available)		582	6.5	6.3
1924				577	6.3	
1925				636	6.9	
1926	120	1.33		680	7.2	
1927	124	1.29		760	7.9	
1928	150	1.53	1.61	755	7.7	8.2
1929	182	1.81		838	8.4	
1930	214	2.10		1012	9.9	
1931	172	1.66		1010	9.7	
1932	158	1.50		1028	9.8	
1933	147	1.38	1.45	924	8.7	9.0
1934	142	1.32		929	8.6	
1935	153	1.41		906	8.4	
1936	137	1.25		931	8.5	
1937	138	1.25		981	8.9	
1938	127	1.14	1.21	953	8.5	8.6
1939	124	1.10		982	8.7	
1940	148	1.30		951	8.4	
1941	130	1.13		899	7.8	
1942	113	.97		841	7.2	
1943	125	1.06	1.06	761	6.5	6.8
1944	106	.89		733	6.1	
1945	152	1.26		768	6.4	
1946	146	1.19		1004	8.2	
1947	146	1.16		952	7.6	
1948	155	1.21	1.13	1004	7.8	7.8
1949	172	1.28		1029	7.7	
1950	112	.82		1068	7.8	
1951	137	.98		1036	7.4	
1952	135	.93		1055	7.3	
1953	149	1.00	.99	1054	7.1	7.2
1954	157	1.03		1104	7.2	
1955	157	1.01		1106	7.0	
1956	171	1.06		1226	7.6	
1957	165	.99		1247	7.5	
1958	198	1.16	1.11	1271	7.4	7.5
1959	167	.96		1287	7.4	
1960	244	1.37		1350	7.6	

TABLE 4 (*concluded*)

		Homicides				Suicides	
Year	Number	Rate per 100,000	Average rate	Number	Rate per 100,000	Average rate
1961	233	1.27		1366	7.5	
1962	265	1.43		1331	7.2	
1963	249	1.32	1.35	1436	7.6	7.9
1964	253	1.31		1586	8.2	
1965	277	1.41		1715	8.8	
1966	250	1.25		1715	8.6	
1967	338	1.66		1841	9.0	
1968	375	1.81	1.75	2021	9.7	9.9
1969	391	1.86		2291	10.9	
1970	467	2.19		2413	11.3	
1971	473	2.19		2559	11.9	
1972	521	2.38		2657	12.2	
1973	546	2.47	2.56	2773	12.6	12.4
1974	600	2.67		2902	12.9	
1975	701	3.07		2808	12.3	
1976	668	2.89		2935	12.8	
1977	711	3.05		3317	14.2	
1978	660	2.81	2.78	3475	14.8	14.0
1979	631	2.66		3357	14.2	
1980	593	2.48		3358	14.0	

Source: For homicides, 1926-60: rates have been calculated by author from figures given in Leacy, 1983: series 221. For homicides, 1961-80: Statistics Canada, Catalogue 85-209, 1980. For suicides, 1921-68: Statistics Canada, *Suicide Mortality, 1950-1968*, Catalogue 84-528:31. For suicides, 1969–80: Statistics Canada, Catalogue 84-203, various years.

the context of the rapid population and economic growth of the western provinces in comparison with the more stable eastern ones.

However, if we try to fit the incidence of public violence into this table, we are clearly in trouble. Consider Quebec: this province experienced profound socio-economic changes during the sixties, but fell below the national average on each of Manzer's "indicators of disruptive socio-psychological conditions." But with the violence of its separatists, students, and union members, it would probably have ranked at or near the top of any comparable table showing provincial rates of public violence. The position of Quebec forces us to call into question either (1) the validity of these indicators of anomie, or (2) the association between anomie and public violence.

(1) Crime rates, in particular, may be poor indicators of deviancy for a number of reasons. First, they are subject to reporting vagaries and definitional changes that can make year-by-year or geographic comparisons suspect (Zay, 1963; Giffen, 1976). Second, crime rates reflect the resources

devoted to the detection of crime. The more policemen there are, the greater the number of crimes that will be detected (McDonald, 1969). Third, the more activities that are criminalized in a society, the higher its crime rate will be (Gurr, 1976: 169). Historical or cross-national comparisons of totals for all crimes may tell us more about the size of the criminal code than the unruliness of the population. And fourth, we know from victimization surveys that crime statistics underrepresent the true crime rate (Hagan, 1977: 44).

Crime rates, then, are an imperfect indicator of the extent of criminal activity in a country. Yet they are not worthless. If we concentrate on the most serious crimes, which seem to be less subject to the problems we have noted, and on long-term trends (in order to iron out some of the year-by-year quirks), real changes in social behaviour should be revealed (Gurr, 1979a: 365-6).

(2) But if we accept conditionally the validity of crime rates as indicators of deviancy and anomie, do they enable us to predict the incidence of public violence? Every possible answer can be found in the literature.

The anomalous position of Quebec in Manzer's table would suggest that there is no relation between deviancy and public violence. This, in fact, is the conclusion reached by Lodhi and Tilly in their historical study of France. The authors (1973: 312) find "no evidence at all that crime and collective violence are interchangeable or even interdependent." The Tillys (1975: 76-83) report that levels of European collective violence were correlated neither with socially disruptive forces that might give rise to anomie, such as rapid socio-economic growth, nor with indicators that anomie is supposedly widespread, such as rates of suicide or major crimes.

However, other studies have found a relation between public violence and crime. In some the relation is negative: as public violence increases, crime rates go down. For example, in the American South, the rise in civil rights demonstrations coincided with a decline in rates of violent crime committed by blacks (Gurr, 1976: 11). A negative relation may reflect the development of an anomic, crime-prone population into an organized collectivity given to public forms of action. Or it may reflect a preoccupation of police forces with public disorder which gives them less time to apprehend private criminals.

Yet other studies show a positive relation between crime and public violence. Thus Gurr (1976: 90) finds that "sharp increases in indicators of crimes of violence and theft usually coincide with episodes of strife" in the four urban centres he studied historically. He suggests that crime and conflict can be expected to coincide both on the standard argument that social strains produce violence-begetting anomie, and also because widespread and prolonged group conflict may itself produce a breakdown of moral order: "People in disorderly times are more likely to do what they feel like doing than what others say is right and proper" (1976: 82-3). Another theory comes from Engels who argued that crime could be understood as a form of working-class revolt. Countries ripest for revolution would have the highest rates of crime (McDonald, 1976: 55).

Criminal statistics in Canada are so confused that it is exceedingly difficult to draw any conclusions from them. The longest series available (stretching back into the nineteenth century but stopping short of recent years)[4] deals with court convictions. However, court convictions are poorly related to actual levels of criminal activity: to secure a conviction, the crime has first to be reported, then the police have to take up the case and lay hands on a suspect, and finally a court has to be convinced of a suspect's guilt. Convictions for more serious crimes – the indictable offences – seem to be somewhat less subject to the vagaries of victim, police, and court behaviour. Table 5 presents the data on conviction rates for indictable offences from 1886 to 1968. Our task is to relate them both to levels of public violence and to suicide and homicide rates in order to gauge their ability to indicate restraint versus anomic periods.[5]

At the time of the Northwest Rebellion, conviction rates in the country were running around 80 per 100,000, and they remained steady until 1893-4 when the rate moved over 100. There is thus no association between the public violence and conviction rates of the 1880s. (Moreover, according to Thorner's [1979: 74] study of crime in southern Alberta, 1878-1905, the Northwest Rebellion would seem to be unrelated to conviction rates even in an area directly affected by it.) Between 1894 and 1904, that is, well after the turbulence at the turn of the century was underway, the rates held steady between 103 and 116. Thereafter they took off to reach a peak of 272 at the start of the First World War. In fact the years 1912-14 are the only ones included in the period under study that meet Gurr's (1976: 83) criterion of a "crime wave" (rates rising on average by at least 10 per cent over three or more successive years). This peak, however, occurred well after the worst of the pre-war public violence was over.

The years of the First World War evidently formed a restraint period. The conviction rate fell from 272 in 1914 to 193 in 1917. After the war the rates rose somewhat but did not return to their pre-war levels. The post-war turbulence does not show up in any marked peaks in conviction rates. For most of the twenties, the conviction rates remained at a relatively low level of around 180. This was also a quiet period for public violence.

From 1927 conviction rates started strongly upwards again to reach a plateau of around 300 between 1931 and 1935. This coincides with rising homicide and suicide trends to indicate that the pre- and early-Depression

4 Court statistics are best used only up to the mid-sixties. Thereafter one or more provinces were not reporting. The series was discontinued after 1973.

5 Rates for violent crimes by and large follow the pattern of the overall crime rate. For the sake of simplicity, I deal only with the latter.

TABLE 5

Convictions for Indictable Offences per 100,000 Population, Canada
  (A) Total Convictions for Indictable Offences, 1886-1921
  (B) Adult Convictions for Indictable Offences, 1922-1960
  (C) Adults Convicted for Indictable Offences, 1949-1968

	A		B		C	
Year	Rate per 100,000	Average rate	Rate per 100,000	Average rate	Rate per 100,000	Average rate
1886	77					
1887	70					
1888	80	80				
1889	89					
1890	82					
1891	82					
1892	83					
1893	94	95				
1894	106					
1895	109					
1896	103					
1897	112					
1898	112	109				
1899	109					
1900	109					
1901	105					
1902	103					
1903	115	113				
1904	116					
1905	127					
1906	133					
1907	142					
1908	171	156				
1909	168					
1910	167					
1911	175					
1912	211					
1913	240	231				
1914	272					
1915	258					

TABLE 5 (*continued*)

Year	A Rate per 100,000	A Average rate	B Rate per 100,000	B Average rate	C Rate per 100,000	C Average rate
1916	239					
1917	193					
1918	213	216				
1919	222					
1920	215					
1921	221					
1922			176			
1923			168	177		
1924			178			
1925			185			
1926			185			
1927			195			
1928			221	224		
1929			240			
1930			279			
1931			304			
1932			299			
1933			308	302		
1934			293			
1935			307			
1936			327			
1937			334			
1938			389	377		
1939			425			
1940			409			
1941			373			
1942			337			
1943			353	353		
1944			355			
1945			346			
1946			381			
1947			350			
1948			323	334		
1949			307		230	
1950			308		229	

TABLE 5 (concluded)

Year	A Rate per 100,000	A Average rate	B Rate per 100,000	B Average rate	C Rate per 100,000	C Average rate
1951			288		207	
1952			288		206	
1953			304	298	199	199
1954			314		202	
1955			295		180	
1956			286		170	
1957			331		191	
1958			368	334	202	188
1959			321		178	
1960			362		198	
1961			391		212	
1962			385		208	
1963			415	394	227	216
1964			396		218	
1965			383		213	
1966			399		228	
1967			376	391	224	231
1968			398		241	

Source: A and B, 1886-1952, are from Statistics Canada, Catalogue 85-201, 1946: 164 and 1952: 148. For 1952-68, the rates are calculated by author from figures given in Leacy, 1983: series Z66. For C, 1949-68, the rates are calculated by author from figures given in Statistics Canada, Canada Yearbook, various years.

years were an anomic period. However, the conviction rates continued to climb in the later thirties. They reached a high point of 425 in 1939, well after the suicide, homicide, and apparently public violence rates had reached their respective peaks.

Once again the war years appear as a period of restraint. The rate fell from 425 in 1939 to 346 in 1945. Suicides, homicides, and public violence were also down during these years. As well, the small post-war upswing in homicides and suicides was matched to some extent by the conviction rates for 1946 and 1947. The fifties, a period of low public violence, constitute another restraint period, with suicides, homicides, and convictions all remaining at low levels.

Around 1960, the conviction rates started to move upwards again. But for most of the turbulent sixties, the increase was neither consistent nor particularly dramatic. One set of figures (adults convicted of indictable offences per 100,000 population aged 16 and over), for example, runs as follows for the years 1960 to 1967: 307, 330, 324, 354, 340, 330, 352, and 341 (Statistics Canada, *Canada Yearbook*, various years).

For more recent years, court statistics on convictions are no longer available; instead there are police statistics on the "crime rate" (all offences reported or known to the police less those which prove unfounded on investigation). The crime rate should be somewhat closer than convictions to the actual extent of criminal activity. I shall look at the crime rate for criminal code offences (both indictable and otherwise) but excluding traffic offences.

Pre-1970 crime rates are suspect because of changing reporting practices during the sixties, but such as they are, they indicate a modest but steady rise during this period of high public violence. Yet, as with the earlier statistics on convictions, we find a striking increase in the rate occurring after the peak years of public violence. The five-year average rate per 100,000 population for the years 1970-4 was 5690, but for 1975-9 it was 7056, a rise of 24 per cent (calculated from Statistics Canada, Catalogue 85-205, various years).

In summing up, I should again stress that these figures are questionable both in themselves (variable reporting practices and so on) and as indicators of the concept under study – the actual incidence of deviant behaviour.

If we make the assumption that they do capture, at least partly, changing levels of deviancy, then we have the problem that they do not consistently coincide with the homicide and suicide rates. There are certainly times when homicide and suicide, crime and public violence are all at a low ebb – the war years, the early twenties, and the early fifties. This gives strong support for Durkheim's theory concerning periods of restraint. It is when we try to fit in Durkheim's anomic years that difficulties occur. While usually tending upwards in these times, conviction and crime rates seem to reserve their dramatic rises for some five to ten years after suicides, homicides, and public violence have reached their peak: in 1910-14 rather than circa 1905; in 1935-9, rather than circa 1930; in the later rather than the early seventies. (Crime rates are discussed further in chapter 9.)

This pattern could be interpreted as support for Gurr's suggestion that we can reverse Durkheim and have public violence leading to anomie. But if this was the case we should expect homicide and suicide rates to peak at the same time as the crime rate, and not some years before as has been the case in Canada. Gurr's hypothesis probably requires public violence of a greater magnitude than Canada has experienced to be applicable.

In short, some relations among crime, public violence, and anomie as indexed by homicide and suicide rates can be discerned. These relations are far from from perfect, in particular the rates tend to peak at different times. Perhaps we should not expect anything better given the great many factors that must intervene between Durkheim's concern for general changes in social morality and the decisions individuals make in selecting their courses of action. Indeed, as we look at alternative explanations for the incidence of public violence, we may decide that these intervening variables are sufficient in themselves to explain the patterns of behaviour observed by Durkheim. Nevertheless, at present the theory cannot be dismissed out of hand, and we must now turn to examine the social and political processes that are said to bring about a state of anomie.

FORCES PRODUCING ANOMIE

In this section I shall be looking at conventional wisdom and several theories, not all of which are derived directly from Durkheim. But, like Durkheim, their authors do specify an association between the breakdown of traditional values and the outbreak of public violence. I shall try to answer the following questions. What is the evidence from other countries that the factor in question does produce anomie, as marked by rising crime, suicide, and homicide rates? What do the Canadian data say? What is the evidence from other countries that the factor at issue is associated with public violence? What do our limited Canadian data on the incidence of public violence suggest?

Immigration. Moving from one country or distinctive region to another is thought to produce anomie as the norms an immigrant learned in childhood crumble in new and different surroundings. Heavy immigration is also sometimes said to dilute the normative structure of the host society so that the native-born also become unsure of appropriate guides to conduct (Bell and Tepperman, 1979: 90-4). This conventional wisdom has been challenged: studies in other countries indicate that migrants tend not to engage in public violence. The Tillys (1975: 236), for example, suggest that protest is not easily organized in unfamiliar surroundings, and American studies show that participants in the ghetto riots of the 1960s were typically those who had been born and brought up in the area rather than recent migrants from the South (United States, 1968: 130-1).

Interestingly, neither the standard approach nor the challenge to it seems to fit the Canadian data. In the first place, there is no consistent relation between rates of immigration to Canada and the incidence of public violence. Admittedly the peak in mainly job-related violence in the early years of the century did coincide with a decade of heavy immigration. Yet the turbulence at the end of the First World War and during the Depression occurred while immigration was at an ebb, and more recently there were higher immigration rates in the quiet fifties than in the turbulent sixties.

Second, from their lowly contribution to crime statistics, Canadian immigrants would seem not to be a particularly anomic group. This is true even for the second generation; as Giffen (1976: 104) points out, "the conventional wisdom that children of immigrants are exposed to cultural conflicts which produce high delinquency rates is not borne out by ... [the] figures." Many immigrant groups in Canada may have avoided anomie because they were not forced abruptly to discard their norms on arrival in this country. There are several possible reasons for this: among them, a national mythology that long encouraged ties to the homeland; a host culture that favours a less demanding "mosaic" over a "melting pot"; structural barriers to assimilation; and a pattern of immigration that often saw extended families and even whole communities, as with the Doukhobors, rather than isolated individuals landing in the country.

Third, the challenge to the conventional wisdom seems nevertheless to be off base. Canadian immigrants have been perfectly willing to engage in public violence. Consider, for example, the Fenian assassination of D'Arcy McGee, the occasional outbreaks of the Chinese working on the CPR line, the Japanese fishermen in violent British Columbia strikes at the turn of the century, the Sikhs aboard the SS *Komagata Maru*, the mainly Italian workers in the Lakehead freighthandlers' strike, the Doukhobors, the British new-comers in the Winnipeg General Strike and the On to Ottawa trek, and the Eastern Europeans in the Winnipeg General Strike and the sitdown strike at Sarnia in 1937.

These selected examples indicate that immigrants to Canada have not been deterred from public violence by their novel surroundings. Yet neither can this turbulence be associated with anomie. Obviously therefore, immigration cannot be fitted into a breakdown theory of Canadian public violence. Indeed, a solidarity theory, which stressed the immigrants' ability to retain sufficient traditional identity to organize for collective action, would seem to be more appropriate. Since Canadian immigrants seem not to be anomic although they have engaged in public violence, the search for anomic groups must turn elsewhere.

Rapid socio-economic change. One theory points to rapid socio-economic change as a destabilizing factor. Olson (1971) has tried to specify how modernization affects the lives of those caught up in it, and many of the effects he identifies concern the disruption of established norms and aspirations. According to him, modernization, among other things, changes traditional patterns of life and work; loosens class and caste ties; weakens the tribe, manor, guild, or rural village; creates unemployment in the traditional industries; and increases expectations as new knowledge, ideologies, and communications permeate the society. Empirical studies, such as the cross-national research of the Feierabends and Nesvold (1969), appear to bear out Olson's thesis. They find that the most stable countries are typically either those which have not started modernizing or those, like Canada, which have already undergone modernization. Unstable countries are often in the process of modernization and are characterized by particularly rapid rates of change.

However, Canadian figures call into question whether rapid change should be associated with anomie. Let us take urbanization as our indicator of change. The proportion of the Canadian population living in cities grew steadily but with marked acceleration between 1901 and 1910 and between 1951 and 1960. In the earlier decade, conviction rates were also on the rise, but the growth during the fifties was accomplished for the most part without any great rise in the suicide, homicide, or conviction rates. Correlations between crime and provincial urbanization rates during the sixties are inconsistent (Bell-Rowbotham and Boydell, 1972: 102-3; Giffen, 1976: 106-7). Notably, Quebec ranked high on the urbanization scale but low on crime and delinquency rates. And then, between 1971 and 1980 we have had the anomic indicators soaring while the country for the first time in its history had a decline in its urban population.

If it seems difficult to establish a link between rates of change and anomie, it is equally hard to see that the thesis – the greater the rate of change, the higher the level of violence – applies within the currently modernized countries or even very well to their historical patterns of growth. Flanigan and Fogelman's survey (1970: 13-15) suggests that, while the initial "take-off" decade may be accompanied by violence, the violence falls off subsequently even while the pace of development is accelerating. Lodhi and Tilly's study (1973: 303-4) of nineteenth-century France finds neither crime nor collective violence to be related to urban growth.

In Canada the pattern is inconsistent. There has been turbulence both during rapid urbanization periods (the early years of the century) and during slow periods (the Depression years). More recently, the growth of Quebec's cities in the sixties has been implicated in that province's public violence (Latouche, 1971: 183-4), but there were provinces with even higher urbanization rates, such as Alberta and Saskatchewan, which had no comparable violence.

The rate of socio-economic change is a factor that has assumed the status of conventional wisdom in many explanations of violence but it does not help to explain the Canadian data. Still even if modernization rates are of little or no importance, especially in a country that has, in technical terms, been modern since before Confederation, it is still possible that more immediate measures that gauge the performance of the economy could be helpful.

Business cycles. It will be recalled that Durkheim postulated that anomie would be produced by the weakening of restraints that occur both in boom times and in depression years. Which of these two situation is more likely to give rise to anomie is the subject of a continuing controversy that is not going to be resolved easily; for it seems that the meaning and consequent impact business cycles have on people have varied over the years and in different countries.

For instance, business cycles apparently have a different effect on crime rates today than they did a hundred years ago. In the nineteenth century, economic downswings were accompanied by rising crime rates. This is no longer the case. Instead, rising crime rates are more typically associated with economies on the upswing, perhaps because relative deprivation is then more acute and because there are simply more opportunities to purloin others' possessions (Lodhi and Tilly, 1973: 301-2; Gurr, 1976: 179). Other factors rendering downswings less anomic could be less condemnatory attitudes towards the unemployed and the establishment of various social welfare measures that mitigate the harshest effects of unemployment.

Yet, even if we restrict ourselves to this century, there remain awkward differences between countries that are unexplained. The Great Depression started for most countries in 1929, and their economies were at their lowest level by mid-1932 (Safarian, 1970: 73-5). This economic nadir corresponds with peaks in suicide rates (Chesnais, 1981: 183-4); for example, in the United States, the suicide rate per 100,000 rose from 13.9 in 1929 to 17.4 in 1932 but fell thereafter. American crime and homicide rates also appear to have reached a peak in 1932 (Gurr, 1979a: 360-1).

The Canadian economy as well started downwards in the second half of 1929, but reached its lowest point somewhat later than in other countries, in 1933. However, in Canada the homicide and suicide rates peaked at the onset of the Depression, in 1930, while conviction rates jumped sharply before and at the onset of the Depression, 1927-30, and did not make another sharp gain until 1938, well after the worst economic years had passed. (Interestingly enough, Canada now seems to be repeating this pattern, although it is too early to be certain since, at the time of publication, some figures are only available to 1980. In 1982 unemployment reached its highest level since the 1930s, but homicides and suicides have been declining since 1977 and 1978 respectively. The crime rate, however, had not abated by 1980.) That crime did not blossom during the worst of the Great Depression years is borne out by Thorner and Watson's (1981: 235) detailed survey of crime in Calgary. Cases before the Police Court there fell "dramatically" from 1930 through 1934, even though the number of police per capita showed a slight rise. The authors (1981: 237) note in particular a sharp drop in liquor-related offences: "In spite of the belief that the psychological need for drunkenness would accompany prolonged unemployment, the Depression appears to have encouraged sobriety." Calgary, at any rate, was plainly not an anomic city during these difficult years.

Recent figures also suggest that anomic behaviour in Canada falls rather than rises during economic downturns. For the years 1950-77, Adams (1981) reports an inverse relation between unemployment and nearly all rates of mortality and psychiatric morbidity; that is, the higher the unemployment rate, the lower the level of homicides, suicides, and first admissions to psychiatric institutions for alcoholism. However American studies, notably the work of J. Harvey Brenner which Adams was replicating, come to the opposite conclusion. In the United States, apparently, rising unemployment rates are accompanied by rising anomic indicators.

Durkheim's theory would thus predict for Canada a high incidence of public violence in the anomic-boom years rather than in the restraint-depression years. But the evidence in support of the theory is contradictory at best. In direct opposition to the theory are Thorner and Watson's findings for Calgary during the Depression. Even though anomic indicators were declining, public violence was much in evidence: "There is little question that Calgary experienced its share of civil strife during the Depression. Battles between police and the single unemployed men, full scale riots and threats to blow up public buildings appear to have been almost annual events" (1981: 234).

Frank and Kelly (1977: 149-51) correlate their Ontario and Quebec collective violence incidents for 1963-73 with income and employment levels. Durkheim's thesis receives some confirmation. The authors report that "en Ontario la violence accompagne l'amélioration des revenus" and that half the cases of above average levels of violence in Quebec occurred during "une situation économique favorable." However, the most violent years in both provinces, 1971 and 1972, fell in years of relatively high unemployment.

Jamieson's study of industrial conflict also lends some support for Durkheim. He observes a high rate of conflict during the boom years at the turn of the century; "two minor nation-wide strikepeaks, those of 1937 and 1943, did appear to have some correlation with the expansionary phase of business cycles"; and "a distinct cyclical pattern [of conflict], in close tandem with the underlying cycle of expansion and inflation of the early and middle 1960's" (1968: 456, 453). Nevertheless, in opposition to Durkheim's thesis, are his findings that earlier major peaks in conflict, 1919-20 and 1946-7, appear unrelated to the business cycle, and "there were later peaks of inflation and economic growth, during 1951 [and] ... 1956 and early 1957, but in neither of these was there a 'wave' of strikes at all comparable to 1965-66 or 1946-47" (1968: 455-6).

Given this contradictory evidence, Jamieson largely dismisses business cycles as an explanatory factor in the incidence of industrial conflict. However, he does adduce other factors, some of which are consistent with an anomic theory. The peaks of conflict in 1919-20, the 1930s, and the 1960s coincided with the entry of a large number of young people into the labour force; and the 1919-20 and 1946-7 peaks could be attributed to "blowing the lid off" as wartime restraints were relaxed. (I shall discuss age structure and war separately below.) As well, the period around the First World War was "an age of rapid technological and economic change and of new radical ideologies that attacked the prevailing system of power, privilege, and values inherited from the Nineteenth Century." Similarly, in the 1930s, "the prevailing system of institutions and ideas was discredited in the eyes of many people, particularly younger workers. Revolutionary ideologies and violent programs of action had a new and widespread appeal" (1968: 475-6). Once more in the sixties Jamieson sees a "wholesale rejection, again largely among younger people, of traditional authority, ethics, morals, and ideologies" (1968: 483). Thus the high conflict periods were those in which established norms were being called into question, with the exception of the 1946-7 peak which, in comparison with the others, tended to have little accompanying violence.

But Jamieson notwithstanding, these periods were not anomic in the sense of being accompanied by rising suicide, homicide, or crime rates. It is probably best to leave his speculative interpretation aside for the moment (since the absence of an indicator for the type of anomie he is discussing forces him to reason backwards from the incidence of conflict) and concentrate on his major conclusion: over the long term, business cycles do not predict the incidence of industrial conflict in Canada. Indeed, coupled with the evidence from Calgary in the 1930s and the inconsistent findings from Ontario and Quebec in the 1960s, Durkheim's theory as it relates to business cycles remains unconfirmed – at least for Canada.

War. Durkheim predicted that "great popular wars" would draw people out of their self-centred apathy into a passionate focusing on the collectivity, so that the number of suicides would drop, although homicides would increase. Besides Durkheim's reasoning, there are other breakdown theories linking war and domestic violence that stress the abnormality and eroding values of wartime. The dislocations during modern wars and in their aftermath may lead to violence if people's traditional patterns of behaviour and expectations are abruptly altered. Further, by teaching large numbers of the population how to handle guns and how to kill and maim the enemy, the inhibitions against violence held in peacetime may be shattered, at least for those in the armed forces. Even for the rest of the population, the omnipresent carnage directed and approved by the state may serve as a legitimating example for the use of violence in their daily lives.

The suicide statistics amply bear out Durkheim's prediction of a falling rate during wartime. The Tillys (1975: 76-8) report that the suicide rate dropped in France during both world wars. In the United States, the rate fell steadily between 1915 and 1921 and between 1940 and 1945. We do not have Canadian figures for the First World War, but the rate declined in each succeeding year of the Second World War.

It is when we come to the prediction of a concomitant rise in homicides, crime, and public violence that the picture becomes confused. Gurr (1979a: 366) argues that "war is the single most obvious correlate of all the great historical waves of crime in England and the United States." Archer and

Gartner (1976: 948) find that most nations involved in one or both world wars experienced sharply rising homicide rates after the war, a pattern that they argue is best explained in terms of war legitimating the general use of violence in domestic society. But Canada does not fit this pattern; in fact it is the only country that did not have sharply rising homicide rates after both world wars. Nor, Gurr notwithstanding, is there any evidence of a Canadian crime wave during or after these wars. Average annual conviction rates for indictable offences per 100,000 population during the war years and the three years before and after them are as follows:

1912-1914	241	PRE-WAR	1937-1939	383
1915-1918	226	WARTIME	1940-1945	362
1919-1921	219	POST-WAR	1946-1948	351

If anything, Canadian wars are associated with troughs rather than peaks in crime. All three indicators, then, homicides, suicides, and crime, converge to point to wartime in Canada as a period of restraint and not one of either anomie or a passionate focusing on the collectivity.

International comparisons reveal no consistent relation between wars and public violence. As Brooks (1979) shows in his historical study of the United States, some wars seem to provoke public violence, while others do not. Rummel's and Tanter's studies (Tanter, 1969: 552), together covering the years 1955 to 1960, yield only a slight positive relation between foreign and domestic conflict behaviour. A longer-term survey, extending from 1800 to 1960, by Flanigan and Fogelman (1970: 5) discovers no relation. In Canada, the end of the First World War was marked by public violence, but the end of the Second World War was not.

Thus, the legitimation of violence and disruption of traditional restraints are arguments that are not generally applicable. Whether or not public violence accompanies or follows a war seems to be more related to the amount of discontent the war has created – such as the feeling that the war is not just, or that its costs are unevenly distributed, or the blow to national pride that accompanies defeat – than to any loosening of restraints against violence.

One partial exception may be made in the case of veterans. When returned soldiers have reason to be discontented, it seems that some of these men who have been taught to use violence against foreign enemies are prone to turning this knowledge against those whom they see as domestic enemies, such as shirkers, "enemy aliens," or profiteers. The violence of some Canadian veterans during and after the First World War provides a possible example, although of course we have no figures on the relative propensity to engage in public violence of veterans and others. However, in explaining rising homicide levels after the two world wars, Archer and Gartner (1976: 956-8) discount the "violent veteran" model since homicide rates climbed among groups, such as women and older people, who were not directly involved in the wars.

Age structure. According to a breakdown theory, young people in our society, and especially young males, form a marginal group as they make the passage from childhood to adult status. At this stage of their lives, they have the fewest commitments in the shape of steady jobs, families, and associational memberships that reinforce norms against deviant behaviour. (It is also argued that structural opportunities to engage in deviant behaviour decline as people grow older or become engaged in steady employment or both; see Dietz's [1978: 18] summary of Herbert Gans's depiction of "routine-seekers" and "action-seekers.") The problems of adjustment are compounded when a "baby boom" comes of age.

The young do indeed contribute largely to some indicators of anomic behaviour. As Gurr (1979a: 367) points out, "all records of crime in Western societies, now and in the past, show that young males are disproportionately represented among offenders." Canada is no exception. For example, in 1966, males aged 16-19 years had a conviction rate for criminal code offences that was well over five times the rate for all Canadians (Bell-Rowbotham and Boydell, 1972: 108-10). Among homicide suspects as well, those under 30 years of age are overrepresented. However suicides are not always concentrated among the young. Historically suicide rates have tended to rise with age.

But what about public violence? From our survey of Canadian incidents in chapter 2, we know that young men tend to be in the forefront of public violence. To take one example, FLQ defendants were on average only 24 years old when they committed their alleged offences. Figures from other countries on the age-sex distribution of participants are unavailable, but anecdotal evidence suggests that Canada is typical in this respect. It could thus be argued that the marginality of youth is associated with their proclivity for public violence, although other factors cannot be ruled out, in particular their greater opportunities to engage in protest activities.

The situation is rather different when a "baby boom" comes of age. Social institutions, from maternity wards, the family, schools, and universities to the labour and housing markets, will not have the resources or capacity to smoothly absorb the increasing demands placed upon them (Easterlin, 1980: 30-2). Some figures give an idea of the dimensions of the problem: in Canada, for every 100 males aged 15-24 years in 1921, there were 131 by 1931; for every 100 in 1961, there were 153 by 1971 (figures calculated from data in Statistics Canada, Catalogue 92-715). Under these circumstances, the transition to adult status can be uncertain and prolonged. Faced with an adult society that is unprepared for them, the young may turn to each other to formulate a rejection of traditional values. Anomic behaviour consequently

TABLE 6

Relative Size of Young Male Population and Suicide Rates, Canada, 1921-81: Percentage Changes

| Years | Percentage change in | | Years |
	Proportion of males aged 15-24 in total population	Suicide rate	
1921/31	+10.7	+64.7	1921-2/1930-2
1931/41	−1.3	−20.4	1930-2/1940-2
1941/51	−18.9	−3.8	1940-2/1950-2
1951/56	−6.0	−1.7	1950-2/1955-7
1956/61	+0.6	+0.8	1955-7/1960-2
1961/66	+14.7	+18.4	1960-2/1965-7
1966/71	+12.9	+34.1	1965-7/1970-2
1971/76	+5.2	+11.0	1970-2/1975-7
1976/81	−1.6	+7.6	1975-7/1979-80

Sources: Age structure of the population from Statistics Canada, 1971 Census of Canada, Catalogue 92-715 and 1981 Census of Canada, Catalogue 92-901. For suicides, see table 4.

rises, particularly among the young, but it may not be simply proportional to the increasing numbers of young people. Rather their questioning of traditional ways may permeate the entire society that is struggling to adjust to their overwhelming presence and thus have the effect of loosening restraints among all age groups.

There is considerable evidence that youthful population bulges are accompanied by rising anomic indicators both among the young and among the general population. Easterlin (1980: 89, 102-8) links the rise in American divorce rates, alcohol and drug abuse, suicides, homicides, crime, and political alienation to the rise in the relative number of young adults. And Gurr (1979a: 369) has found crime increases of 300 or 500 per cent occurring with a 50 per cent growth in the size of the youthful population.

The Canadian figures also point to the same conclusion. Table 6 shows the percentage change in the contribution of young men aged 15 to 24 years to the total population and, for comparative purposes, the percentage change in the average suicide rates around the census years. Despite the influences of wartime and economic cycles, the suicide rates are still plainly moving up and down in concert with the size of the youthful population. The last few years appear to be an exception, but the suicide rate has in fact been falling since 1978.

The most recent youthful population bulge also appears to have had an impact on anomic behaviour across society. Naturally enough, the young themselves are most affected by the social strains. And so, reversing the traditional pattern, we find that for every one suicide in 1961, in 1976 there were 4.7 among the 15-19 year olds and 3.3 among the 20-24 year olds. Yet every age group up to age 60 (that is, those most affected by the impact of the bulge on social and economic institutions) recorded an increase (Health and Welfare Canada, 1981: 38-9).

I have seen no cross-national or historical studies that deal with the impact of age structure on public violence.[6] But it seems this variable cannot be ignored in any explanation of the incidence of Canadian violence. We have already noted Jamieson's association of industrial conflict with youthful population bulges and his argument that the spirit of rebellion kindled by the young evoked a general calling into question of traditional norms. We can take the turbulent 1960s as a prime example of the coincidence of public violence with a "baby boom" coming of age. As well it might be noted that young males have historically made up a somewhat larger proportion of the population in Quebec than they have in the country as a whole – a factor that may contribute to an explanation of that province's high rates of public violence.

The frontier and isolated communities. Clark describes the many forms of frontier protest. The political reform movement, religious sectarianism, vigilantism, medical quackery, mob rioting, tax evasion, smuggling, and political apathy are all "means of resistance by a frontier population to the interferences of an outside society in its affairs" (1962: 219). He discerns a repeated process of rapid development as new fields of economic exploitation are opened up which outrun the integrative capacity of established social organizations. "Social problems," "social disorganization," and "anomie" emerge in the face of weak institutional controls, novel environmental influences, and a heterogeneous population largely made up of young men and a greater share than usual of misfits, incompetents, and the independently minded.

Of related interest is Kerr and Siegel's (1954) cross-national survey of the propensity to strike in various industries. They find the most strike-prone to be: coal-mining, metal mining, maritime (shipping and stevedoring), lumber, and textiles. What workers in these industries have in common is that they tend to live in geographically isolated communities or in social isolation from other workers. Very often these communities are one-industry towns dominated by the employer, in which the frontier-related anomie identified by Clark can easily develop.

6 See McNeill (1982: 310-16) for some suggestive ideas on the interrelations among demography, industrialization, and the outbreak of war.

Kerr and Siegel do not include Canada in their study, but their thesis does seem to fit the Canadian experience. The industries they name are precisely the ones that have been primarily responsible for strikes and for most violent strikes as well. In addition, the argument helps account for the high levels of violence in British Columbia before the Second World War. Jamieson (1968: 105-6) observes that much of the province's industry was carried out in frontier areas which attracted "the more restless and dissatisfied elements, the *déracinés*, from other regions," and that the province "specialized to an extreme degree in the types of industries" associated by Kerr and Siegel with distance and social isolation. Other isolated communities of Canadians that have erupted into violence include Red River and Batoche, the repatriation camps in the United Kingdom at the end of the First World War, and the Sons of Freedom villages in the remote, interior valleys of British Columbia.

Nevertheless, the thesis linking the frontier or isolated community with anomie and violence is not wholly convincing. In the first place, not all such communities have been afflicted with problems. At the least, this would indicate that factors other than social or geographic isolation do play a role of some significance. In particular, we need to explain why remoteness would seem to have produced at the most general level a more violent frontier in the United States than in Canada. Second, indicators of anomie that would confirm Clark's argument are largely unavailable (although it might be noted that currently the highest suicide rates in Canada are to be found in the Far North). And third, there is Tilly's finding (1978: 66-8) that the Kerr-Siegel thesis does not apply to France and Italy; he contends that the data are better explained by a solidarity theory emphasizing the joint interests and opportunity to mobilize in these communities.

Native peoples. Indicators of anomie suggest that Canada's small native population (some 3 per cent of the total population) contains a high proportion of anomic individuals. Among Indians, Inuit, and half-breeds, suicide rates are at least double those of the general population. In 1976, natives made up nearly 9 per cent of inmates of federal penitentiaries, nine out of ten of whom reported committing their offences while under the influence of alcohol or drugs. Their hospitalization rate for injuries resulting from accidents or violence is four times greater than that for all Canada (Statistics Canada, 1980: 173-5; Health and Welfare Canada, 1981: 39).

Anomie and private violence are related in native society, since violent crimes against the individual make up a high proportion of native offences. But there would seem to be little association with public violence. The two Riel uprisings cannot be adduced to support the latter linkage; for Red River and Batoche at the time of the risings were culturally integrated communities acting in defence of traditional values, not anomic communities where these values had already crumbled. It was only after 1885 that the demoralization of the native and half-breed populations occurred. Since then, they have been involved in few incidents, and these, moreover, have been typically associated with strong local groups acting together to preserve traditional rights and practices.

CONCLUSION

Students have discerned within violent crowds a breakdown of existing restraints on behaviour. According to breakdown theorists crowds are a microcosm of a process which can occur among a broader community or whole society and which helps to explain rising levels of public violence. Government leaders and royal commissions in Canada have subscribed to a breakdown theory, and there is no *a priori* reason not to do so, so long as the breakdown of restraints is seen as one contributing factor to be considered along with others, including the culpability of government agents and the grievances of the violent.

Nevertheless, a consideration of the forces that have been identified as producing anomie in other countries reveals the breakdown-of-values explanation of Canadian public violence to be inadequate. Anomie has been prevalent among the native peoples of Canada, but they have rarely engaged in public violence, whereas immigrants who are not exceptionally anomic have engaged in violence. Rapid socio-economic change has not been consistently related to either anomic indicators or outbreaks of public violence. Economic upswings seem to produce more anomie than downturns, but public violence has occurred in good years and bad. Wars are clearly associated with declining anomie, but have had an inconsistent effect on levels of public violence. Only in the case of the age structure of the population, and frontier or isolated communities do anomic situations coincide with public violence. In both these cases, alternative explanations to be considered in the following chapters may supplement or supplant the breakdown-of-values thesis.

One reason for the disarray of the breakdown-of-values thesis is undoubtedly the quality and nature of the data. As previously mentioned, such data tend to be of a dubious nature, both in themselves and as indicators of the concepts under study. Using national averages to measure the response of individuals to the world around them is particularly dangerous.

A second reason for the disarray is Durkheim's underlying theory. There are two problems. First is the evidence that it is not universally applicable. Thus, the whole section of his theory dealing with suicide and homicide rates moving in opposite directions does not apply in Canada; wars have not produced high homicide rates in this country; and business cycles appear to have a different effect here than in the United States. To take such differences into account, one or more variables would have to be added to Durkheim's equation, including probably the influence of culture on our interpretation of the social phenomena he mentions and what we consider to be the right response to them.

The second problem with Durkheim's theory is more basic. It was noted that, while countries with low homicide and low suicide rates (situation 3) were also low on public violence, countries with high homicide and high suicide rates (situation 4) were not disproportionately likely to fall among the high violence countries. Similarly, over the years in Canada, we can readily find situation 3 periods with low public violence, but it is more difficult to discern situation 4 periods with high violence. Both the 1930s and the 1960s were indeed turbulent periods when the anomic indicators were relatively high, but on closer examination we find a need to build in as yet unexplained leads (anomic indicators peaking before public violence in the 1930s) and lags (anomic indicators peaking after public violence in the 1960s). Perhaps in these two cases the timing and impact of the youthful population bulges were different. At any rate, we cannot simply call the years when homicides and suicides were at their peak the most turbulent.

However, the source of this second problem lies mainly in the muddled concept of anomie which has been used by different theorists to embrace several different situations, not all of which are conducive to public violence. There is the anomie of *every-man-for-himself*: the weakening of social restraints on ambitions and expectations leads to a tooth-and-nail struggle for personal advantage. In this situation, lawlessness and homicides could be expected to rise and perhaps also suicides among the losers in the race. There is the anomie of *withdrawal*: aspirations and ambitions are abandoned. This is the situation of helplessness, of withdrawal from the concerns of society in which despair and alcohol can lead to high suicide and homicide rates. And there is the anomie of *social ferment*: the weakening of restraints reopens questions of social justice and the proper institutions for society. While traditional social, economic, and political values may be under attack, I do not see any necessary connection, either as cause or as effect, to a concomitant crumbling of ethical values that would lead to higher crime, suicide, or homicide rates (aside from the casualties of public violence).

One might logically expect these forms of anomie to give rise to different kinds of violence. The anomie of every-man-for-himself should produce violence motivated by personal ambition; for example, private or criminal violence, some quasi-public violence in the shape of family feuds, and on occasion some public violence, such as coups, which affect the lives of all members of society even if they are the handiwork of self-seeking individuals. The anomie of withdrawal should only elicit private violence since the demoralized no longer have the will or capacity for public protest (chapter 8 elaborates on this point). It is the anomie of social ferment – that is, the anomie that is least well depicted by the classic indicators of anomie – that one would expect to be most closely linked with public violence. For in this situation, issues of public importance are in contention, and individuals have the capacity to organize with others to promote the causes they espouse.

In the face of all these problems, it would be simple to dismiss the breakdown theories of Durkheim and others, and yet this would be hasty. Despite all of its insufficiencies, Durkheim's theory remains suggestive. The theory, however, requires further refinement and better indicators. In particular, there is an urgent need to find the indicators and the sources of the anomie of social ferment.

Inflation, war, isolation within society, and the like have all been treated in this chapter as possible conditions that can undermine values and thereby produce public violence. There is another way of linking them to violence: they can be treated as hardship variables that cause feelings of bitterness and discontent, that in turn prompt a resort to violence regardless of values and social restraints. This perspective is the subject of the next chapter.

CHAPTER SEVEN

The Growth of Discontent

The root cause of violence is commonly taken to be discontent of one form or another. Aristotle believed that an outraged sense of justice lay behind all political revolutions. Marx thought that the progressive immiseration of a class would lead it to violence. Gurr and the Feierabends trace the origins of aggression to the frustrations of men and women in not achieving the values they believe they can or should achieve (sometimes inelegantly referred to as the want:get ratio).

That some kind of discontent lies behind many acts of violence is scarcely in question. The problem is that we are all more or less discontented with some parts of our lives, but only infrequently do we manifest this discontent in violence. However, a good deal of theoretical and empirical effort has gone into specifying the kinds of discontent that are typically associated with violence. The results can be roughly grouped into economic, social, and political areas.

THE DISCONTENTS ASSOCIATED WITH VIOLENCE

Economic discontents. Around the end of the eighteenth century, one of the most common manifestations of violence in Europe was the food riot. A scarcity or rise in price caused by poor harvests, inefficient distribution, or greedy middlemen could provoke an immediate and violent response. The violence was limited, predictable in form, almost polite. The commodity in question – bread or cheese, for example – would be forcibly seized from farms, stores, or warehouses, put on sale at a popularly established "just" price, and the proceeds returned to the legal owners. Today very few people in western nations live as close to the subsistence level as did eighteenth-century rioters. However, threats to our purchasing power are still a strong source of discontent. Crop failures that lead to high food prices, price rises of imported commodities resulting from currency fluctuations, and unilateral hikes imposed by powerful international cartels and corporations gnaw at the temper of a nation. Over the last decade, inflation was usually ranked high when pollsters asked people what concerned them the most. The "hyperinflations" of the twentieth century, for example in Germany after the First World War, have wiped out middle-class savings and made a mockery of working-class wages, and have been directly linked with subsequent political turmoil.

Perceived threats to the right to earn a living have also been a potent source of discontent. After the food riots of the eighteenth century came the Luddites of the first half of the nineteenth century. The Luddite disturbances centred around machine wrecking by workers displaced from their jobs by technological developments. Other causes of unemployment have similarly led to violence then and since: foreign imports undermining a local industry; the closing down of no longer profitable mines and mills; trade superseded by changes in fashion, technology or, as in the case of seal hunting, public morality; or an economy, dependent on the export of raw materials, depressed by declining commodity prices. In the agricultural sector, farmers have been faced with natural disasters such as drought and pestilence, lack of control over the selling price of their produce, and – a notoriously provocative factor – changes in the traditional land tenure system that seem to threaten the farmers' means of making a livelihood. General economic downturns, such as the worldwide depression of the 1930s, are sometimes identified as another source of violence-begetting discontent.

Over the last one hundred years, violence in industrialized economies has centred characteristically on the questions of union recognition and the right to collective bargaining. With the passage of legislation establishing union rights, such discontents have faded. However, strikes over wages and working conditions still occasionally spill over into violence, especially when a company tries to carry on production by importing strike-breakers. Unionization campaigns, resistance to them, and interunion jurisdictional quarrels have also been occasions for violence.

The distribution of wealth in society can give rise to discontent: highly inequitable distribution has been blamed for creating civil disturbance by thinkers ranging from Aristotle to de Tocqueville. In a present-day study, Russett (1964) has taken one measure of wealth, land distribution, and found inequality to be positively associated with violence, especially in agricultural societies where land was the major source of wealth.

Social discontents. Status is the measure of the standing and respect accorded to an individual in the community. As such it is a valued object. Declining status groups such as the lower middle class have resorted to violence in defence of their position. So have groups aspiring to greater status such as native groups in colonial societies. "Rank disequilibrium" and "status inconsistency" are terms used to describe a situation in which people are high on one indicator of social worth, for example income, but low on another, such as political power. Such discrepancies are said to provoke particularly virulent discontent (Galtung, 1964).

Another social value is the sense of belonging to a community such as a religious or ethnic group that provides meaning and direction to our lives. Perceived threats to the community's life are apt to provoke deep resentment. Membership in non-ascriptive organizations (for example, trade unions, interest groups, self-help and fraternal organizations) also gives valued feelings of participation, direction, and an ability to influence the course of our lives by joining together with others. In societies where such organizations are poorly developed, what Kornhauser (1959) has called "mass societies," there is said to develop a characteristic anomie and sense of vulnerability and powerlessness. This anomie is in itself a matter of discontent, but it also predisposes the expression of discontent through violence since alternative channels of expression are absent.

The presence of competing communities within a nation-state is strongly correlated with outbreaks of violence. Values in such states are often seen in zero-sum terms, so that each group feels threatened by the other. Ascriptive barriers interfere with intergroup communications; misunderstanding and prejudice can consequently flourish. The presence of small, visible minorities opens the way to scapegoating – the venting of all one's discontents on usually helpless victims. Attempts in these segmented societies to apply universalistic, democratic norms, such as equality under the law and majority rule, may leave a weaker group with a sense of being persecuted.

Discrimination, involving the curtailment of opportunities and status slights, is a deeply resented and widespread condition, especially in segmented societies. Barriers between classes, castes, sexes, races, and linguistic or ethnic communities are omnipresent and assiduously maintained by the historically favoured and entrenched group. These prejudices are deeply resented by the victims, particularly when the legitimations of the existing system begin to be called into question.

Political discontents. For individuals to feel that they are playing an effective part in the political system (and also in other organizations like trade unions) they need to believe that they can significantly affect the outcome of decisions and can become part of the political elite. Conversely a sense of political inefficacy results from a feeling that decisions are made without reference to the individual's wishes and that the elite is inaccessible. Thus discontent can arise when elections and other prescribed channels of influence are lacking or are believed to be ineffective, and when there is no circulation of elites, no regular alternation between the "ins" and the "outs." Discontent is believed to be particularly high among the intrinsic elite – those "outs" who by birth or other qualifications believe elite positions should rightfully be theirs. Where elite positions are few in number, as in countries ruled by a small coterie or a charismatic leader, the situation is exacerbated. Colonialism forms an extreme case of non-participation, since key decisions affecting the country are not even made within its borders. Further, in reaching these decisions, the interests of the imperial power predominate, thus giving rise to the corrosive sense of being exploited.

Another source of political discontent is the failure to follow prescribed norms of political behaviour. These include both formal constitutional precepts and the informal understandings of the rules of the game. Examples are seizures of power, failure to call elections, the banning of a political party, breach of civil liberties, and the neglect of informal norms governing minority access and representation. Typically such actions deprive a government of the willing support and co-operation of the citizens, or a substantial body of them, thereby compelling the government to resort to coercion to secure compliance with increasing frequency. Coercion in turn promotes further alienation of support and discontent, and thus becomes even more indispensable as the means of governing. Johnson (1966: 29-33) has labelled the process "power deflation."

Certain political conditions are notorious fomenters of discontent. Three in particular stand out: attempts to extend government control over previously unaffected groups; changes in taxation laws; and the imposition of conscription. Rubenstein (1970) analyses a number of American revolts in terms of resistance to expanding governmental controls. Refusal to pay new taxes formed the prelude to both the English Civil War and the American Revolution. Conscription gave rise to rioting in revolutionary France and sparked one of the bloodiest single incidents in American history: the New York draft riot of 1863 which left over a thousand people dead.

Incompetent or inefficient governments are another focus of discontent. In his study of the four "Great Revolutions" (the English, American, French, and Russian), Brinton (1965: 251-2) characterizes the pre-revolutionary regimes as incapable of acting effectively. Rigid attitudes among the elite that prevent them from adapting to a new era, administrative machinery that is unresponsive or inadequate, an officialdom that is riddled with corruption – all can render a government unable to perform the tasks expected of it. Basic among these tasks is the provision of law and order; citizens may become profoundly discontented when they feel their lives and property are insecure. A belief that the government is failing to protect its population can prompt citizens to take the law into their own hands, resulting in violence in the form of vigilantism and lynching.

THE EXACERBATION OF
DISCONTENT

The listing of sources of discontent may seem to provide a quick answer to the question of when people resort to violence. However, while all the discontents mentioned have given rise to violence on occasion, none has done so consistently. The imposition of conscription, for example, has often been the cause of rioting, but it has also often been introduced without open resistance. Researchers have tried to link discontent more closely to violence by specifying particular circumstances or characteristics of the issues involved that might make the discontent especially keenly felt, and the ensuing conflict difficult to resolve peacefully.

Some have emphasized the importance of relative as opposed to absolute deprivation. Relative deprivation is the feeling that one is poorly off in relation to other individuals or groups with whom one can be reasonably and properly compared. A peasant is poor in relation to a prince but because he does not see himself in the same frame of reference, when the prince's fortunes wax or wane, the peasant is unconcerned. Again there is no relative deprivation if an affliction is seen to be universal with none prospering while others suffer, as for example in a major economic depression whose deleterious effects are felt throughout a society. Yet two groups of workers or the population in different economic regions of a country (or in neighbouring countries) may well draw comparisons between themselves. The discontent of the less advantaged group will be compounded by what they consider to be the invidious discrepancy existing between their own position and that of the more fortunate group.

Davies's (1962) J-curve theory of revolution specifies another exacerbating condition. The theory postulates that the discontentment which arises from a sudden, sharp reversal following a long period of progressive amelioration is felt particularly keenly. The theory combines two early formulations on the causes of revolution. De Tocqueville (1955: 177) had suggested that revolutions occur when conditions are improving. Some improvement creates the expectation of further improvement; and "patiently endured so long as it seems beyond redress, a grievance comes to appear intolerable once the possibility of removing it crosses men's minds." But Marx and Engels, in *The Manifesto of the Communist Party*,[1] had argued that revolution would follow a long downswing in conditions – the progressive immiseration of the proletariat – until the workers had nothing to lose but their chains. However, Davies points out that impoverished people do not actually make revolutions;

---

1 However, in *Wage Labour and Capital*, Marx also suggests that during an economic upswing wages will rise but the position of the capitalist will improve even more. Workers will consequently feel a growing sense of relative deprivation. Cited in Davies (1962: 5).

they are too caught up in the daily struggle for survival to have any energy left over to invest in toppling regimes. Rather he says the crucial variable is the balance between men's expectations and the actual satisfaction of these expectations. Expectations will probably always run higher than satisfied needs, but the two should not become dangerously out of line during a period of gradual improvement. A rebellious frame of mind does arise when expectations based on past achievements continue to rise while the capacity to satisfy them suddenly drops. Such blocked progress causes people to fear "that ground gained over a long period of time will be quickly lost" (1962: 8).

Gurr (1970) has added a number of glosses to the J-curve theory. He points out that expectations and satisfactions need not become imbalanced during a long period of decline, such as experienced by the North American Indians, and that an imbalance can occur not only when the capacity to satisfy expectations drops, but also when some extraneous factor, such as a new ideology or the example of another country, creates a sudden increase in the population's aspirations. In a nutshell, Davies and Gurr argue that people can tolerate their discontents under both improving and declining conditions, but they will become exasperated when their aspirations exceed society's ability to satisfy them, due to an abrupt shift either upwards of what they desire or downwards of what they can achieve.

Discontent is also said to be particularly strong when it centres around a value to which much importance is attached. It is thought that there is a universally applicable hierarchy of values such that some values always tend to be more salient than others. Thus Gurr (1970: 71) hypothesizes that "in any heterogeneous population, the intensity of relative deprivation is greatest with respect to discrepancy affecting economic values, less with respect to security and communality values, least with respect to participation, self-realization, status, or ideational coherence values." Certainly the preservation of life itself is, with only rare exceptions, our primordial goal. When it is threatened, the associated discontent may result in an immediate resort to violence in self-defence.

However, an alternative argument stresses that conflicts fought for personal, material advantage are not the most intense. Rather, those that involve concepts of justice and liberty, or symbols representing a group's identity, are, as Coser (1956: 118) says, "likely to be more radical and merciless than those that are fought for personal reasons." The participants are imbued with a sense of self-righteousness and moral fervour; they tend to be intransigent because accommodation would be a betrayal of the cause or group; and by pursuing an abstract goal or fighting an objectified opponent, they are freed from the personal considerations that might restrain their conduct.

Instead of determining salience by the content of the values, a constructive alternative is to identify those circumstances that seem to turn any value into a salient one. Gurr (1970: 71-3) suggests two such circumstances. First, people will be more prepared to fight for values that are almost within their grasp than for those that are only faint hopes for the future. Second, the greater the amount of effort previously invested in achieving the value, the greater its salience. Similarly, Coser (1956: 114) argues that conflicts in which the participants make personal sacrifices for the cause and identify closely with it, so that the group becomes an extension of their own personality, will be particularly intense ones.

Besides salience, two further characteristics of values that make conflict over them more bitter are their divisibility and reversibility. When a value is indivisible, that is, when all the benefits accrue to one camp with nothing left over for another, then its allocation will be much more strongly contested than when the nature of the value enables a division of spoils. And when the allocation is irreversible, so that a decision on it today is binding into the future, then the struggle to achieve the value will be more intense than, say, in the case of elections in which defeated political parties can live in hope of a more favourable outcome the next time they go to the polls (Oberschall, 1973: 50-1).

Conflict over an indivisible value is characteristic of a class of zero-sum games or situations of pure conflict. In these games the interests of the two parties are diametrically opposed so that there is no possible outcome in which both parties could secure some gains (if A gains $+1$, then B is left with -1). Non-zero-sum or mixed-motive games are those in which both parties can end up winners, even if one gains more than the other (if A gains $+2$, B may still obtain $+1$). Oberschall (1973: 53) notes that zero-sum games "violate all the basic principles of equity, fair exchange, and mutual benefit upon which most social relations are founded" and that conflicts involving them will probably be more bitter, intense, and difficult to regulate than those involving mixed-motive games. Take, for example, a revolution in which all the perquisites of the established elite are under attack. Since the revolutionaries would leave the elite with nothing, the latter tenaciously resists, much more so than were reformers to strip the elite of some but not all of its privileges. Similar are Gamson's (1975: 41-4) "displacement" groups: those seeking to displace one or more opponents rather than merely trying to change their policies or organization. Opponents may be willing to bargain over policies; they are unlikely to acquiesce in their own removal. Also of relevance is Coser's (1956: 73-5) distinction between groups which carry on a conflict within a framework of consensus and groups which are contesting the very basis of consensus. Compromise is only possible in the former case; the groups recognize their interdependence and do not try to drive each other off the stage.

The number of issues involved in a conflict is also thought to influence its bitterness. Everyone plays several roles in society, the family, the community, the job, and so on. Discontent may arise independently in several of these relationships. When this happens the total experienced discontent will probably be profound, and any additional grievance may be the "last straw" that pushes the individual into rebellion (Gurr, 1970: 67). As opposed to individuals or groups with multiple discontents, there is also the case of a society afflicted by several focuses of discontent: for example, farmers with crop failures combined with urban workers facing unemployment and armed forces upset by budgetary restrictions. "Dysfunction must 'metastasize' beyond one substructure" before revolutionary violence breaks out (Johnson, 1964: 9). Oberschall (1973: 49) also notes that "periods of social turmoil and political upheaval almost always result from combinations of economic and political grievances that are widely distributed but nevertheless centered in different social strata and groups. It is this multiplicity that taxes the institutions of conflict regulation to their breaking point." Conflicts are particularly bitter when this multiplicity of issues builds up within a community distinguished by ethnic or other criteria. In these cases the integrative benefits derived from cross-cutting cleavages are lost, and conflict comes to centre on the basis of consensus by which the community has agreed to form part of the wider society: attempted secession or civil war may result (Coser, 1956: 76-80).

Discontent is not thought likely to give rise to violence as long as people can still hope and plan for better times. They may believe, for example, that enterprise and diligence will enable them to get ahead, that the problem is only temporary, or that they can better their lot through migration, education, or making use of alternate channels of political influence (Gurr, 1970: 73-9). An obvious corollary of this is that discontent will be exacerbated if opportunities are circumscribed by discrimination, inability to migrate, or limited skills. People in isolated communities may feel deprived of alternative opportunities when they lack easy access to the outside. In a society as a whole, the elite or very structures of the society may be seen as requiring removal before progress is possible.

Finally, Coser (1956: 68-71) argues that conflict is more passionate the closer the relationship between the contending parties. Brinton (1965: 251) also suggests that "revolutions seem more likely when social classes are fairly close together than when they are far apart. 'Untouchables' very rarely revolt against a God-given aristocracy." Being almost equal is more exasperating than being far apart because the goal of complete equality is almost in one's grasp and the closeness intensifies the sense of relative deprivation. But Coser goes further than this in saying that conflicts in closely tied groups, such as family quarrels or feuds within sects, are especially bitter because of the parties' personal involvement in the relationship. Opponents are accordingly accused of disloyalty and perceived as a threat to the group's very existence. In contrast, where cohesion is low, the conflict can be carried on at a less emotional and intense level.

DISCONTENT IN CANADA

There are two methods of determining how well these various focuses of discontent and exacerbating characteristics predict the outbreak of violence in Canada: identify all the occasions on which they have arisen and then see how often violence has resulted; or work backwards from an incident to find the existence of discontent behind it. The former method is problematic since there is always doubt concerning the validity of the objective indicators that must generally be used to identify the subjective sense of discontent, or more specifically of relative deprivation or frustration. The latter is used by most analysts of violence although, since discontent of some kind can always be found, the "procedure has the advantage of almost always producing a fit between the data and the theory, and the disadvantage of not being a reliable test of the theory," as Tilly (1978: 207) observes in his criticism of Davies and Gurr.

I shall briefly examine both procedures. First, I make an impressionistic list of the focuses of discontent and exacerbating conditions that have obtained in Canada. Such an exercise also serves to introduce the stress points and problem areas of Canadian society. Second, I shall study two previous attempts to relate the incidence of recent Canadian violence to the rise and fall of discontent. I shall also examine some manifestos put forward by violent Canadians over the years to see what the people actually involved in violence have had to say about their discontents.

Some judgment is required to draw up a list of Canadian discontents since it is not difficult to find a Canadian example for practically all the factors mentioned. The following features of Canadian society, taken from the works of historians and other social scientists, emerge as the dominant sources of discontent.

First, the nature of the economy must be considered. Canada has always earned its way in the world largely through the export of foodstuffs and unfinished raw materials. It has had little control over either the demand for them or their price. Beaver pelts, fish, wheat, lumber and pulp, metals and ores are industries that have all risen and fallen according to world demand, with unsettling effects on the economy as a whole. Recession and growth have followed each other with bewildering succession. The Canadian economy could thus be seen as creating a series of J-curves, with the sudden drops producing discontent as expectations based on previous good years are shattered. However, an alternative argument, which is more consistent with the figures given in the last chapter, is that the perennial economic instability has produced a "boom or bust" psychology whereby downturns become accepted as inevitable but discontent rises during upswings as people scramble to get what they can while the going is good. This psychology is also fostered by the temporary booms resulting from the spectacular construction projects running through the country's history, from the building of the CPR to the James Bay hydro-electric complex. "The very magnitude of such operations", as Jamieson (1973: 104) points out, "has tended to have unsettling effects upon industrial relations over entire regions."

Extracting raw materials for export has usually meant that workers must live in isolated camps, often run as company towns far from the major cities. Such isolation can be demoralizing in itself, but it also cuts off alternative employment opportunities. There has been a repeated process, as described by Clark (1962: 3-19), of frontier communities – founded on timber, mining, or farming – passing through an initial stage of anomic disorganization followed by a gradual building up of organizations adapted to frontier conditions. Metropolitan society then attempts to extend its control over the frontier regions. Bitter resentment follows at what is regarded as interference in the new society's desire to go its own way.

Canada has relied heavily on foreign capital, first from Britain and later from the United States, to exploit its staples and finance its construction projects in a land continental in size but with a scattered population. To some, this control of the Canadian economy by outsiders has been an affront to national pride. A more tangible result has been the frequent exclusion of Canadians from economic decision-making on such matters as the retention of profits in Canada, expansion, and the development of a home-grown technology. The dispersed population over such a vast area has also meant that many economic sectors – banking, for instance – have been dominated by a few, large firms. Much of the economic power within the country has thus been concentrated in the hands of a small group of people. Accordingly Canadians as exporters, consumers, and employees have very often felt themselves powerless in relation to the dominant economic forces in the country.

Regional economic disparities have been a persistent feature of the economy. In terms of per capita income, Ontario, British Columbia, and more recently Alberta have stood above the national average. The Atlantic provinces and Quebec have just as persistently fallen below it. These disparities may be a source of relative deprivation, especially if for cultural or other reasons migration is not an acceptable alternative. Another source of discontent arises from the fact that the various regions have distinctive industrial structures so that national economic policies have an unequal effect on the different regional economies. Thus tariffs have fostered the development of manufacturing centres in Ontario and Quebec, but the Prairie farmer is left feeling that the rest of Canada has been developed at his expense when he compares prices for manufactured goods at home with those across the border in the United States. Indeed the perception of many poorer provinces that they are exploited colonies of Ontario – the sense that the economic dice are perennially loaded in that province's favour – has been a persistent source of resentment. Generally economic development in Canada has been seen as a zero-sum game; a gain for one region is not viewed as strengthening the national economy but as a direct loss to the other regions.

Another area in which Canadians experience relative deprivation is in comparison with the United States, a richer and economically far stronger country whose example is inescapable because of physical proximity, the penetration of the American media, and the recruitment of Canadian workers into American-based unions. Historically, prices have been higher and wages lower in Canada than in the United States. Wage parity with American workers has long been sought but only achieved by a few Canadians belonging to the more powerful unions.

Some features of the Canadian union scene have been notable sources of discontent. First, the right to collective bargaining was not established until quite late in Canada, mostly in the 1940s. As a result, disputes centring on union recognition have been prevalent until recently. Second, Canadian governments have established lengthy and cumbersome procedures for collective bargaining with the object of avoiding industrial conflict. However, the resulting delays and rigidities have been criticized for creating more discontent than they alleviate (Jamieson, 1973: 125-8, 133-42). Third, the Canadian union structure is modelled on that developed for the much larger American economy, and most Canadian unionists are members of American-based unions. Canadian locals are consequently very often weakened by their small numbers and are far removed from the centres of union decision-making. They may very well feel that their particular problems are lost sight of in the union bureaucracy. And fourth, the Canadian union structure has been complicated by regional, nationalistic, and ideological divisions. Interunion competition to secure members has on occasion produced bitter resentment.

The distribution of wealth in Canada is unequal. Since the Second World War, the richest fifth of the population has absorbed some 40 per cent of income, while the poorest fifth has received around 4 per cent (Gillespie, 1976: 436). While such a distribution is common among western nations, and Canada is far from having the worst record (Cromwell, 1977: 294-5), the imbalance is glaring and might be expected to evoke deep resentment.

There has never been in Canada a class system in the European sense. Canadian workers have not endured the prolonged oppression, status slights, and curtailment of opportunities which in the last century welded English workers into a cohesive, conscious class. Early attempts to impose a stratified society in New France and Upper Canada collapsed in the face of frontier conditions. Neither has there ever been a base for working-class consciousness in a large rural proletariat, such as was required by the sheep-rearing stations of Australia (Brady, 1958: 10). Instead Canadian agriculture has grown from the base of the family-owned farm. Where working-class cohesion has obtained in Canada, it has tended to be in those regions, notably British Columbia, where the early economy was not dependent on agriculture but rather on the activities of large lumber and mining companies. The weakness of Canadian class consciousness can be viewed positively as reflecting the relatively modest oppression and alienation that has been experienced by Canadian workers in the past. An unfortunate result of this, however, is that they have found it difficult to organize in pursuit of their class interests.

The demographics of the Canadian population have also worked against the development of a cohesive class structure. Awareness of class interests is impeded by the scattering of the population over a large area and by the mobility of Canadians (including the possibility that long existed for the most discontented to emigrate freely to the United States). Compounding the problem is the heterogeneity of the population. One source of division is religion. Roughly half the population is Catholic with the remainder divided among the Protestant churches and other faiths. Historically, religious differences have provided focuses for discontent, but as the importance of religion in everyday life has declined, so too have expressions of religious bigotry.

An enduring source of heterogeneity has been ethnicity. Over the last fifty years about 20 per cent of the Canadian population has been made up of immigrants. The presence of such a large group of newcomers has provided Canadians with more opportunities than most for the expression of prejudice. The immigrants' drive to secure employment has sometimes undermined the efforts of the native-born labour force to achieve improved working conditions. Some groups have adhered to their traditional ways, and their resistance to assimilation has aroused suspicion. Others have simply provided convenient targets for the expression of xenophobia or have served as scapegoats in the venting of frustrations. Adding to the ethnic heterogeneity are Canada's indigenous peoples – the Inuit, Indians, and Métis groups. As contacts with whites have increased, native people have seen the traditional means of making a livelihood virtually destroyed, and the cultural basis of their society eroded.

The most significant division in Canadian society is that between French-speaking and English-speaking Canadians. Centred in Quebec is roughly one third of the population, which maintains its adherence to a language and culture different from that of the majority. Francophone discontent arises from relative deprivation and the curtailment of opportunities. Even within Quebec, the average income of French Canadians has been lower than that of most other groups and few have reached senior positions in industry or the federal government, at least until recently. Studies conducted in the 1960s show French Canadians to have been well aware of their inferior position (Johnstone, 1969; Roseborough and Breton, 1971). Partly as a result of this awareness Quebec underwent a period of rapid socio-economic change during the sixties, a time known as the Quiet Revolution. In particular the educational system was reformed so as to equip more French Canadians for upward mobility. New and greater expectations were aroused that could only be partly satisfied (Guindon, 1975). The very rapidity of change was disorienting to many. However, the impact of the reforms and of provincial and federal policies to open up senior positions to francophones is now becoming apparent (Olsen, 1977: 210).

Yet French-Canadian grievances are not simply material ones. There is also the related yet distinct issue of pride in one's group or national identity. Nationalism produces the desire for self-determination – to be *maîtres chez nous* – and a corresponding impatience with outside control and interference. Since self-determination can cover not simply cultural areas but any field of policy, nationalism widens the possibilities for confrontation. The historic French-English conflicts in Canada have revolved around the resentment experienced by French Canadians when English Canada has used its majority position to push through decisions and policies inimical to the minority, notably the hanging of Louis Riel and conscription in the two world wars.

Whether the discontents of the francophone worker stem from his ethnicity or his class position has been confused by the issue of nationalism. The effect has been to dissipate the potential power of a united working class. But Canada is a classless society only in the sense that class consciousness is poorly developed, not in the objective sense that every Canadian starts with an equal opportunity to reach the highest positions available. Porter (1965) and subsequent analysts have identified various elites containing a relatively small number of people who have gathered unto themselves a disproportionate share of the country's wealth and power. By means of an exclusive corporate network, a small group has spread its influence far in the economic field. As well, it interpenetrates the political elite either through direct involvement or kinship ties. These elites can be identified partly by ascribed characteristics such as ethnicity: those of British origin are overrepresented relative to the proportion in the general population. Porter observes that if Canada is heterogeneous – a mosaic rather than a melting pot – it is also very much a vertical mosaic with some groups persistently enjoying a more advantaged position than others.

Many of the dominant companies in Canada are branches of multinational corporations. Access to their top positions will consequently be restricted by policies established in head offices outside the country. But for many of the Canadian-born members of the country's elites, entry is a matter of inherited status. In Porter's (1965: 292) study, some 20 per cent of the economic elite had fathers in the same elite; nearly all came from upper- or middle-class families. Inherited advantage is not confined to the top elites. Several studies have shown that advanced education, which is the key to upward mobility, is obtained disproportionately by the children of parents with high incomes or high education or both. Indeed it has been suggested (Porter, 1965: 49-56, 165-98; Lipset, 1970: 40-3) that up until the fifties Canada had only a small number of places for postsecondary school students, that courses were preponderantly academic rather than vocational (immigrants being relied upon to make up any resulting deficit in skills), and that the educational system thus served to curb upward mobility and maintain the elitism of Canadian society. Since then universities have greatly expanded and the vocation-oriented community colleges have been developed, so that the considerable gap that once existed between Canadian and American enrolment figures has been progressively narrowed (Hiller, 1976: 141).

Nor is the Canadian social structure with its elite groups and restricted mobility opportunities atypical. Some recent studies have suggested that it is still probably less dynamic than in the United States, but more so than in many other countries, including many western European ones (Tepperman, 1975: 188-91). Nevertheless, inequality of opportunity does exist in Canada, notwithstanding a widespread belief in the possibilities of individual advancement (Marchak, 1975: 12-15). When such a belief is revealed to be unfounded, discontent can only be further embittered: for example, for working-class children forced out of school at an early age, immigrants unable to secure work in line with their qualifications, and minority group members encountering discrimination and prejudice.

At various times Canadian political institutions have been subjected to a number of criticisms. The main thrust of the complaints has been the insensitivity of the system to particular interests. Opposition parties have been handicapped by gerrymandering, manipulation of the franchise, and delays in redistributing seats in line with population movements. Cairns (1968) suggests that the electoral system, in which the candidate securing the plurality of votes in a single-member constituency is elected, is inequitable as compared to some form of proportional representation. Under the present system, parties often gain a disproportionate number of seats relative to their popular vote, small parties with a broad geographic base are at a disadvantage, and large blocs of voters are effectively disenfranchised. In recent years, for instance, the non-Liberal vote in Quebec and the non-Conservative vote in Alberta have run as high as 50 per cent but have been translated into few if any seats.

Several movements for electoral reform have surfaced in Canada. For example, after the First World War the Progressives and farmers' parties advocated various measures and sought to tie elected representatives more closely to their constituents' wishes in an effort to undermine what they conceived to be the domination of the political system by the "big interests." Their proposals failed partly because parliamentary democracy calls for disciplined parties in the legislature responding to party interests rather than constituency demands.

In theory, those elected representatives who form the cabinet determine government policy and answer for the activities of the public service in the legislature. In practice, it is said the mandarins of the public service tend to dominate cabinet ministers, and the cabinet in turn relies on party discipline to dominate the legislature. Obviously this varies depending on the extent to which ministers have their own policies that they are determined to pursue and the relative standing of the parties in the House of Commons. But even under the most favourable circumstances, the influence of elected representatives is limited and only some interests are given an effective voice.

A second method of making the system responsive is to create a cabinet so that each of the country's major regions and ethnic groups have a representative within it. However, the custom has broken down in those critical times when large areas have declined to return any members of the government party. This brings us to the third mode of representation, the federal system.

By permitting the subnational units to go their own way, federalism removes from the central government what would be an intolerable burden of trying to achieve a consensus on issues over which the regions differ strongly. It is accordingly a means of dissipating regional discontent. Yet it also creates a constant push and pull between the federal and provincial governments; desired policies may be barred or delayed by constitutional provisions; and provincial governments appeal to and reinforce local sentiment so as to acquire greater legitimacy for themselves. Federalism is thus also a source of conflict. For a federation to function effectively, there must be a willingness to co-operate and seek consensus, a recognition that there are both national and local interests that must be met, and a sense that local interests are not exclusively championed by the provincial governments but are represented as well in the national institutions. In all these respects, Canadian federalism has recently suffered.

The participation of working-class Canadians in politics is largely confined to voting. With only a few exceptions, members of parliament come from upper- and middle-class backgrounds. Other segments of the political elite – the judiciary, federal and provincial cabinet ministers, and the upper levels of the public service – show a similar bias (Olsen, 1977: 212-13). Following American practice, the dominant Canadian trade unions have traditionally hesitated to throw themselves into the electoral fray, the assumption being that unions can influence governments more effectively as an interest group rather than, as in the United Kingdom or Australia, by working directly towards the election of a government sympathetic to their interests. Since parliamentary institutions are apparently less susceptible than American ones to the influence of organized groups, Canadian labour has thus tended to fall between two stools. Yet the interpenetration of the economic and political elites has eased the access of Canadian business to the government.

The key cleavage in Canadian politics has always been region rather than class. Regionalism is a reflection of the country's diversity, but it is also reinforced by the country's political institutions, notably the electoral system, parliamentary government, and also federalism. While Canada has historically been dominated, and integrated, by a political elite, the working class has been comparatively powerless and divided. This is so not only because of its history and internal divisions, but also because many of the policy fields immediately affecting it, such as labour and social welfare legislation, are constitutionally within the provincial sphere of responsibility. Thus the attention of the working class is often focused on the separate provincial arenas, and inducements to organize nationally are lessened (Smiley, 1972: 92).

Political practice in this country has generally been characterized by an adherence to the "rules of the game." However, there have been some breaches of the conventions and legalities that offend our sense of justice. The belief that a section of the country should not be forced into a policy over its strong objections by a numerical majority has occasionally been set aside, as in the conscription crisis of 1918. The civil liberties of small minority groups have been infringed (for example, the fate of Japanese-Canadians and of religious sects in Quebec during the Second World War). Radical political groups have had their activities circumscribed (for instance, the harassment of the Communist Party in the interwar years and the banning of the FLQ in 1970). Such groups have not been included within the ambit of the national dogma that the country must be run on the principles of conciliation and co-operation. The dogma applies mainly to French-English and federal-provincial relations, but even within these areas the search for consensus has been pursued with varying diligence and success on different issues and under different governments. Again when reality has parted company from the ideal, there has been extreme bitterness.

Finally, Canadian governments can be looked upon as reasonably efficient, even in the frontier areas. Today they possess sophisticated bureaucracies, staffed mainly on the merit principle, and spend a substantial proportion of the GNP in administering complex welfare programs. (But note that the welfare state came relatively late to Canada, largely because of federal-provincial complications.) Corruption is used in attempts to circumvent local ordinances or to secure government contracts, but does not so pervade the system that even the simplest services become dependent on the bribery of public officials. Occasional word leaks out of dishonest policemen or judges involved in "fixing" traffic tickets. However, the administration of justice is not notably less honest or competent in Canada than elsewhere, although the antics of the RCMP against Quebec separatists have dealt a blow to the force's prestige. The impartiality of the police in strikes, particularly in earlier years, has also been questioned.

There are, then, many possible grounds for discontent in Canada. Among the more important are: an unstable economy; regional economic disparities; frontier conditions; the overwhelming presence of the United States; an unequal distribution of wealth; the weakness of the working class and the dominance of a political-economic elite; barriers to social mobility; the heterogeneity of the population; the dominance of Ontario and Quebec at the expense of other regions; the unrepresentativeness of the political system; and federal-provincial conflict. Clearly many of these factors bear absolutely no relation to the incidence of Canadian violence. There are few, if any, incidents, for example, arising from discontent attributable to regional economic disparities, the American presence, or federal-provincial relations. Even when some relation can be discerned, it is usually an uncertain and inconsistent one.

In some cases, what we can objectively determine to be hardships have not been subjectively perceived as such. In others, even perceived hardships have been acquiesced in because they have not been thought to be remediable or necessarily inequitable. And in others, where injustice has been perceived, recourse has been had to the established institutions of conflict-regulation rather than to violence. Perhaps we shall one day achieve a better specification of which discontents are violence-begetting ones. Yet so many factors intervene between the onset of discontent and the outbreak of violence that the former may never reliably predict the latter.

Another possibility is that the discontents of Canadians are pale shadows of those experienced by other nations. An optimist could argue that the lack of correlation between discontents and violence in this country simply shows that Canadians have rarely had cause enough to get fighting mad. Put differently, Canadians are relatively peaceful because they have reason to be basically contented with their lot. There is a measure of truth in this, especially when we place the life led by Canadians in an international context.[2] On a world-wide scale, multiple dysfunctionality, frustrating conditions, and dashed expectations have been used with some success to explain varying levels of violence among nations (see, for example, Gurr, 1968). Social analysts in Canada sometimes seem to be labouring under a compulsion to prove that Canadians are every bit as oppressed and deprived as any other people. These pessimists are taken aback by what they judge to be the unnatural quiescence of the population. Certainly everything is not perfect in the peaceable kingdom; some Canadians, if not Canadians in general, have had cause to feel profound discontent. Perhaps we can identify the relation

2 See the previously cited works by Cromwell (1977) and Tepperman (1975). Chapter 9 refers to studies showing Canada to be among the least repressive nations in the world. See also tables on such factors as GNP per capita, literacy, and infant mortality in Taylor and Hudson (1972) and others.

between discontent and violence more successfully if instead of moving from discontent to violence we start with the violence and move back to find the discontent underlying it.

VIOLENT CANADIANS AND THEIR DISCONTENTS

Two Canadian studies that have examined violence and discontent are by Latouche (1971) and by Frank and Kelly (1977). Latouche attempts to explain the high levels of violence in Quebec during the 1960s by examining various sources of discontent. First, using figures on the birth rate, urbanization, and school attendance, he shows that Quebec experienced a period of rapid socio-economic change during the early 1960s. Second, even with these changes, Quebec did not notably improve its position in relation to the other provinces with respect to infant mortality, unemployment, and personal income per capita. However, relative deprivation was probably not significant since Quebec was far from being the worst-off of the provinces and there was a steady improvement in conditions within the province throughout the decade. Third, Latouche looks at the Davies-Gurr J-curve theory which he believes offers a more convincing explanation. Quebec government expenditures increased rapidly in the early 1960s, especially in the health and education fields. Popular expectations were aroused. But by 1966 the government had been hit by financial constraints. The revenue from taxation had decreased, as had public and private investment in the province and the province's share of the gross national product. The system could no longer satisfy the expectations of the people or allay their fears that what had been gained would not soon be lost.

Frank and Kelly attribute 45 per cent of the collective violence incidents they found in Ontario and Quebec, 1963-73, to immediate economic issues such as wages and working conditions and 41 per cent to political issues. The remaining 14 per cent covered random incidents of violence such as drunken brawls and motorcycle gang rampages; these were classed as "issueless." Roughly four out of five of the economic incidents took place in the context of strikes, and strike violence usually erupted, at least in Ontario, "as a result of scabs or non-striking workers attempting to cross picket-lines" (Jackson, Kelly, and Mitchell, n.d.: 261). Political questions were raised in the form of violent demonstrations. A surprisingly large number – 35 (14 per cent of the total) – involved foreign policy issues, including protests against the actions of other countries. These were the years of the Vietnam War.

However, Frank and Kelly emphasize that the combined figures for Ontario and Quebec are almost meaningless given the differences in the two provinces' patterns of collective violence. Four-fifths of the incidents animated by foreign policy concerns occurred in Ontario, and the economic violence of this province was exclusively for immediate economic gains. In Quebec, by contrast, much more of the violence centred on domestic political issues, with the separatist movement providing an umbrella for the many Quebeckers who had come to challenge the status quo and sought radical reform of their society. Even the Quebec economic incidents were less often restricted to bread-and-butter issues; rather they tended to be ideological and politicized to the extent that contract negotiations for immediate gains might become entangled in questions of Anglophone economic domination. Jackson, Kelly, and Mitchell (n.d.: 256) conclude: "In Quebec, collective violence was a part of the nature of politics: it was ideologically based and functionally relevant. In Ontario, most of the violence was either irrelevant to the larger society or relevant to only a very small segment of it."

The differences between the provinces are further illustrated when the incidence of collective violence is related to economic indicators. In Ontario as unemployment rose, so too did the number of incidents; in Quebec the pattern was not so obvious. Frank and Kelly also use an "indice du paradoxe économique" that combines measures of unemployment and income levels. This index was regarded as being a sensitive predictor of violence since a rise in it indicates the existence of a growing number of unemployed in a precarious economic situation faced with the few groups who managed to secure advantageous wage settlements. In Ontario, again, violent strikes – but not demonstrations – did increase as the index rose. In Quebec the opposite occurred: the number of violent strikes was unrelated to the index, but there was a moderate positive correlation between it and the number of violent demonstrations. The authors (1977: 151) suggest that the political cultures of the two provinces are such that economic injustice is seen as properly remediable only by economic means – a strike – in Ontario, whereas in Quebec broader collective actions are permissible. Nevertheless, the generally far weaker relation in Quebec than in Ontario between the levels of all forms of collective violence and the economic indicators shows that in Quebec nationalist and linguistic issues were superimposed on economic ones in motivating people to collective violence.

Like Latouche, Frank and Kelly work backwards from the incidents to seek out indicators of discontent. Thus they do not report on income and employment levels, the only two factors they consider, in other provinces and at other times. However, their study is valuable, not only because it was the first published work to report on a systematic collection of incidents in more than one province, but also because it shows how discontent-fomenting forces, such as unemployment, are apparently perceived and acted upon differently in different settings.

However, in speaking of economic and political motivations, the authors are too abstract. A better way to capture the reality of people's discontents is to examine the written documents released by violent Canadian groups.

Generally, they contain not one but several grievances, each of which tends to be quite specific. Thus the December petition to Ottawa that preceded the Northwest Rebellion of 1885 demanded:

more liberal treatment for the Indians: scrip and patents for the half-breeds: responsible government, representation in the Dominion Parliament and Cabinet, provincial control of natural resources, modification of the homestead laws, vote by ballot, a railway to Hudson Bay and reduction in the tariff for the white settlers. It also contained a long complaint, obviously prepared by Louis Riel himself, of the treatment of the North-West delegates in 1870 and the non-promulgation of the promised amnesty. (Stanley, 1961: 306-7)

Another example of multiple, specific grievances is provided by the 1935 program of the On to Ottawa trek. The relief camp strikers demanded:

1. That work with wages be instituted at a minimum of 50 cents per hour for unskilled workers and trades union rates for skilled work on the basis of a six hour day, five day week with a minimum of 20 work days a month.
2. That all workers in the relief camps be covered by the Compensation Act and that adequate first aid supplies be carried on the job at all times.
3. That the National Defence and all military control with the system of blacklisting where men are cut off from all means of livelihood be abolished.
4. That democratically elected committees be recognized in every camp.
5. That there be instituted a system of non-contributory unemployment insurance based on the "Workers Bill of Social and Unemployment Insurance."
6. That all workers be given their democratic right to vote.
7. That section 98 of the Criminal Code, Sections 41 and 42 of the Immigration Act, vagrancy laws and all anti-working class laws be repealed. (Cited in Hoar, 1970: 11)

It is not surprising that the various platforms should contain several itemized discontents, for the main purpose of these documents was to build support for the movement. The more grievances mentioned, the greater the number of people who may be enticed to join it. The total document thus represents the extent to which people with different grievances may be expected to support each other. A good example of this coalition-building function of manifestos is provided by the 1970 FLQ document which covers a wide range of grievances. Quotations from it are given in figure 5.

The FLQ manifesto is quite specific concerning the people to which it is addressed. It refers to workers in particular named factories who are on strike; it even gives the names and addresses of individuals – "Mrs Lemay of St-Hyacinthe [who] can't afford little trips to Florida, as the crooked judges and MPs can with our money." But it is rather less specific on who or what is to blame for all the discontents it is seeking to orchestrate. It points the finger

FIGURE 5
The FLQ Manifesto, October 1970

... The Front de Libération du Québec wants the total independence of the Québécois, brought together in a free society, purged forever of its band of voracious sharks, the patronage-dispensing "big bosses" and their servants who have made Quebec into their private preserve of "cheap labour" and of exploitation without scruple.

The Front de Libération du Québec is a movement not of aggression, but of response to aggression – the aggression organized by high finance through the marionettes of the federal and provincial governments ...

We believed, once, that it was worth the effort to channel our energies, our impatience ... within the Parti Québécois; but the Liberal victory shows clearly that what is called a democracy in Quebec is, and always has been, nothing but the "democracy" of the rich. The Liberals' victory in this way is nothing but the victory of the Simard-Cotroni election riggers. As a result, British parliamentarism is finished, and the Front de Libération du Québec will never let itself be diverted by the electoral crumbs which the Anglo-Saxon capitalists toss into the Québécois lower courtyard every four years ...

Yes – there are reasons for the Liberal win. Yes, there are reasons for unemployment, for poverty, for slums, for the fact that you Mr. Bergeron of Visitation Street, and also you Mr. Legendre of Laval who earns $10,000 a year, you do not feel free in our country, Quebec.

Yes, there are reasons, and the men of Lord and Cie know them; the Fishermen of the Gaspésie, the workers of the North Shore, the miners of Iron Ore, of Quebec Cartier Mining, or Noranda Mines, they also know those reasons. Also the decent, honest working people of Cabano whom they tried to screw one more time know lots of those reasons ...

We have had our fill of Canadian federalism which penalizes the dairy producers of Quebec to satisfy the needs of the Anglo-Saxons of the Commonwealth; which maintains the decent taxi drivers of Montreal in a state of half-slavery ... ; which carries out an insane import policy while throwing into the street, one by one, the small wage-laborers in the textile and shoe industries, the most downtrodden in Quebec, for the profit of a clutch of accursed "money-makers" in their Cadillacs; which classifies the Québécois nation as one of Canada's ethnic minorities ...

We live in a society of terrorized slaves, terrorized by the big bosses ... Terrorized by the capitalist Roman Church, ... by payments to Household Finance, by the advertising of the masters of consumption ... ; terrorized by the closed precincts of knowledge and culture called universities ...

Working people of Quebec, begin today to take back what belongs to you: take yourselves what is yours. You alone know your factories, your machines, your hotels, your universities, your unions; do not wait for a miracle organization ...

Let all those, in every corner of Quebec, scornfully dismissed as "lousy French" and

FIGURE 5 (*concluded*)

---

drunkards, take up with vigor the battle against the club-smashers of freedom and justice, and strip their power to harm from the professionals of hold-ups and fraud: bankers, "businessmen", judges, sold-out politicians ...

We are Québécois working people and we will go to the end. We want, with all the people to replace this slave society with a free society, functioning of itself and for itself, a society open to the world.

Our struggle can only be victorious. Not for long can one hold in misery and scorn, a people once awakened. Vive le Québec libre! Vive les camarades prisonniers politiques! Vive la révolution Québécois! Vive le Front de Libération du Québec!

(Translation by Canadian University Press. By permission.)

---

at big bosses, high finance, Anglo-Saxon capitalists, the system, Canadian federalism, U.S. millionaires, the capitalist Roman Catholic Church, technocrats, cigar puffers, and so on. Some specific villains are singled out: Trudeau, Bourassa, Drapeau, Steinberg, Bronfman, etc. But these are abstract villains; they are not people the ordinary Quebecker had come in contact with.

While symbols are obviously important in mobilizing people to act upon their discontent, there is generally nothing symbolic about the actual discontent they experience. As Piven and Cloward (1977: 20) point out, people feel deprived and oppressed in relation to actual circumstances. It is a particular assembly line or a particular foreman that galls them, not monopoly capitalism. An example of discontent at the personal level is provided by the Quebec City riots of 1918. While conscription was the general issue, the immediate impetus to the outbreak was the behaviour of certain Dominion policemen attempting to enforce the Military Service Act. In the House of Commons *Debates* (1918: 391, 407, 426), these agents of the government were variously characterized as bullies, drunken brutes, and bribe-takers. The coroner's jury investigating the four deaths squarely blamed the riot on "the tactless and grossly unwise fashion in which the Federal police ... did their work" (Hopkins, 1919: 463-4). In other words, at the root of the social scientists' indicators of economic or political discontent, there is often a personalized grievance that ignites and focuses this discontent.

In Canadian manifestos there is an interesting conjunction between economic and political discontents. Specific economic ills are mentioned, and then the lack of political means to redress them is deplored. Thus the On to Ottawa trekkers wanted elected camp representatives and the right to vote as well as work with wages. The FLQ sought an independent Quebec as well as a more equitable socio-economic system. Another good example is the manifesto (28 July 1884) produced by Riel's lieutenant, W.H. Jackson, and addressed to the citizens of Prince Albert:

We state the various evils which are caused by the present system of legislation showing:

1. That they are caused by the facts that the Ottawa legislators are responsible to Eastern constituents, not to us, and are therefore impelled to legislate with a view to Eastern interests rather than our own ...

2. That the legislation passed by such legislators has already produced great depression in agricultural, commercial, and mechanical circles ...

We give the complete list of our grievances, but instead of asking the redress of each of them separately, we ask the remedy to the root of the evil, i.e., Provincial Legislatures with full control over our own resources and internal administration, and power to send a just number of representatives to the Federal Legislature ... (Cited in Stanley, 1961: 301)

With the exception of the FLQ manifesto, all the documents cited were written before any violence had occurred. Without a control group of platforms from movements that did not resort to violence, it is not possible to determine whether the platforms of violent groups are in any way distinctive. A comparison might show that the violent groups tended to emphasize discontents that were large, zero-sum, or otherwise difficult to settle, that the very number of the grievances mentioned reflected the existence of "multiple dysfunctionality," and that their emphasis on political power was characteristic of what Tilly (1979: 88, 109) has identified as the particular violence-proneness of groups rising or falling in the polity.

Given that most of these manifestos were written early in the movements' career, they naturally have little to say about violence. W.H. Jackson counselled that all constitutional means be exhausted lest moral support be lost and warned that the local press were circulating wild rumours "seeking a pretext for placing the country under martial law and so goad the people into a false step" (Stanley, 1961: 302). The FLQ, on the other hand, had already turned to violence before the appearance of its manifesto. It urged others to follow its example and provided them with a justification for doing so: they would not be the aggressors but only responding to the aggression and terrorism they believed the system inflicted daily upon the Quebec people.

CONCLUSION

This chapter has examined the classic sources of violence-begetting discontent, suggesting which of these obtained in Canada, and looking at the particular discontents which have been associated with violence in this country. Such a procedure reveals only a tenuous relation between discontent and violence. Many of the grievances that have produced violence in other countries did not do so in Canada, perhaps because they were not experienced as severely here. Others are clearly not consistently applicable, as is evidenced in the different results of Frank and Kelly's (1977) "indice du paradoxe économique" for Quebec and Ontario. In some cases, discontents have been passively accepted, while in others they have been regulated by the country's political institutions or manifested in peaceful reform movements. Sometimes the theories seem to be too general to capture the specific circumstances that convert a dispute into a violent confrontation. Plainly many factors intervene between the growth of discontent and the outbreak of violence.

Yet if discontent is not a sufficient condition for violence, is it even a necessary one? It seems not. First, it has to be remembered that other motives can underlie violence. In particular, there is the use of violence as a means of coercion. The Black Donnellys, for instance, employed violence in order to terrorize the population of Lucan into compliance with their demands; and the violence of nineteenth-century elections was used to disrupt opponents' campaigns. Also, despite the suggestion in this chapter that behind violent acts are to be found grimly disappointed people, it should be noted that violence can also take place in a good-humoured atmosphere. In his eye-witness account of the Quebec City riots of 1918, C.B. Power (Ward, 1960: 83) notes that "there were times when the comic aspect, accompanied by hilarious laughter from thousands of spectators, turned the whole matter almost into a slapstick Hollywood show." Or consider this memory of the 1935 Regina riot and the On to Ottawa trek:

But it wasn't all that much of a riot. The papers played it big but it wasn't all that much. A lot of guys just thought it was a lark, a chance to yell at cops and snap a lighted cigarette in their faces and then run like hell ... [The trek] was a free ride for some, both ways. A lot of fun, a chance to break the monotony for others. I let off a little steam and so did a lot of others and we were fed pretty well. (Cited in Broadfoot, 1973: 366)

Second, discontent is not a necessary condition for violence because many incidents erupt, not from the actions of protesting civilians, but rather from the actions of governmental agents. A classic riot scenario has a peaceful demonstration to protest grievances broken up by police trying to clear the streets. Discontent produced the demonstration, but not the violence; that was the result of police using violence as a means of coercion. Any civilian resistance has self-defence rather than discontent as a dominant motive.

The long-standing assumption that discontent in one form or another is the basic cause of violence was particularly prevalent in the American studies of violence that burgeoned in the 1960s. At that time sympathy for blacks, students, and war-resisters at home and anti-colonial movements abroad impelled researchers to stress that those who took up arms had more than enough just cause and to demand that the general public listen closely to what they were saying rather than dismissing their actions as criminality, amorality, or crowd hysteria. It is a valid point: if people risk life and limb for a cause, they must be accorded the dignity of careful attention to their pronouncements.

Whatever their limitations, discontent theories thus provide another essential component to an explanation of violence. They provide a framework for classifying and analysing the motivations of the violent. For example, in considering the issues in a dispute it can be asked whether exacerbating conditions are present and consequently whether the dispute is especially liable to turn violent, whether scattered focuses of discontent exist concurrently, whether grievances have become elevated into disputes about the existing structures of power, or whether isolation and discrimination have curtailed alternative opportunities. The *ex post facto* delineation of discontent may not be sufficient to prove that discontent caused the violence, but any analysis of an incident will be poor and truncated unless it takes into account the ideas of the discontent theorists.

CHAPTER EIGHT

Solidarity Theories

The theories concerning breakdown and discontent examined in the last two chapters concentrate on individuals, and therefore tend to attribute actions to a variety of psychological states: excitement, alienation, anomie, frustration, and the like. By contrast, solidarity theories question both this approach and its empirical base. They emphasize not the individual, but people working in groups to attain a common objective.

Instead of the miserable and confused specimens that populate breakdown and discontent theories, solidarity theories give a more dignified view of men and women rationally pursuing their interests in the company of their fellows. Indeed solidarity theories argue that, as a simple matter of fact, the anomic individual or the one most pressed by hardship does not figure largely in violent movements. Rather, participants typically can look beyond their own misery and recognize the like condition of others; they are full of hope; and they possess the material and intellectual resources that will enable them to work with others in achieving a better future.

Solidarity theorists are prepared to grant that conflict rises during historical crises, such as wars and depressions. But they reject the linking mechanisms proposed in theories of breakdown or discontent. It is not that these crises produce a crumbling of normative restraints or increase discontent. Rather it is that they produce an abrupt shift in the risks, rewards, and resources – the three R's that form the backbone of solidarity theories – that temporarily favours the activities of conflict groups. At these times, the authorities have little in the way of unused resources to divert to social control, so that it becomes more convenient to bargain with the group than to fight it; the group consequently runs less risk of repression and enjoys the likelihood of higher rewards from its activities.

Another characteristic of solidarity theories is that they often pay little direct attention to violence and its causes. They tend to concentrate on how "conflict," "opposition," or "challenging" groups are formed and maintained, and deal only incidentally with the choice between violent and peaceful tactics which is often ascribed to factors of secondary importance to them. Tilly (1978: 182-4), for example, sees no essential difference between violent and non-violent conflicts. The former tend to be better documented, and thus there is some justification for focusing on them as tracers of the wider body of collective activity. Yet what the solidarity theorists do say about violence is often illuminating, and not all of them play down the subject. For instance, Oberschall (1973: 332) argues that violence is a proper subject unto itself and cites Weber in support: "The treatment of conflict involving the use of physical violence as a separate type is justified by the special characteristics of the employment of this means and the corresponding peculiarities of the sociological consequences of its use."

This chapter starts with a review of the classic issues in solidarity theories. How are groups, both violent and non-violent, mobilized? What are the different types of groups? How do they maintain cohesion? Who are the leaders and the rank-and-file? The chapter then turns to those features of groups that have been tentatively linked to violence as well as considering a fine Canadian example of the world viewed from a solidarity perspective. The chapter will be concluded with a comparison of the contribution that breakdown and solidarity theories have made to an understanding of violence.

MOBILIZATION

Mobilization is "the process of forming crowds, groups, associations, and organizations for the pursuit of collective goals" (Oberschall, 1973: 102). The minimum to instigate this process is the development of group consciousness, that is, an awareness of a community of interests and that co-operative action against external targets is possible and desirable. Mobilization is most readily achieved when it builds on an already extant group consciousness, whether that group is communal or associational.

Ease of communications is another facilitating factor. Geographically concentrated people are more easily mobilized than a scattered population. Similarly, institutions that assemble previously isolated individuals aid mobilization: such as peasants who become linked in large commercial agriculture programs, workers united in large factories and isolated communities, or the poor brought together at the offices of relief agencies. An example of this effect in reverse is the married unemployed in Vancouver in the 1930s, who rioted when they had to assemble at one centre to get relief, but who did not when the relief was distributed to them at their homes. Mobilization becomes exceedingly difficult when the free flow of communications is disrupted: "The importance of freedom of association, speech, and, in general, of oppositional activity based on civil liberties cannot be overemphasized in a theory of mobilization" (Oberschall, 1973: 138).

Another impetus to mobilization is any loss of legitimacy by the existing system. Piven and Cloward (1977: 7-8, 12) argue that lower-class protests are structurally precluded most of the time because social institutions enforce political docility. A series or combination of dislocations, representing profound changes in the larger society, are necessary if the poor are to overcome their culturally bred sense of shame and blame others for what comes to be recognized as their collective plight. Elites can contribute to this reappraisal by publicly displaying division within their ranks. (Cf. Brinton's [1965: 251-2] finding that inefficient government machinery and loss of faith and division within the old ruling class are common conditions in prerevolutionary societies.)

Coser (1956: 37-8) also treats legitimacy as a "crucial intervening variable" between feelings of hostility and actual conflict: "When a social structure is no longer considered legitimate, individuals with similar objective positions will come, through conflict, to constitute themselves into self-conscious groups with common interests." Loss of legitimacy occurs when social changes induce a shift in reference groups. Thus, in India intercaste conflict used to be "rare because lower and higher castes alike accepted the caste distinctions." But the change from agriculture to industry, and the concomitant opening of opportunities for mobility, "have been instrumental in inducing the negatively privileged groups to change their definitions of self and others."

Coser's argument is closely paralleled in Guindon's (1975) explanation of the rise of Quebec separatism. Guindon points to the economic changes in that province since the Second World War. Rapid urbanization created a new French-Canadian middle class as urban bureaucracies expanded and fresh channels of upward mobility developed. During his lifetime, the conservative provincial premier, Maurice Duplessis, was the *bête noire* of this new class. However, subsequent provincial governments espoused its interests, so that hostility had to be shifted to an external target, the federal system. The sentiments expressed by the separatists had long been current in Quebec society, but, before the 1960s, they had been confined to marginal intellectuals. Thus Lionel Groulx first voiced the slogan "maîtres chez nous" forty years before it was officially adopted by the provincial Liberal party. Only after 1960 did his views "become the unifying ideology giving political cohesiveness" to the new middle class (1975: 342).

But does the terrorist FLQ fit this analysis? In some respects it does not. Marc Laurendeau (1974: 97) contends that the terrorists were by no means all of new middle-class origins. And, especially in the later sixties, the movement embraced the cause of working-class liberation. Nevertheless, the development of a self-conscious group aware of oppression and the illegitimacy of existing institutions appears to have been a necessary precursor to the terrorist movement. It was only after participation in the seemingly ineffective separatist organizations, such as the RIN, that some of the separatists turned to violence.

"Mobilization" is also used, for example by Tilly (1978), in the wider sense of accumulating and marshalling any and all of the necessary resources to carry on a conflict. Such resources extend at a minimum to a mobilized group – "mobilized" being here used to designate the process of group formation. High membership commitment is only one requirement of the group. Others include the recruitment of intellectuals, allies, sponsors, defence lawyers, and individuals with organizational and leadership experience. The group also needs ideas (myths, ideologies, and traditional lore) and material objects (money, weapons, printing presses, and a headquarters).

Solidarity theorists place a heavy emphasis on the gathering of resources, urging that it is a key determinant of a group's success. Resource accumulation cannot be taken for granted; it represents a long, uncertain struggle for a group challenging a well entrenched elite. Hence comes the importance of disaffection among the elite. Only when internal differences prevent the elite from fully using its own resources or cause some of its members to transfer their resources to the challenging group is the balance of resources likely to swing in favour of the challenger. Solidarity theorists further argue that a group that is poorly endowed with resources initially cannot grow unless it receives an injection of resources from the outside, for example, when urban-based members of a political party move to organize a rural population.

Resource mobilization is one of the most illuminating of the concepts used by solidarity theorists. It captures well what conflict groups attempt to do in their day-to-day activities. It emphasizes that the other party to the conflict, often enough the government, also has to assemble and commit resources in order to fight off any challenge. A revolutionary situation is accurately described as one in which two or more contenders draw into their conflict more and more of a society's resources. It directs attention to whether a group's resources can be mobilized with ease or only with great difficulty – the activation factor. And it raises the interesting question of the substitutability of resources – of where and when a shortfall in one resource, say manpower, can be compensated for by an abundance in another, say wealth or membership zeal. At the moment, beyond postulating the existence of a group that is mobilized in the narrow sense of possessing a group consciousness as a minimum condition for conflict, solidarity theorists are unable to rank the various resources in order of importance or to distinguish the essential from the desirable. Clearly, this is an area that requires further theoretical and empirical work. In particular, the concepts of activation and substitution need further refinement if one is to understand better the occasional successes of apparently resource-poor groups.

TYPES OF GROUPS

I shall concentrate on four of the many possible variables for classifying groups. The first is the extent to which the group is formally organized. At one extreme is the spontaneous group in which prior organization is altogether absent; at the other is the group with a written charter, a formal membership list, a centralized authority structure with a hierarchy of offices, and a full-time bureaucracy. The second variable is the extent to which a group operates clandestinely. Third is whether the group is an inclusive one which anyone interested can join or an exclusive one in which membership is limited and accorded only to those meeting special criteria established by the group. Clandestine groups are invariably exclusive ones, but open groups may or may not restrict membership. The fourth variable is the size of the group and overlaps the above three: large groups tend to be formally organized, to operate openly, and to be inclusive. Nevertheless, the converse does not necessarily apply: small or middling-sized groups may or may not be formally organized, open, and inclusive.

The literature indicates that students of conflict groups have found many other variables to use in classifying groups. For instance, Oberschall (1973) asks whether a group has a communal or an associational base and in what way it is linked to the upper strata of a society. Coser (1956) adds the degree of membership commitment must be specified and distinguishes groups that are engaged in a continuous struggle with the outside world ("sects") from those that are not. Gamson (1975) looks at the goals of the group (Does the group pursue multiple issues or a single one? Does it seek to displace opponents or does it have more modest goals?) and the extent to which it secures coalition partners or outside help.

Rather than wrestle with a formal taxonomy of conflict groups, it seems better to focus on three recurring types in incidents of violence. First is the *spontaneous* group. In mobilizing, it draws on its own resources without benefit of outside help. It has no prior formal organization or continuity of leadership; indeed there may be no visible leaders at all. Lack of organization implies open operations and an inclusive membership. Its size varies upwards from a small street-corner gathering to a city-wide or, in the case of rural uprisings, province-wide movement, but its lack of organization again points to a localized rather than a national revolt. Second is the *vanguard* group. Usually operating clandestinely and with an exclusive membership, it comprises a small band of highly committed, tightly organized individuals who hope to lead a latent group into mobilizing. Third is the *mass membership* group. Formally organized, open, and inclusive, its aim is to recruit as many members as possible to the cause.

Many solidarity theorists regard spontaneous group action as a waste of effort: organization, not anarchism, is what counts. (This point is elaborated later in the chapter.) But should the organization take the form of a vanguard party or a mass membership movement? There is a long tradition of heated debate on the issue. The question divided the Bolsheviks and Mensheviks in tsarist Russia, just as it did the communist parties and guerrilla *focos* in Latin

America during the 1960s. It resurfaced in Quebec in the debate between the proponents of the terrorist group, the FLQ, and the supporters of a mass political party, the PQ.

Oberschall (1973: 144-5) suggests that institutionalization and internal organization depend on:

the reaction of the authorities and their success in containing or repressing the movement. A movement that is illegal and that has to operate in secrecy to protect its members will develop a different organizational structure than a similar movement operating in a liberal environment. Movements that seek to expand their membership base as opposed to those wishing to maintain their hold over an already mobilized membership must by necessity be organized along different lines. The degree of heterogeneity of members reflected in ethnic, class, religious, and regional composition, as well as the availability of historical models and outside resources, all have an impact on internal organizational processes.

Organizational decisions are, however, determined by the way movement members perceive their world, which is not necessarily the world as it actually is. Often two or more movements organized on different principles exist side by side, for example the FLQ and the PQ, as a result of varying perceptions of the nature of the society within which they must work.

The choice of organization is an important one since the group's chances of success depend heavily on having an organization appropriate to the task before it. The choice also has important implications for the likelihood of the use of violent tactics, for violence is more often found with some types of groups than with others. I shall return to this point in the discussion below on organization, success, and violence.

MAINTAINING COHESION

For groups to act effectively, they must maintain solidarity. The resources of the group must be co-ordinated and be capable of activation where, when, and how it seems appropriate. Factional disputes have to be avoided if the energies of the group are not to be dissipated. Group consciousness by itself does not ensure cohesion. Olson (1968) puts his finger on the problem, when he states that individuals in any large group pursuing collective goods can, with perfect rationality, leave it to others to do the hard work. A collective good is one that cannot be feasibly withheld from some – the idlers, the free-riders – if others are to enjoy it. For example, campaigns against a tyrannical government, or for extended suffrage, or for higher wages are such that their success must benefit all the members of the group irrespective of their contribution to the campaign: all the tyrant's subjects, all the women voters, or all the workers in a particular plant. Free-riders will reason that their lone contribution will make no difference one way or another to the success of the campaign and that consequently they might as well stay at home with purse and person intact.

To overcome the free-rider problem, a group must offer non-collective or private benefits or be prepared to apply coercion. Non-collective benefits provide an individual with an incentive to join and remain with the group. Membership itself may provide satisfaction in the form of fraternity, self-esteem, and identity. Special services may be offered members, such as the private insurance schemes instituted by many early unions, or the promise of jobs and facilities for social gatherings given by the Orange Lodges.

Fear and despisal of the world outside the group may also be fostered so that members hesitate to leave its protection. This may have been a factor in maintaining cohesion among the Doukhobors. After joining an opposition movement or taking part in its illegal activities, members may believe that they will not be allowed to rejoin "straight" society since the authorities will always mistrust them as dangerous radicals and a criminal record will bar them from employment. They thus see no possibility of leaving the group. As Benjamin Franklin warned during the course of the American Revolution: "We must all hang together, gentlemen, or most assuredly, we shall all hang separately" (cited in Bell, 1973: 107).

Selective incentives are invariably accompanied by ideological appeals for solidarity. Rhetoric, slogans, and songs are employed to urge members to loyalty. Rituals – the mass parade, sharing of food and drink, particularities of dress and speech, oaths – all serve to emphasize the group's community of interest and identity. These are all efforts at what Gamson (1975: 57) labels "persuasion." He stresses their importance, so long as they are used in conjunction with selective incentives. In his sample of challenging groups, those that relied only on appeals to loyalty were far less successful than those that employed them in addition to selective incentives.

The nature of a group's organization is also sometimes thought to affect cohesion. The existence of a bureaucracy may help to co-ordinate action. However, Gamson (1975: 92) argues that a bureaucracy serves the necessary function of maintaining commitment among members that can be activated when necessary, "but it guarantees nothing with respect to the problem of internal conflict." The latter problem, he believes, is best solved by centralizing power. According to his study, decentralized groups were far more likely to be afflicted by factional splits than those with centralized power, but whether or not a group was bureaucratized was unrelated to factionalism. Yet centralization is perhaps only possible in groups with a low tendency to factionalism in the first place. At any rate, Coser (1956: 79-80) argues the opposite case: loosely structured groups are least susceptible to breaking apart because they permit the expression of dissent within the group.

Thus the existence of the group itself does not have to be called into question by dissidents seeking to make their point.[1]

Leaders play a key role as "the architects of organization, ideology, and mobilization for the movement." In particular, a charismatic leader "can build a cohesive movement by directly orienting the loyalties and commitments of members to himself personally rather than through the groups and group leaders that were in existence at the time of the creation of the movement" (Oberschall, 1973: 146, 144). Dissident leaders often invest more in a movement than they can hope to gain from the achievement of its goals. By devoting their lives to a cause and by taking considerable risks to promote it, they seem to contradict Olson's portrait of individuals in groups rationally pursuing their interests by doing as little as possible. There are two balancing factors in the leaders' calculations of risks and rewards. First, their chances of advancement outside the movement are typically low, either because they come from groups prevented from gaining access to power in the wider society or because, in joining the movement, they have burned their bridges behind them. Second, dissident leaders are political entrepreneurs much like leaders in legitimate organizations. They not only enjoy directing a campaign, but they are investing for the future, hoping that their present commitment will pay off in terms of power and other rewards once the movement is successful.

Cohesion may also be fostered by the very fact of engaging in conflict. According to Coser (1956: 87-95), conflict reinforces the identity of the group by delineating a sharp distinction between "us" and "them." It also mobilizes the energies of group members and raises morale. Even conflict within the group, providing it does not concern the group's consensual basis, is functional in removing tensions, coping with dissidents, and re-establishing unity (1956: 80). However, groups engaged in a continued struggle with the outside rarely tolerate internal dissension (1956: 103).

Georges Sorel early recognized the importance of carrying on uncompromising conflict in order to maintain group cohesion. Writing at the turn of the century, Sorel was enraged by the efforts of the French middle class to reach accommodation with the workers. The former, he believed, would sap the revolutionary consciousness of the workers and prevent them from carrying out their historical role, as laid down by Marx, of overturning capitalism and the state. The workers' task was to re-establish clearly the class cleavages in society, and do so by engaging in acts of violence that would force the middle class to perform its allotted role and reject the possibility of social peace.

---

1 It might be suggested that Quebec and western separatism in Canada is the product of federal government attempts at centralization. If the separatists believe the political system has become too centralized to give adequate expression to regional interests, then quite logically they challenge the system itself.

"Everything may be saved, if the proletariat, by their use of violence, manage to re-establish the division into classes, and so restore to the middle class something of its former energy" (1961: 98). Violent conflict, in short, exorcizes obfuscating accommodation and strengthens the unity and sense of purpose of both antagonistic groups.

However, Coser (1956: 92-5) adds a proviso to this general thesis that conflict enhances cohesion. He notes that intergroup conflict "has often led to anomie rather than to an increase in internal cohesion." Group disintegration occurs when "internal cohesion before the outbreak of the conflict is so low that the group members have ceased to regard preservation of the group as worthwhile, or actually see the outside threat to concern 'them' rather than 'us.'" In these circumstances, the only alternative to disintegration is some form of despotically enforced unity. Coser offers two examples of the process. First is the impact of the Great Depression on families: those "lacking internal solidarity before the depression responded apathetically and were broken up, whereas solidary families actually were strengthened." And second, he contrasts the effects of the Second World War on the French and British social structures: in Britain the war increased social cohesion, but in France social fissures widened "to the point of a breakdown in consensus even concerning the most basic question of all: whether France was to continue as an independent national unit ... The only alternative to disintegration then came to be the 'despotism' of the Pétain regime."

Similarly in Canada during the First World War, the low internal cohesion of the nation at the start of the war was further exacerbated by the conflict. The "us" (Canadians) versus "them" (Germans) division was considered irrelevant by many in French-Canadian and labour circles. The breakdown in consensus was indicated by the debate on the Francoeur resolution in the Quebec assembly questioning the value of maintaining Confederation and the Borden government's increasing resort to coercion. The Second World War also revealed signs of strain in Canadian society, but far less seriously than the First. Initial cohesion was probably stronger; unlike Borden's in 1914, Mackenzie King's government in 1939 had strong French-Canadian representation and was largely able to keep that representation during the course of the war. The government was thus able to maintain some credibility as the leadership of a united country against the Axis powers. In both wars, there was industrial conflict, but the conflict declined over the course of the Second World War and rose during the First. In the earlier conflict many workers believed that labour was being forced to bear a disproportionate share of the war burden; strikes were bitter and often violent; and radical doctrines of revolutionary socialism captured some support. In the Second World War, the government finally protected labour's right to organize and bargain collectively; it set in motion important measures of social reform; strikes though often protracted were rarely violent; and the CCF was present to integrate left-wing discontent into the political system. In short, the Second World War, unlike the First, saw French-Canadian and labour protest largely worked out within a relatively solidary community, and the country emerged from the war united and strong.

Another proviso that should be added to Coser's thesis that conflict enhances cohesion is that the conflict should not end in the utter defeat of one side. If it does, the hope that fuelled the cause will be dissipated, and the prestige of those who directed the movement will be in question. One Canadian example is the disintegration of the Métis community after its defeat in the Northwest Rebellion. Another is provided by the Winnipeg General Strike. In Bercuson's assessment (1974: 30), "the defeat of the strike assured the weakening of those unions and labour leaders who had championed its use and who had called it ... Much of the vitality of a labour movement grown powerful and energetic during four years of war was sapped in the grinding and hopeless struggle of the six-week confrontation at Winnipeg."

Finally, coercion. As shown, Coser considers despotically enforced unity the only means of unifying a disintegrating group. Johnson (1966: 32) also sees coercion as a replacement for consensus during a power deflation. However, many other theorists argue that coercion is not a substitute for consensus, but must always be present if groups are to cohere. Thus Dahrendorf (1959: 165-7) urges that authority relations imply the existence of sanctions to compel obedience from the occupants of subordinate roles. Olson specifies that large groups providing collective goods, such as trade unions and the state, have to compel participation. He points out (1968: 13), for example, that despite the indubitably valuable collective goods the state provides and the great powers of persuasion it commands, "no major state in modern history has been able to support itself through voluntary dues or contributions ... Taxes, *compulsory* payments by definition, are needed."

Irrespective of their relative merits, both views – coercion as a substitute for waning consensus, and coercion as a constant requirement for group cohesion – point to the importance for group survival of the ability to coerce recalcitrant members into line. Coercion may take a non-physical form, such as the threat of excommunication or the loss of the selective benefits that attracted the member into the group in the first place. Very often, however, it assumes a physical form. For example, during the relief camp strikers' sojourn in Vancouver in 1935, solidarity was enforced by a picket squad that prevented any individual strikers leaving town. Applicants for relief were compelled to hand over their transport passes; outgoing trains were searched with "the occasional flying human bundle hitting the dirt at a quick run"; those resisting the squad might end up in hospital (Liversedge, 1973: 65-6).

Selective benefits, persuasion, perhaps a centralized structure, leadership, conflict with external groups, and coercion can all be used to combat factionalism and apathy, the two bugbears of collective action. Of the two, apathy appears to be the more deadly to a group's chances of success; for while factionalism can degenerate into fruitless infighting, it does have its positive side, as Coser (1956: 47, 80) points out. The group that is too successful in its campaign for solidarity may lack the excitement and new ideas generated by internal argument, its leaders may lose touch with the rank-and-file, and in general it may fall prey to what Oberschall (1973: 259) calls "the conservative tendencies inherent in large-scale organizations."

LEADERS AND FOLLOWERS

Given a dissatisfied collectivity, some of its members will join a protest movement and others will simply refuse to participate. Among the participants, some will become leaders while the great majority will remain in the rank-and-file. Much attention has been focused on these differences. There are three strands of thought.

The oldest is the psychological tradition beloved of breakdown theorists which asserts that there are definite differences between participants and non-participants and also between leaders and followers. Participants are seen as suffering from alienation, anomie, or marginality, and the movement offers them acceptance and a chance to regain their self-respect. Their commitment is consequently intense. Indeed, the more they are called upon to sacrifice for the movement and the more they project their own personalities into it, the greater their sense of exhaltation and commitment becomes (Coser, 1956: 114). These "true believers" are not contrary or contentiously minded individuals. Rather they are seekers of security, purpose, and order who willingly embrace both demands for total obedience to the leadership and an elaborate, hierarchical organization, replete with special uniforms and grades of initiates, so as to build up their own sense of belonging. Leaders come from a similarly dispossessed background, but they have special personal characteristics that differentiate them from their followers. These are summarized by Leiden and Schmitt (1968: 81-3) as including vital qualities of will, courage, and the ability to concentrate on essentials; a fanatical belief in themselves and their cause; and personal magnetism.

The psychological tradition has fallen into disrepute because of its scant empirical backing. In reaction to it came the "everyone-the-same" school of thought whereby little was thought to distinguish joiners from non-joiners and leaders from followers. Brinton (1965: 120), for example, argues that the revolutionary leaders and followers he studied "were not in general afflicted with anything the psychiatrist could be called in about ... [They were] more or less a cross-section of common humanity."

Further empirical studies revealed that this conclusion was also too simple. Even if psychological distinctions were irrelevant, there were noteworthy sociological differences. Overrepresented among participants and leaders of social movements were members of the free professions, especially lawyers and students. They were also usually young and male. Movement leaders differed from the rank-and-file in coming from higher social strata and from among those already in leadership positions in pre-existing communal or associational groups.

Solidarity theorists account for such irregularities in terms of the three R's: risks, rewards, and resources. Isolated, uprooted, or atomized individuals in mass society do not have the education or experience that produces activists and leaders. Furthermore, their lack of economic autonomy renders them extremely vulnerable to the agencies of social control, so that the risks of involvement in a dissident movement far outweigh any possible rewards. In contrast are the members of the free professions. Their education endows them with intellectual and organizational skills, and they usually have an initial economic resource base and clientele to draw upon. If their mobility is blocked by discrimination, dissidence promises to be rewarding. Even if they are repressed (which leaves them little alternative but continued dissidence), they probably have a well-to-do family to fall back upon, and connections with associations and elite groups to help protect them from the harsher punishments that might be meted out to less well-situated individuals (Oberschall, 1973: 164-5).

The key point stressed by solidarity theorists is that their portrait of joiners and leaders of dissident movements is essentially the same as that which applies to the joiners and leaders of legitimate groups that work within the existing political system. Both sides require similar skills and resources. Lawyers, for example, are overrepresented both among revolutionary leaders and among leaders of legitimate political parties. Whether individual lawyers work within the existing system or attack it from the outside has nothing to do with their psychology, but everything to do with whether the system blocks their mobility and how it responds to their grievances. If dissident leaders sometimes behave erratically, this is because of the strains of the job, not because they were psychologically flawed individuals in the first place.

On paper the distinctions among the psychological, everyone-the-same, and solidarity theories are clear enough. It would seem that we have only to inspect the data on actual leaders and followers to see which of the theories best fits the facts. Yet the data do not always support one theory to the exclusion of the other two. Consider the various treatments of the FLQ, for example. M. Laurendeau (1974: 96-8) argues for an everyone-the-same interpretation: the felquistes were a cross-section of the population with representatives from all social classes. On the other hand, Morf (1970) relies on psychological factors. And indeed the FLQ seems to have served a psychological purpose in providing goals, fraternity, and sense of self-worth to some of its members. This is revealed by the sense of belonging and joy in acting together reported by an interviewer of the earlier terrorists (cited in M.

Laurendeau, 1974: 91), the elaborate organizational charts cited by Pelletier (1971: 212-14), the participants' chequered school and work histories, and the prior rejection and alienation they experienced in trying to work in Anglophone-dominated organizations (especially the then largely Anglophone armed forces). However, a solidarity theorist would point to the same language-of-work problems as shifting the risk:reward ratio in favour of participation in an opposition movement and would see the resort to conspiratorial terrorism as a response to the repression handed out to those embracing Quebec nationalist and socialist ideas. Yet if the FLQ was the product of repression, how to account for the coexistence of the PQ and its equally non-violent, non-conspiratorial predecessors?

A solidarity theory offers a better account of the PQ than of the FLQ. It predicts that the leaders and followers of opposition movements will be drawn largely from those who are well integrated with their collectivity and who are already actively participating in various causes, and that the leaders will tend to be well educated and with previous leadership experience. PQ reliance on the new middle class and its leader, René Lévesque, tranferring from a cabinet post in a provincial Liberal government to leading his own political party, neatly fit the model. But none of the felquistes had been in any sort of leadership position before. Its two main leaders, Charles Gagnon and Pierre Vallières, came from lower-class backgrounds. I shall argue below that it was precisely their remoteness from power and consequent inexperience and misunderstanding of what could be achieved through legitimate political channels that drew them into a terrorist strategy.

None of the three theories, then, offers a complete account of who was drawn into and who became leaders of the FLQ. All three also fail to explain the case of the Sons of Freedom Doukhobors. The Sons of Freedom seem to be easily classed as "true believers." Indeed, Woodcock and Avakumovic (1977: 328) do point to some psychologically distinguishing marks. They speak of "the surges of mass emotion," "alienation," and "tense psychological states [created] by the atmosphere of fanatical communities." However, a true believer seeks organization and hierarchy, and would consequently be very uncomfortable with the Doukhobors' anarchistic and egalitarian tenets. Moreover, the Sons of Freedom were not atomized or rootless individuals; they were, rather, intensely involved in the life of the community. The everyone-the-same theory also does not fit the facts, for there were differences between the Sons of Freedom and the rest of the Doukhobor community. Apart from their "tense psychological states" and commitment to the group, they were also the Doukhobors with the fewest economic and educational resources. This was partly a matter of deliberate choice. Even so, their resourcelessness, according to a solidarity theory, should have rendered them incapable of sustained protest. Yet the more wealth and education Doukhobors have accumulated, as with the "right-wing" independents, the less they have committed themselves to the group or participated in its collective protests. The activists that remain today have little formal education and are materially deprived (Woodcock and Avakumovic, 1977: xii).

The solidarity theory does seem to fit the two Métis revolts of the last century rather well. The Métis communities at Red River and Batoche were segmented from the rest of Canadian society and had their own thriving religious and economic organizations. Differences of status and wealth existed within them, and the leaders of the resistance movements came from among the previous leaders of the community. Louis Riel's father managed a prosperous household and had acted as a community leader. Riel himself was sent east to further his education, and there he found opportunities for a career outside the Métis community closed to him. After leading the first resistance in 1869-70, he was labelled a traitor and murderer, and any possibility of his playing a role in the wider Canadian society was lost. The deprivations and harassment he experienced after the Red River affair undermined his mental stability though he was not insane either before or during it. He did display some of the traits attributed to revolutionary leaders such as determination, impatience, belief in himself and his cause, personal magnetism, and political skills in building cohesion. As his religious thinking developed in the years after the Red River rising, he became a fanatical believer in his role as a prophet. By 1885 he was a charismatic leader in the strict sense, basing his authority on the anointing of the Holy Spirit as made manifest in miracles, revelations, prophecies, and sanctity (Flanagan, 1979: 184). The tale of the Northwest Rebellion is often told simply in terms of Riel and his charismatic hold on his followers. Yet this version neglects the role of such local leaders as Gabriel Dumont and Charles Nolin and the rational means and ends calculations of many participants who, suffering very real grievances to which the government was apparently blind, saw an opportunity to right their wrongs by following Riel.

These Canadian examples show that theories regarding participants and leaders need further refinement. The everyone-the-same theory is of little use, no doubt partly because Canadian dissident movements have been narrowly based and are not the nation-encompassing revolutions studied by Brinton. We can see traces of psychological factors at work but they offer only a partial explanation. Solidarity theories carry us some way towards an understanding, but they are not very helpful in explaining how dissatisfied people are drawn to different groups with variant strategies and goals.

One line of inquiry that is promising has been suggested by Tilly's (1978: 87-8) examination of the resources that people are willing to expend to gain various collective goals. He notes that:

Groups differ considerably in the relative values they assign to collective goods and to the resources which must be expended to acquire them ... Some groups value a given collective good so highly that they are willing to incur what other groups regard as net losses in order to achieve their cherished objectives.

The latter he labels the "zealots," a label which would seem to fit the Sons of Freedom and the felquistes. Tilly does not go on to specify the characteristics of zealot participants. Perhaps they are psychologically different from those who join other groups, but perhaps as well, as was briefly suggested earlier for the FLQ, they are people with a particular combination of resources. In contrast to Oberschall's formulation which stresses the similarities among all movements, of whatever legal or political status and employing whatever structures and tactics (which he treats as largely a function of the regime's response to the movement), we could start by assessing the resources possessed by different groups. Some will have the ones stressed by Oberschall: an assured economic base, education, political skills, and leadership, which enable them to work within the existing system or to establish a counter-polity in a revolutionary situation. Those possessing such resources will probably participate in a movement where their advantages can best be put to use. However, groups without the resources Oberschall mentions are not totally resourceless. Indeed, their very lack of resources may be an advantage of sorts. They are not closely linked to the existing regime and have nothing to lose and everything to gain by joining a dissident movement. They become zealots, not counting the risks and rewards of participation as others might do, and their self-sacrificing idealism compensates for their lack of other resources. They are attracted to precisely those movements that rely on fervour, not wealth or political skills: to terrorism rather than to the construction of a mass membership party. (See Breton's [1972: 45-9] point that the splitting off of the radicals from the Quebec separatist organizations left the radicals further than ever from channels of influence and forced them to adopt "extraordinary means.")

ORGANIZATIONAL STRUCTURE, SUCCESS, AND VIOLENCE

In explaining violence, those who have delineated solidarity theories play down or reject outright the factors we have considered in the previous chapters. Discontent, culture, ideology, or the breakdown of moral restraints are all dismissed as inconsequential. Instead they stress that violence involves an interaction of two or more parties, one of which is often the governmental authority. Whether violence erupts in a conflict depends as much on the behaviour of the other, often governmental, party as on the actions of the protesters themselves. The role of governments will be examined in the next chapter. Here I concentrate on the organizational characteristics of spontaneous, vanguard, and mass membership groups that solidarity theorists claim to affect both a group's chances of success and its propensity to engage in violent tactics.

Let us take first the violence of spontaneous groups. Oberschall (1973: 325) rejects in a few words the older tradition of crowd analysis that emphasized irrationality and emotions. Instead he endorses the approach adopted by Turner and Killian (1972) which "stresses the heterogeneity of composition and response in a crowd, the impact of the actions of the agents of social control upon the behavior of crowds, the fact that the risk and reward structure for a group situation differs from that applicable to individuals, and the emergence of appropriate models and norms of behavior disseminated within a crowd by communications processes . . . [and] continuity between usual group behavior and behavior of individuals in a crowd." Oberschall places special emphasis on the risk/reward structure for crowd participants. As the numbers involved in a crowd go up, the risks for the individual go down; the police may be overwhelmed and anonymity ensures against official reprisals. The rewards also increase "because one gets immediate public approval and social support" from other participants (1973: 327). From this arises the curious fact that a rainstorm will more effectively curtail crowd violence than anything the police can do. When it rains, the crowd thins out, and would-be violent participants find themselves uncomfortably exposed and with diminishing support. That Canadian incidents of collective violence cluster in the warmer months of the year (Frank and Kelly, 1977: 148) can be similarly explained. In the depths of winter, even though discontent may be high (unemployment, for example, usually reaches its peak in January), people stay at home and do not collect in sufficient numbers to establish the necessary risk/reward structure for violent crowd action.

However, in contrast to Turner and Killian, Oberschall tends to dismiss the violence of crowds as insignificant. All that is necessary for such collective action, he argues (1973: 311) is communication among the participants and a common culture to ensure a similar interpretation of events. These minimum conditions can give rise "to only short-term, localized, ephemeral outbursts and movements of protest such as riots. For sustained resistance or protest an organizational base and continuity of leadership are also needed" (1973: 119). Hobsbawm's (1965) comparison of peasant movements in Andalusia and Sicily buttresses the argument:

Just because modern social agitation reached the Andalusian peasants in a form [anarchism] which utterly failed to teach them the necessity of organization, strategy, tactics and patience, it wasted their revolutionary energies almost completely. Unrest such as theirs ... would have sufficed to overthrow régimes several times as strong as the rickety Spanish governments of the time; yet in fact Spanish anarchism ... never presented more than a routine police problem to the authorities. It could do no more:

for spontaneous peasant revolt is in its nature localized, or at best regionalized. (91)

In certain parts of Sicily the non-anarchist teachings of the [town-based] Socialists ... [produced] permanent peasant movements, capable of outlasting oppression and utilizing even non-revolutionary periods (101)

Their original millenarian enthusiasm has been transmuted into something more durable: permanent and organized allegiance to a modern social-revolutionary movement. (105)

Oberschall also argues that the more organized the contending parties are, the less is the likelihood or magnitude of violence between them. This is partly a matter of alternative resources. A large, well organized group has many resources to draw upon whereas "terrorism, bombings, and assassinations are resorted to by weak groups who already know their lack of mass support and their inability to generate more of it by other means and who therefore have nothing to lose by violence, especially if they have already been discredited in the eyes of the public" (1973: 309-10). But, more importantly, high levels of organization are inherently inimical to violence: "To begin with both sides have a stake in conciliation; agreements that are reached are more likely to be enforceable and adhered to; the probability of unplanned incidents resulting from a lack of control over the rank-and-file is lower" (1973: 340).

Others have drawn a similar connection among organization, violence, and success. One Canadian who did so was André Laurendeau (1973: 62) who helped create the League for the Defence of Canada whose purpose was to get out the Quebec "non" vote in the 1942 conscription referendum. He assessed the situation in the province at the time as follows: "Several of us ... knew that part of Quebec opinion would rebel but that it was leaderless and unstructured. There was danger of anarchy, and if this was the case the revolt would be more violent and less effective. These forces had to be channelled." And in their study of "street politics" in Ontario and Quebec, 1963-1975, Frank and Kelly (1979: 600-3) find that "random violence" was typically associated with poorly organized, less successful groups. By contrast, the more organized groups were both more successful in gaining political status and more given to routine and disciplined forms of collective action.

For these observers, then, a successful movement is an organized one; and a large organized movement is less likely to engage in violence than small or spontaneous groups. But these are highly contentious propositions. While Piven and Cloward (1977: x-xii) agree that organizational complexity inevitably serves to restrain violence, at the same time they argue it predestines a movement to failure. Activists have traditionally sought to build up a structured organization with mass membership, believing this to be the best means of securing concessions from the elite. However, in practice, elites actively cultivate lower-class organizations so as to entice insurgent masses into normal political channels and thereby dissipate the energies and élan of those mobilized. Time is wasted in fruitless discussions of the finer points of doctrine and tactics; leaders become preoccupied with preserving their own power and hesitate to gamble their organizational gains in "wild" action; and they become entangled in the existing system, growing dependent upon it for the prestige and minor concessions by which they maintain their position. Elites feel threatened and hence respond effectively to lower-class protest only when it is in the form of insurgency, and for this formalized organizations and articulated social change goals are not required (1977: 5).

But is organization necessarily inimical to violence? The answer is plainly no in the case of persistently violent campaigns which, as Gurr observes (1970: 292), cannot carry on without a high degree of organization. Coser (1956: 92) makes much the same point in arguing that a group engaged in warfare "must differentiate its tasks in order to struggle effectively, and in continued struggle will feel the need for further differentiation and hence centralization." Warfare, both by regime and anti-regime forces, requires the organization of recruits, supplies, and information and a general staff to direct and co-ordinate the conflict. Small conspiratorial groups dedicated to violence also cannot survive without a tight organization to ward off infiltration, create and maintain arsenals, direct operatives to appropriate targets, provide refuge for them afterwards, and so on. It was the inferiority of Riel's organization in 1885 in relation to that of the government that as much as anything ensured the prompt suppression of the Northwest Rebellion.

Another qualification relates to the growth and development of organizations. Among mass membership groups, we may expect violence to be more prevalent in the early years before the movement is fully accepted by outside agencies, has established control over its membership, and built up an organizational stake it hesitates to endanger. Violence may also be more likely to occur in "overmature" organizations where the leadership is too distant to be able to control the membership or to be adequately responsive to their needs. Jamieson (1968: 68, 469-70, for example) gives examples of both cases among Canadian unions.

Notwithstanding Oberschall on the conservative tendencies of large organizations, there is not a necessary connection between the degree of organization and the probability of violence erupting. Rather, large organizations acquire the ability to control the outbreak of violence. On this both Gurr and the Tillys are in rare agreement. According to Gurr (1970: 293, emphasis added), "competent leadership and complex organization may be used to minimize rather than increase political violence, *depending* on the commitments and tactical calculations of the leaders." And the Tillys (1975: 71) write:

As associations become more prominent in the struggle for power, the people who lead them gain a certain ability both to move their followers around and to calculate the probability that one action or another will lead to violence. They therefore acquire some of the same control over the frequency of violence that the state ordinarily possesses. So the number of violent incidents at a given point in time is a function of the intensity of the political struggle and the tactics of the contenders.

Thus, in organized groups, violence may occur if and when the leadership deems it helpful to the cause. Even when rank-and-file outbursts are unplanned, the leadership can take advantage of the situation to strengthen their bargaining position (Nieburg, 1962: 871).

In Canada there are repeated examples of protest leaders judging violence to be dysfunctional to the achievement of the movement's goals and consequently counselling against its use: Riel restraining his troops in 1869-70 and 1885; the leaders of the Winnipeg General Strike, the On to Ottawa trek, and the Oshawa strike; and Vallières ultimately advocating the dissolution of the FLQ. Take, for example, the following incident from the Oshawa strike of 1937, as related by Abella (1974: 107):

That morning, the company sent several trucks to pass through the picket line in front of the plant gates. There the strikers were gathered seven deep and refused to let the trucks through. Within minutes, Mayor Hall was on the scene and, jumping on top of a car, urged the men to let the trucks in "because your leaders have ordered you to do so." The strikers ignored Hall and began rocking the trucks. It seemed that the riot [Premier] Hepburn had predicted was finally underway. At just this moment [UAW organizer] Thompson arrived, jumped up beside Hall and shouted: "General Motors has been trying to arouse some sort of disturbance to get an excuse for bringing the Mounties in here and taking power out of your hands. Why let them?" ... Thompson reminded the men that "as long as you maintain discipline you have the public on your side and you can't lose!" The men cheered lustily and the trucks only had to fight their way through an army of catcalls and huzzahs to get into the plant.

If Canada has a generally low incidence of violence, this must be partly attributed to the efforts of movement leaders to avert, rather than encourage, outbreaks. The leaders' pacifism reflects a perception of the surrounding society as one that is intolerant of violence and supportive of governmental attempts to quell it.

Factionalism is another organizational variable that has been associated with violence. Oberschall (1973: 339-40) argues that violence increases with factionalism because the rank-and-file are less disciplined; conservative tendencies are not given a chance to build up around vested interests; and radical leaders shun conciliation in favour of heightened conflict in order to garner more followers. Once a movement has split into separate organizations, for example, the divisions among the Doukhobors, and the split in the Quebec separatist movement into the PQ and the FLQ (Breton, 1972: 34-41), this also is thought to increase the likelihood of violence. According to Tilly (1978: 219), it is the number of contenders in a conflict, holding constant the number of people involved, that increases the chances of violence erupting "because the number of mutual tests of position between contenders likely rises exponentially with the number of contenders." However, I doubt whether violence need be associated with factionalism any more than it is with the level of organizational complexity. In fact, in Gamson's (1975: appendix d) sample of American conflict groups, factional movements were somewhat less prone to engage in violent tactics than were solidary ones.

As we have seen, Oberschall not only suggests that poorly organized or unorganized groups are more likely to engage in violence, he also disparages the significance and achievements of these groups. Other writers, with more idealism and less economic rationalism in their views, have seen these incidents more positively. They point out that it is typical of mass insurrections of the mobilized to produce their own organizations and leadership spontaneously, and they regard this as evidence of the capacity inhering in all individuals to work with others to take control of their own destiny. Arendt (1965: 262-3) notes that the professional revolutionary dedicated to the violent overthrow of the regime, with his paraphernalia of party organizations, has been with us since the French Revolution. But, she notes, "the outbreak of most revolutions has surprised the revolutionist groups and parties no less than all others, and there exists hardly a revolution whose outbreak could be blamed upon their activities." Instead the revolutions repeatedly produced, without "any conscious imitation or even mere remembrance of the past" (1965: 260), a form of popular self-government through a system of councils (*communes*, *soviets*, or *Räte*) which "sprang up as the spontaneous organs of the people, not only outside of all revolutionary parties but entirely unexpected by them and their leaders" (1965: 252). The revolutionaries, like the politicians of the established regime, thought in terms of the nation-state and securing "power" by gaining control over the means of violence. In contrast, the council system represented a new form of government by direct democracy, with "the direct participation of every citizen in the public affairs of the country" consciously and explicitly sought (1965: 267).

Another instance of spontaneous organization sometimes occurs in religious sects. These, says Coser (1956: 91), "may have such strong cohesion that each member of the group participates in the exercise of control tasks and that there is no need for centralization of these tasks in the hands of a few." This would seem to be particularly applicable to sects like the Doukhobors whose theology calls for the rejection of organized structures, both state and ecclesiastical, in favour of allowing individuals to act according to their conscience. Woodcock and Avakumovic (1977: 327-8) believe that:

The theory of an organized and enduring terrorist conspiracy ... stems from the attempts by police officers and lawyers to impose a convenient logical structure on an illogical situation. The erratic nature of Sons of Freedom activity, the waves of depredations followed by periods of calm, the bitter internal feuds, the surges of mass emotion ... all suggest a group fighting against logical organization, which is an attribute of the world they hate.

Yet another instance of spontaneous organization is the emergence during disturbances of what Rudé (1964: 251) calls riot captains. These are the men whose suggestions and guidance the mobilized group accepts in the heat of the moment. They are usually anonymous, and their authority is purely local and temporary; they pass unnoticed among their fellows on the morrow. Although Rudé (1964: 252) suggests that with the coming of industrial society riot captains tended to be supplanted by openly acknowledged, professional militant leaders, they are probably still to be found in most spontaneous incidents even if their anonymity and temporary leadership make it difficult to single them out. Another reason why little attention is paid to them is that governments are predisposed to reject the possibility of spontaneous leadership and prefer to blame a pre-existing conspiratorial organization for the disturbance. Government members, just like revolutionaries, seem unable to accept the notion that an individual is capable of spontaneous, self-directed action outside the bounds of any organization. One example of the official search for conspiracy flying in the face of the reality of spontaneous leadership is provided by the demobilization camp riots in England after the First World War. The suggestion was made that Bolsheviks were behind the violence. "This was nonsense," says D. Morton (1980: 351). "There was no conspiracy. Like other riots, the Kinmel affair had no plan and many leaders – soldiers whose anger, excitement, or assertiveness led them to play prominent but transitory roles."

It should be noted, however, that all these spontaneous movements were eventually repressed outright or replaced by formal organizations. If the revolutionary does not start revolutions, he nevertheless seeks to use the occasion to establish his organization in power and to destroy the competing council system. For example:

When, finally, during the Kronstadt rebellion, the *soviets* revolted against the party dictatorship and the incompatibility of the new councils with the party system became manifest, [Lenin] decided almost at once to crush the councils, since they threatened the power monopoly of the Bolshevik party. The name "Soviet Union" for post-revolutionary Russia has been a lie ever since, but this lie has also contained, ever since, the grudging admission of the overwhelming popularity, not of the Bolshevik party, but of the *soviet* system which the party reduced to impotence. (Arendt, 1965: 261)

To Arendt, the *soviets* and other spontaneous council systems were glorious experiments in freedom, and their repression a tragedy. Most solidarity theorists, however, would simply dismiss this as hopelessly romantic. In their vision of the world what counts is power, which is gained by amassing and controlling resources. One such resource is a disciplined rank-and-file that will follow the directions handed down by the organization's leadership, and not dissipate their energies in spontaneous actions of their own.

Finally, an observation concerning the success of campaigns that include violence. Empirical evidence is scattered, sparse, and contradictory. For example, Tilly (1978: 183) notes one study showing that on average violent strikes were less successful than non-violent ones in Italy, while another study dealing with France came to the opposite conclusion. Gamson (1975: 79-80) addresses the question directly and finds in his sample of American protest movements that those which did use violence were more successful than those which did not. However, he declines to say that violence led to the success. Rather:

Violence should be viewed as an instrumental act, aimed at furthering the purposes of the group that uses it when they have some reason to think it will help their cause. This is especially likely to be true when the normal condemnation which attends to its use is muted or neutralized in the surrounding community, when it is tacitly condoned by large parts of the audience. In this sense, it grows from an impatience born of confidence and rising efficacy rather than the opposite. It occurs when hostility toward the victim renders it a relatively safe and costless strategy. (1975: 81-2)

Gamson's thesis directly challenges the common notion that violence is a last resort of groups and governments that have tried and failed with other means of influence:

Groups that are failing for other reasons and authorities that are being forced to respond by rising pressures generally do not turn to violence. This is why, in my interpretation, violence is associated with successful change or successful repression: it grows out of confidence and strength and their attendant impatience with the pace of change. It is, in this sense, as much a symptom of success as a cause. (1975: 82)

Gamson is overstating the case. Violence is often used after nonviolent means of redress have been tried and found wanting. Nevertheless, when a group demonstrates to itself and the world that violence is the only alternative left, it is providing itself with a justification for violence that would mute "the normal condemnation that attends to its use." A strong group facing an unpopular target does not have to go through this process.[2] And because it is

---

2 At least not to the same extent. Where the normal condemnation of violence is high, even a strong group may feel impelled to make a token effort at conciliation. Canadian governments, for example, have usually tried at least to talk to challenging groups before repressing them.

strong, its violence will probably be more successful than the last-resort violence of weaker groups.

Gamson's general thesis is well illustrated by the governmental violence in the closing stages of the Winnipeg General Strike. It was only after the solidarity of the strike had begun to crumble and when the government felt that it had won the battle for public opinion that it pounced upon the leaders of the strike and violently broke up the June 21 demonstration. Indeed, Gamson's interpretation of violence as "moving in for the kill" from a position of strength can well be applied to the general history of Canadian violence. Canadian governments have enjoyed an overwhelming advantage vis-à-vis protest groups both in material resources and public support. They have used violence and successfully put an end to virtually all challenges to their authority. By contrast, protest groups in Canada have been weak, and their leaders have counselled against the use of violence lest it dissipate the few resources and limited public support the group has managed to muster.

Similarly, in the economic sphere, Jamieson (1973: 6-9) attributes the traditionally lower incidence of industrial conflict and violence in Canada, as compared to the United States, in part to the organizational weakness of the Canadian workers. Yet Jamieson would also seem to counter Gamson's argument that violence arises out of an attack by a stronger party against an unprotected target when he suggests (1973: 5) that "Canadian employers ... until recently have been in a comparatively stronger position vis-à-vis organized labour than were their counterparts in the United States, and hence perhaps have not felt impelled to resort to such devious and at times violent means to resist unions." However, Gamson is not saying that the strong necessarily attack the weak. The strong may regard violence as unnecessary, or they may consider it improper and subject to reproval by other elite groups. Perhaps more to the point, Canadian employers long relied on government forces to uphold laws largely favourable to them. As a result, unlike American employers in the glory days of laissez-faire who created or hired private armies to do their bidding, Canadian employers rarely had direct control over the means of violent action against their adversaries.

In short, in Turmoil events, one party launches violence against another if and when it believes this will hasten its success. In Internal Wars, an armed group launches battle at a time and using resources that it believes will produce a successful cost/risk outcome. The same mechanism applies in Conspiracy events, but in a closed, sect-like atmosphere beliefs about the chances of success and estimates of outside support may become unrealistic. Believing that God is on one's side or that one's success is historically inevitable can supplant the careful weighing of odds. Such groups may "move in for the kill" from an objective position of weakness, while subjectively believing in their own infallibility.

In dealing with the Sons of Freedom and the FLQ, then, we have a choice of interpretations. Earlier we suggested that these groups resorted to terrorism after having rationally reckoned their lack of alternative resources, and the consequent feelings of impotence produced a "nothing to lose and everything to gain" assessment favouring a strategy of conspiratorial violence. The alternative interpretation is that they resorted to violence because they believed, with no actual justification, that they commanded the resources that would bring success. While divergent on paper, perhaps both processes are involved in the founding and operation of a terrorist group. Without the belief in ultimate success, those without resources would never take to arms in the first place. Their reckoning of the objective situation turns them to a closed, sect-like organization. Once this structure is in place and the sect members are cut off from society, they reinforce each other's belief in ultimate success and ignore contradictory evidence indicating their inefficacy and lack of public support.

A PARTICIPANT'S ACCOUNT OF THE ON TO OTTAWA TREK

The British Columbia Relief Camp Workers' Union, the relief camp strike, and the ensuing On to Ottawa trek provide a good example of the development and maintenance of a protest movement. The value of the example is all the greater because we have a history of the movement written by an active participant, Ronald Liversedge (1973), who sees the movement and its times from a perspective similar to that of a solidarity theorist.

Liversedge is not a believer in spontaneous mobilization. He notes the situation in Sudbury during the winter of 1930 where for lack of organization he found the unemployed "frozen into apathy" (13). In contrast, on the West Coast, the Communist Party had been active "organizing and leading the workers" (16), including the single unemployed. The latter produced "no paper organization, but a real live, functioning body" (17), operating out of a hall on Vancouver's Cordova Street. From it two or three men were sent out to each of the camps "to act as organizers or camp stewards" (37).

Liversedge believes that unity is strength and he attributes the high level of cohesion obtained during the strike and trek to a number of factors. First of all, the unity was engendered by the continuing conflict with the authorities and the "comradeship built out of hardships shared, out of the physical defense of each other against police clubs on freight trains, picket lines, and demonstrations" (28). Leadership was another factor: for example, there was Arthur Evans, "a brilliant strategist" (101), Fred Grange "with invaluable organizational talents" (32), and Matt Shaw whose sincerity and brilliant oratory "made possible a unity of all the common people" (25). Then again there was the emphasis on persuasion or education. Life around the hall on Cordova Street was "continually educational" (28); the relief camps were above all schools, with "more men reading Marx, Lenin, and Stalin, than there were reading girlie magazines" (39); "educational forums" were conducted on the boxcars during the trek eastwards (103). The purpose of all these efforts was to generate political and class consciousness that would heal all divisions, including ethnic ones: "This was a period which buried racist expressions, and the old appellation of 'Wop' or 'Bohunk' was never heard" (28).

The use of physical coercion to maintain unity was mentioned earlier. The threat of expulsion was also employed. At one point, some highspirited newcomers were told to "get back into line there, or get the hell off the trek$" (102) As well, there were selective incentives to attract and keep members. Applicants at Cordova Street could get help with the relief authorities, aid in securing medical treatment, and protection from eviction (17).

The factor making for cohesion that Liversedge stresses most is formal organization. For example, councils for the unemployed were set up in each city block. These had elected chairmen, committees, and delegates to the central body of unemployed. A few men from the Single Unemployed Men's Association were allotted to each "to boost and give strength" to them (31). These councils "broke down isolation of the people from each other, bringing the people together and teaching that unity is strength. In some parts of the city a Block council would comprise a veritable League of Nations, working amicably together in a common cause" (32). Similarly, when the relief camp strikers congregated in Vancouver, a "semi-military" (58) structure was set up, with the men divided into three divisions and then organized into groups of twelve within them. The group kept together. "The men got to know each other, and to trust each other in emergency, and there was a loyalty and *esprit de corps* built up in the groups" (67). The division and group structure was maintained throughout the strike and trek.

Organization requires and creates good communications. Requests for assistance could be passed up the delegate system, and decisions handed down. Once the Relief Camp Workers' Union was in place, "nothing ever happened to individuals or groups that wasn't known within a couple of days in every camp in the province" (49). Information was passed through reports that were sent from the camps or conveyed by men moving in and out of camps and who reported in at the Vancouver headquarters. For a time, Liversedge was editor of the union paper, the *Relief Camp Worker* which "was looked forward to in the camps and was a good organizer" (52).

Generally it was an easy task to organize the unemployed. Liversedge refers to "a splendid type of young man" (25) arriving at the West Coast. They were "class conscious and rapidly becoming politically conscious" (19). There was no defeatism, "no 'lost generation' philosophy about these men; they assumed the right to fight against subjection, and calmly refused to be intimidated" (38). Elsewhere he notes that "enthusiasm begets enthusiasm, organization under those circumstances is contagious" (63). Evidently anomic despair was not prevalent. Liversedge says "a few of the young fellows took to crime," but for most "through all this confusion, the unemployed organizations were like a beacon light, pointing the way out" (25). He mentions only two organizational failures, both involving older more apathetic men: at Sudbury, as noted above, and at an ex-servicemen's relief camp in British Columbia where "it would have taken a far better organizer than I ever was to have stirred up those middle-aged war veterans. They were tired and disillusioned" (51).

Solidarity was sought not only among the unemployed but with those who still had jobs and the common people in general. The unemployed sent delegates to other unions, refused to allow any of their members to become strike-breakers, helped other strikers on their picketlines, and generally took every opportunity to present their program to the public at large. Liversedge celebrates "the solidarity, the unbreakable unity" between the relief camp strikers and the common people: "The people as a whole took the camp strikers as their own, extended the protection of their vast numbers to them in meetings and demonstrations on the streets, and at the same time recognized and acknowledged, in the wonderful organization, self-discipline, and exemplary conduct of the camp workers, a force whose example could lead to the realization of their own aspirations" (63).

The long-range goals of the Relief Camp Workers' Union included negotiations with the federal government to abolish the camps and institute work with wages. But Liversedge also refers to "the long-range objective of the union" being "the building of a province-wide, united, disciplined organization" (38). Indeed he is more concerned with organization-building than with specific goals, which often seem to be mentioned only in the context of their ability to unite men behind them. It is not the fact that men are rallying to the slogan "work with wages" or chanting "the Battle Hymn of the trek" ("Hold the Fort") (89) that interests him so much as the fact that large numbers were assembled to chant and sing in disciplined unity. Thereby a new power was created, "a formidable force" (103).

Liversedge's organizational urgency stems from his assessment of the society he lived in. He believed it to be sharply divided. On the one side were the "rulers of Canada, the big capitalists" who speaking through "their" parliaments and "their" newspapers made it clear that "working people would have to bear the burden of the depression." On the other side were "the unemployed workers and generally impoverished people" equally determined to have an adequate living and prepared to fight for it. "And so the forces were joined" (15). As Liversedge saw it, he was engaged in a war, "the war of the depression, a class war" (24). Concessions would never be freely given by the authorities; they would have to be forcibly extracted, and this would only be achieved by a large, disciplined organization.

How did the power of what he calls "mass militant action" (23) work in practice? There were a number of elements, including disruption and ensuing pressure on the authorities. Parades and demonstrations, for example, while they served intangible group-maintaining functions ("to keep up the morale of our forces, enhance our *esprit de corps*" [74]), also provided more tangible rewards in the form of publicity and pressure: "The whole city would be aroused, letters to the press and parliaments, thousands of phone calls to the Mayor and alderman, church groups protesting the police brutality, downtown merchants protesting, traffic tie-ups, a whole string of effects that took a long while to die down" (23). Another element was the implicit threat of violence. Liversedge mentions one incident on the trek at Calgary when he encouraged a reluctant delegation on its way with the words: "Any delegation elected here tonight will not go to the city hall alone. There will be fifteen hundred organized, tried, disciplined men on the street backing you up. There is no cause to fear" (96). The mass would protect its spokesmen. The mass itself relied on numbers for its own protection. Thus Calgary the following morning was "a three-ring circus" with thousands of spectators pouring into the downtown area. "This was reassuring to us, the more the merrier, or as we knew from past experience, the more the safer" (97).

Yet if the threat of violence was implicit, its open expression was avoided both to evade official repression and to retain popular sympathy. Clashes with the police were shunned because "our objective was not civil disturbance, but the abolition of the slave camp system" (74). And indeed the movement did seem successful in controlling the amount of its own violence, especially given the contemptuous attitude of the membership to the police. The strikers "rather welcomed a brush with the police than otherwise" since the police were regarded "as clubbers of hungry women and men, and, therefore, of a very inferior type" (29). When violence did occur, Liversedge squarely blames the police and not the disciplined strikers for its outbreak. The fracas in the Hudson's Bay Company store started when police attacked the strikers who had meant to leave the store quietly; order was finally restored in Vancouver, not by any action of the police or mayor, but when "the camp workers lined up in their divisions and in the interests of peace, marched off the streets" (76). Regina was a "disgraceful police riot," though Liversedge found it a pleasure to work with the newly disciplined recruits to the trek "in restoring order out of the chaos precipitated by the federal police" (103).

Individual criminal activity was also shunned. For example, a man caught stealing relief camp equipment, who argued that "as we were fighting the slave camp system, what difference did it make which method we used," was met with the reply that "any action which lowered the prestige of the union must be condemned, that individual action of that kind was harmful to the aims and purposes of the union and it could be a provocation, and finally, it was not the purpose of the union to serve as a shield for larceny" (40).

Liversedge consistently emphasizes the importance of discipline, by which he means the ability to act resolutely and peaceably in concert with others and in accordance with orders. A disciplined body was a powerful one. Undisciplined action, in contrast, would alienate popular support: "Group leaders talked earnestly to the boys, on the necessity to maintain discipline. The common people were behind us, and we [had to] conduct ourselves so as to maintain that backing" (93). It would also dissipate energies and distract the movement from its major objectives. Liversedge attributes to inexperience the early "spontaneous actions, individual camps going on strike at different periods, anarchistic actions" (38), and records the union president chiding one group of precipitate strikers: their action "was unfortunate in that it was a small minority action, and all such actions delayed the general strike against the slave camps, which was our ultimate aim" (43). Finally, any lack of discipline would have left the movement dangerously open to repression. Thus, the newcomers to the trek, who were "to say the least, very raw ... in contradistinction to our own standard of organization and discipline, which had taken a few years of experience to build" (99), had to be swiftly convinced "of the necessity to conform to our standard of discipline"; for "we knew from experience that there would be attempts to disrupt our organization, in all probability an attempt sooner or later to smash us physically" (100).

In short, Liversedge paints a noble and inspiring portrait which highlights the cohesion, organization, and discipline of the unemployed movement and the solidarity of the common people. However, it must be balanced against less roseate pictures drawn by other eyewitnesses who were not caught up in his enthusiasm for the organization. See, for example, Broadfoot's oral history of the depression (1973: especially ch. 9 and 33) and Gray's account of the camps and trek (1966: 147-60).

CONCLUSION

Solidarity theories make three main contributions to an understanding of violence. First is the stress they place on violence as the product of an interaction between contending groups: the conduct of both parties to an affray must always be considered. Very often the government is one of the parties, and its decision to conciliate or coerce probably determines whether there is violence.

Second, solidarity theories direct our attention to the risks, rewards, and resources of different kinds of groups. The mass membership group accumulates resources, particularly those of organizational and numerical strength. As a result it can limit and control its resort to violence to situations where the risks are least and the rewards are greatest. The vanguard party can also direct its violence. Typically it does not have the resources of a mass membership group, and its members judge the risks of challenging the regime to be so high that they veil themselves in secrecy and engage in hit-and-run, conspiratorial violence. The spontaneous organization has few resources and is consequently unable to mount a sustained challenge or maintain discipline over its members' actions. Its risk:reward ratio for violence is favourable only when large numbers are gathered in the streets.

Third, solidarity theories call into question the conventional wisdom of violence as the last desperate resort of the weak. Weak and failing groups may seem to be acting out of desperation, but it must be remembered that they are interacting with more powerful and successful bodies that are capable of attacking them from a position of strength. While it is often difficult to make out who instigated a violent engagement, a solidarity theory would point the finger at the stronger group. Even when a failing group does initiate violence, its makes more sense to attribute its actions to a miscalculation of the risks and rewards than to what amounts to an impulse to self-immolation.

Nevertheless solidarity theories also have their problems. Violence is generally a subordinate issue in them. Nor, unlike discontent theories, do they give much attention to the goals that lead people to organize. The role of misperceptions, happenstance, emotion, and morality in violent conflicts is submerged in the prevailing concern with the rational calculation of ends and means. Leaders and followers are not necessarily endowed with the resources prescribed by solidarity theories. Spontaneous groups receive short shrift. Indeed both the spontaneous and the clandestine, sect-like group tend to be treated as deviant cases characterized by premature action and miscalculations resulting in objectively irrational behaviour. Solidarity theories are most applicable to mass membership groups – the very groups that, revolutionary armies apart, are the least associated with violence.

Solidarity theories take the mobilized group, rather than a society, as their unit of analysis. They do not predict how many mobilized groups one would expect to find in a given society or why mobilized groups are more or less numerous in some periods than others. (Their contradictory explanations of social ferment in terms of the balance of resources available to governments and challenging groups are examined in the next chapter.) Consequently, they reveal little about a society's average levels of violence or the variations in the incidence of its violence. To say that mobilization occurs more readily when existing structures lose their legitimacy is unhelpful unless the loss of legitimacy is first explained. Solidarity theorists do make occasional concessions to cultural, breakdown, and discontent theories. For instance, Gamson does speak of the "normal condemnation [of violence] ... being neutralized," Piven and Cloward do refer to dislocations and profound changes in the surrounding society, Oberschall mentions norms in crowd behaviour, and Hobsbawn refers to the extent of unrest. Yet these are only glancing references to issues that need to be addressed fully in a study of violence.

Moreover, solidarity theories are not readily verifiable because of the paucity of available indicators. Consequently, as the Tillys say (1975: 8), "they slip into circularity with extraordinary ease because it is so tempting to consider the development of protest both as the consequence of solidarity and as the very evidence of solidarity." To adequately test solidarity theories, we should have to find measures of the sort of variables Liversedge mentions: the activity of organizers, the quality of leadership, popular support for protest activities, the amount and quality of education and communications, and morale within the group.

One promising indicator, however, is trade union membership. A solidarity theory would predict that violence would increase as more workers were mobilized and drawn into the union movement. Precisely this relationship has been found for France (Tillys, 1975: 82). In Canada though the evidence is contradictory. The three periods of high union growth – during and after the First and Second World Wars, and from 1971 to 1976 – were indeed periods of considerable industrial conflict and, in the first and third cases, of violence. However, periods of slow growth or declining membership – 1921-6, 1931-6, and 1956-61 – encompass the particularly violent Depression years; while the notable peak in industrial conflict and violence in the sixties was not accompanied by any surge in union membership. The diverging Canadian evidence is thus too confused to give clear support to either a straight solidarity theory or one of its refinements (formal organizations restrict the resort to violence).

However, solidarity theories, like the others we have been considering, are incapable of explaining on their own the entire subject of violence. While they contribute largely to our understanding of violence, they still need to be supplemented by other theories. Consequently we should not expect a neat correlation between solidarity factors and violence any more than we should expect breakdown factors to show a consistent relation with violence.

Yet if the correlations are ambiguous, does this mean that there is no basis for preferring either a solidarity or a breakdown theory? This question has been best answered by the Tillys (1975: 8-9):

Some compromises immediately come to mind. One is the idea that breakdown and solidarity are different phases of the same process, that each movement of protest develops from breakdown to solidarity or vice versa. A second is the suggestion that there are different varieties of violent protest, some growing out of breakdown, some growing out of solidarity. A third is the notion that "breakdown" and "solidarity" are two names for the same phenomenon as seen from very different angles: what the conservative experiences as breakdown the radical senses as the growth of new forms of solidarity.

Each of these three "compromises" can be found in Canadian history. The Depression years, for example, saw the unemployed movement progressing from a state of breakdown to the creation of a new solidarity. We can compare some of the anomic incidents related in Broadfoot (1973) with the violence that grew out of the activities of the Relief Camp Workers' Union. And we can contrast R.B. Bennett's view of the trekkers as misguided young men unaware of what they were doing with Liversedge's account of discipline and organization.

The Tillys' third "compromise" reminds us that we can expect any incident, both at the time of its occurrence and in later analyses, to be explained by some people according to breakdown theories and by other people according to solidarity theories. The two theories have different implications for the labelling of the incident as public or private violence. Breakdown theories stress the deviant aspects of the violence – how it differs from "normal" political action in "normal" circumstances. Solidarity theories, by contrast, search for the similarities between established groups and dissident ones with their recognized leadership, open membership, large and disciplined numbers, and a developed platform. Because spontaneous and vanguard groups lack one or more of these attributes, they may be considered as somewhat less public in nature than formally organized bodies, although not as private or deviant as when they are explained in terms of breakdown variables.

We noted in chapter 4 that sympathy for a group is associated with a public definition of its actions. We can now suggest as a corollary that sympathy for a group will also be associated with an interpretation of its actions in terms of a solidarity theory. Conversely, a breakdown interpretation will tend to be favoured among those with fewer empathetic ties to the violent. It is a matter of some consequence which interpretation gains widespread acceptance; for a solidarity theory confers political legitimacy on a challenging group while a breakdown theory withholds it. Which gains the upper hand is not simply a matter of the facts of the case, but also very much an exercise in political power turning on who has the superior means of disseminating and enforcing his interpretation. Since governments are generally unlikely to feel much sympathy for a challenging group, it is not surprising that they interpret its actions in terms of breakdown variables (see chapter 6). Moreover, since governments have powerful means of disseminating their opinion, it is also not surprising that, in the received wisdom on the causes of anti-governmental violence, breakdown theories predominate over solidarity theories.

CHAPTER NINE

The Role of the Government

GOVERNMENTS AND VIOLENCE

Governments are inextricably connected with violence. Violence is related both to the functions of governments and to the means they use to carry out these functions. Among governmental functions, one of the oldest and most basic is to protect citizens from the violence of foreign invaders. Citizens today also expect governmental protection from criminal attacks on their lives and property and from the wanton disruption of their everyday lives and institutions by groups widely regarded as deviant.

Another basic function of government is to prevent violence by providing peaceful means of settling conflicts. Many governmental institutions are designed to fulfill this function. Civil courts adjudicate disputes between citizens. Various other tribunals, like those set up under the Industrial Disputes Act, attempt to reconcile divergent interests. Elections settle who should govern. Parliamentary forums enable different viewpoints to be heard. Convention requires that various interests be represented in the cabinet.

Yet, as the previous chapters have indicated, governments often cause the civilian violence that is directed against them. Their injustice, incompetence, intransigence, and impermeability can provoke citizens to take up arms. The provocation may be more immediate, as when citizens are enraged by arrests or attempts to break up a demonstration, or more immediate still when governmental *agents provocateurs* have been at work. Governments could also be said to create the opportunity for public violence by the very nature of their institutions: election brawls, prison riots, army mutinies, and assassinations all require the existence of a government.

Many governmental functions inevitably give rise to conflict and hence to the possibility of violent resistance. To carry on, a government has to extract resources from its citizens, both financial (in the form of taxes of one sort or another), and sometimes manpower resources (in the form of conscription or labour contributions to various public works). These naturally create resentment, particularly when traditional exactions are made more onerous to provide for an expansion in governmental activities. Such expansion itself creates discontent when it involves the takeover of previously autonomous local units. The growth of the nation-state has involved both the centralization of power and the extension of governmental control to new areas, and neither process has taken place without violent resistance.

The citizenry is not an undifferentiated mass, but consists of socio-economic groups with varying ability to influence the government to carry out its functions on their behalf. The government accedes to the demands of at least some of these powerful groups because it needs their support, but in doing so it incurs the resentment of the groups at whose expense the decision is made. Groups rising in power try to attract governmental recognition; declining groups try to fight off the challengers. The "struggle for established places in the structure of power" is, according to Tilly (1979: 87), the most immediate cause of violent protests.

Conflicts also arise within governments themselves. Governments should not be seen as monolithic entities pursuing clear-cut objectives. Rather they are made up of ambitious people, differing like the rest of us in their hopes and fears, competence, highmindedness, and notions of what a government should be doing. Governmental agencies are often at loggerheads as they push and pull for institutional advantage or the advantage of the groups they represent: the executive struggles with the legislature, the federal with the provincial, one department with another. Intragovernmental conflict is related to public violence either when the army turns its guns against the present rulers or when internal division encourages outside groups to attack. Divisions within the government have marked the onset of the great revolutions and civil wars.

In carrying out its functions, a government has basically three means at its disposal. First, it can depend on the willing co-operation of its citizens. Where it exists, the belief that a government's lawful edicts should be obeyed is an invaluable cultural inheritance, handed down from one generation to the next. Governments also actively intervene to manipulate public support in their favour. For example, by statements of authoritative individuals, control over the schools, and support for "right thinking" churches and news media, governments can influence socialization so as to discourage citizens from resisting the government or resorting to violence. The manipulation of opinion tends to be particularly heavy-handed during wars and when revolutionary regimes are hastening to build their legitimacy.

Second, governments secure compliance by manipulating the rewards at their disposal. A dissident group can be promised economic reforms such as special taxation privileges or favourable investment strategies, or political reforms such as the extension of the franchise or a devolution of government powers, or personnel reforms when unpopular members of the government are retired. Governments can also co-opt a group by institutionalizing its participation in government decision-making. As well, its leaders can be placed on the government payroll, and jobs for its members found through patronage or expanding the bureaucracy.

Third, governments secure compliance by manipulating the risks they attach to undesired behaviour, that is, through coercion. As noted above in chapter I, coercion is the infliction of penalties for disobedient behaviour, and violence is that form of coercion where the penalty is personal injury or property damage.

Physical coercion, according to Weber's famous definition, is the specific means peculiar to the nation-state. While in the past this means was used by various institutions, today "we have to say that a state is a human community that (successfully) claims the *monopoly of the legitimate use of physical force* within a given territory ... The right to use physical force is ascribed to other institutions or to individuals only to the extent to which the state permits it" (Gerth and Mills, 1958: 78). When this governmental monopoly is called into question by rebel groups, the overall legitimacy of the government is directly impugned. It is generally agreed that, without the capacity to inflict violence, governments cannot survive. People will accede to government blandishments or threats only when they believe these to be ultimately backed up by the sword.[1]

The government's capacity to inflict violence is embodied in its police and military forces. The nation-state today claims the sole right to recruit and maintain such forces. Their existence is primarily justified on the grounds that they are necessary to carry out the governmental function of protecting its citizens from the depredations of others. However, they are also used to enforce governmental decisions that favour one group over another and to ward off attacks on the government. These roles can become confused. We may be told, for instance, that the government is only protecting us from criminal or maladjusted elements when the police are used to break up a challenging group.

Violent coercion, then, underlies the other means of government control and can be employed in the service of all the various functions a government performs. However, it raises a number of questions to which we now turn: When do governments manipulate risks rather than rewards or opinion? What are the legal and other constraints on using coercion? How effective is coercion in securing compliance? And is there a relation between levels of coercion and levels of dissidence?

---

1 This is not to say that governmental control is limited to coercion. As Arendt (1969: 50) points out, all governments depend on an irreducible minimum of uncoerced support, and particularly the support of the armed forces.

CONCILIATION VERSUS COERCION

A government that seeks to conciliate a dissident group has first to recognize it. Recognition involves acknowledging the group's right to exist and to plead its case before the government and to the general public. After recognition, a conciliatory government may go further and negotiate with the dissident group. A non-conciliatory government, by contrast, can refuse recognition and label the dissidents criminals or rebels.

Recognition and negotiations are potentially costly to a government. It may have to admit past mistakes and promise future rewards. There is no guarantee that the group will not rudely reject the government's conciliatory gestures or that it will adhere to any bargains it strikes with the government. Expectations of further progress may be aroused that are beyond the government's ability to satisfy. Coercion, however, is a much more attractive alternative. According to Oberschall (1973: 252), it is "the cheapest and most immediately available means of control to the authorities."

Nevertheless some governments do try to conciliate rather than coerce dissident groups. There are a number of considerations that can influence a government in favour of conciliation.

The influence of public opinion. Coercion may be a source of embarrassment and weakness to governments if they base their claim to legitimacy on the consent of the governed. The public may also pressure a government to settle its differences with a dissident group so that the normal round of daily activities can be resumed (Oberschall, 1973: 263). When dissidents have at least some support, a government may feel impelled to tread warily in dealing with them. Turner (1969: 818-19) has suggested that there is a "folk concept of social protest" and that groups acting in accordance with it are most likely to attract public support. To fit the cultural model, a violent group must, among other things, be seen as representative of a wide constituency, not as individual trouble-makers, conspirators, or fun- or profit-seeking rioters. The group should have well documented grievances which it has tried previously to remedy by non-violent means, and its violence should be seen to be restrained and exceptional.

In Canada, however, it seems that on balance public opinion has been more supportive of coercion than conciliation. As we saw in chapter 5, the country has high standards of public order, and there has generally been strong public support for the government to use coercion to maintain these standards even at the expense of civil liberties.

The degree to which a dissident group appears threatening to a government. Low-threat groups will tend to be ignored or dealt with by routine anti-crime measures, while high-threat groups will be seen as rebels requiring extraordinary coercive measures. Conciliation is most likely to be applied to groups falling between these two extremes: that is, groups that are sufficiently threatening to prompt a government to deal with them but not so much so that they scare any thoughts of benevolence out of the minds of government members (Turner, 1969: 820-2). The degree of experienced threat is partly the product of the dissidents' own means and goals. A revolutionary program, accompanied by assassinations and attacks on government installations, is going to make any government the prey of uneasy fears.

Another element is the government's estimate of the "contagiousness" of the dissidence, that is, the movement's capacity to attract further recruits, to expand the area of rebellion, and to escalate the intensity of the conflict. Canadian governments have shown themselves to be particularly susceptible to this fear. They have been alarmed not so much by the actual extent of the initial violence but by the prospect of the outbreak triggering off an ever-expanding circle of chaos. They have repeatedly used the metaphor of a fire that needs to be quickly extinguished before it spreads (Torrance, 1977: 477-9).

An incident may also seem to be too threatening to permit conciliation when it promises widespread economic disruption. This fear will probably be more pronounced in a country like Canada with its unstable economy at a competitive disadvantage to neighbouring countries and dependent on outside investment for further development. For example, the Northwest Rebellion was seen to require prompt suppression if the opening up and settlement of the Canadian West was not to be endangered and if the money to complete the CPR was to be raised in England. As well, the program of the dissidents may appear to pose a particular economic threat. Thus, in Winnipeg in 1919, the disruptive potential of general strikes and the One Big Union was keenly felt by government members.

The degree to which the government needs the support of the dissident group. If a government needs the co-operation of dissidents, it will favour conciliation over coercion. Perhaps the dissidents control economic resources the government wishes to tap, or perhaps an election is approaching and the government needs their votes. Conversely, weaker groups whose support a government can dispense with are more likely to be coerced into line. Canadian governments have generally been called upon to deal with weak, fragmented groups which they have felt no need to conciliate. A major exception, to which we return below, is the Red River community during the first Riel rising. A cabinet document urged that "every other course should be tried before resort is had to force," for "if life were once lost ... the seeds of hostility to Canada and Canadian rule would be sown, and might create an ineradicable hatred to the union of the countries, and thus mar the future prosperity of British America" (Canada, House of Commons, *Sessional Papers* (1870), No. 12: 143).

The degree of value-discrepancy between the government and the group involved. Goode (1972: 516) proposes that the less this discrepancy, the more likely is conciliation to be favoured since conciliation is only possible between actors sharing common ground. When dissidents and government are far apart in their ideas and objectives, the latter will probably see coercion as the only means of control to which the group will respond. A good Canadian example is provided by governmental attempts to control the Sons of Freedom Doukhobors. The Freedomites' values differed drastically from those of the surrounding society; and they made clear their theologically based opposition to any co-operation with the worldly authorities. Accordingly, governments proceeded with massive coercive measures, including wholesale arrests, forcible removal of the children, and the building of special prisons and schools, even though the group was "uncontagious" and the costs involved were high.[2]

Difficulties in the way of applying coercion. When coercion is not feasible, a government has to rely on conciliation. For instance, without means of transport, a government would find it impossible to move troops to a troubled area. This occurred during the winter months of the Red River rising. In a mutiny, a government may not have loyal troops at its disposal. In some instances, a government may doubt that the troops will follow orders and fire on their fellow citizens. During wartime, it may not be possible to divert troops to maintain civil order.

For Canadian governments, this factor has only obtained on rare occasions. In addition to the Red River incident, there were some doubts expressed at the turn of the century whether a militia recruited in the cities could be relied upon during labour disputes (D. Morton, 1970: 420). During the Terrace mutiny of 1944, the Minister of Defence told the Prime Minister:

If the troops began to resist he had not the soldiers or the men to enforce law and order. He added that what he could do was to call out the Militia in aid of the civil power but its men were for the most part employed in munitions and the like and that would mean cutting down supplies of ammunition and create other difficulties as well. He thought they could be trusted to do their entire duty, but it was a matter of trust. (Pickersgill and Forster, 1968: 252)

The incident was swiftly settled by a conciliatory gesture.

2 Holt (1964: 8) suggests the Doukhobors cost the Canadian taxpayer a minimum of $20 million in compensation for their acts of destruction and to cover police and court costs.

The resources available to the government for conciliation. At some periods governments are more able to afford conciliation than at others. As Tilly (1978: 207) suggests, during a period when governmental resources are expanding there is more to go around; "the polity tends to admit challengers more easily because the relative cost to existing members is lower." When the resource pool ceases to grow or contracts, a government has the choice of "(1) greatly increasing the coercion applied to the more vulnerable segments of the population in order to bring up the yield of resources for reallocation or (2) breaking commitments where that will incite the least dangerous opposition."

However, Tilly's idea that a government conciliates when it has slack resources has to be balanced against Gamson's (1975: 111-22) argument that a government in crisis periods such as wars and economic depressions seeks out support and tends at least to grant recognition to protest groups even if it has not the resources to satisfy all the group's demands. Another factor favouring conciliation in crisis periods would be public opinion pressuring both parties to moderate their demands and settle their differences in the face of the national emergency.

The historical record does not clearly favour either Tilly's or Gamson's argument. In Canada, governments were generally coercive in the First World War and the Great Depression, but conciliatory during the Second World War. It would thus seem that the resources available to the government for distribution is a poor predictor of whether coercion or conciliation will be chosen. In boom times a government may not feel the need to conciliate even if the cost of doing so is then borne more easily. And in tight periods, even if the government wants to conciliate, it may not control the necessary resources.[3]

Governmental concern for national integration. When preserving national unity is a first consideration with governments, conciliation may be favoured over coercion. From such a perspective, it is not the ideal policy which should prevail, "but the policy which can appeal on the whole to all sections of the community" (Sir Wilfrid Laurier, cited in Skelton, 1965: II, 127). In contrast, a government bent on achieving some great national objective – the settlement of the Canadian West, the building of the CPR, or winning the First World War – may become impatient with dissident groups and coerce them into submission rather than allow itself to be distracted from its goal.

3 See also Jamieson's argument (discussed in chapter 6) that levels of industrial conflict are unrelated to business cycles in Canada. Industries in boom times and those able to pass on increased labour costs may be more ready to accept union demands. However, the level of conflict does not necessarily decline because other unions may be encouraged to make increasing demands. Conversely, industries in downturns and marginal operations in general probably will refuse to accept union demands, but whether conflict follows this refusal would seem to turn on the unions' perception of what is possible under the circumstances.

In the light of all these factors, it is not surprising that governmental recognition of dissidents has been rare in Canada. They have instead been labelled criminals. There is, however, one proviso to this labelling pattern. At least for the major incidents, the government has usually distinguished between the movement's leadership and its rank-and-file participants. It is the leaders who are accused of criminality. They are blamed for inciting their followers to illegal actions and are deemed to be acting for illegitimate purposes of political or personal gain. The rank-and-file, however, have generally not been labelled as criminals or riff-raff, apart from a few individuals prominently engaged in acts of violence. Rather they have been seen as well-intentioned enough, but misled, misinformed, and carried away by the excitement of the moment. They have been manipulated by their malevolent leaders. As such they cannot be recognized by the government since they have no valid grievances but only artificially stirred up discontents. Accordingly governments have sought to nullify the pernicious influence of the leaders, or as one minister crudely put it during the On to Ottawa trek, "somehow the leaders should be got at and if possible got out of the position of leading these unemployed" (R.J. Manion, cited in Liversedge, 1973: 191). While the membership has been left largely unscathed, the governments have concentrated their attention on the leadership, using bribery, arrests, imprisonment, exile, and, in the case of Riel, execution to neutralize their hold on their followers.

Governmental preoccupation with the leadership is well recognized within dissident circles. For example, Liversedge (1973: 75) refers to "the old, heavy, primitive mentality of the police throughout the ages, of 'get the ringleaders,' forgetting that the system had made ringleaders of us all." Nevertheless leadership is a scarce commodity (Oberschall, 1973: 158), and consequently removing the leaders from circulation does inflict severe damage on a protest movement. Only in small sects do membership and leadership coincide (Coser, 1956: 91), although strongly institutionalized conflict groups may also be able to withstand the loss of individual leaders. This is part of the reason why solidarity theorists attach so much importance to organization if the group is to persist.

I have narrowed the discussion by treating coercion and conciliation as simple alternatives. In fact there are degrees of both, and a government may combine the two in its response. Typically in Canada governments have resorted to levels of violent coercion that are fairly modest in comparison with the deliberate policy of terrorization and wholesale slaughter that have occurred in other countries. And at the same time they have not relied wholly on coercion to defuse potential difficulties. Usually some attempt is made at least to establish communications with the dissident group. There have also been quite frequent efforts to bribe the dissidents into giving up their agitation through offers of money, jobs, or immunity from prosecution. As well, public opinion has been manipulated, mainly through statements to the press and in the House of Commons, to ensure that the dissidents' actions are seen to be illegal and ineffective.

The first Riel rising is the major exception to this general policy of refusing recognition and relying mainly on modest levels of coercion albeit in combination with various other means of control. This is a particularly interesting incident, first, because the government changed its tactics during the course of it, and second, because it can be compared to the similar 1885 rebellion in which the government persisted in using the criminality label. Originally the government in 1869 dismissed the affair as the work of a misinformed and overexcited rabble who would soon disperse of their own accord. When the incident persisted, the government was forced to change its assessment and chose one of straight deviancy, stressing that only particular sections of the community were involved and that they were under the influence of personally ambitious and traitorous leaders. At this stage, since geography and climate precluded the use of the armed forces, the government concentrated on trying to buy off the malcontents with offers of money and jobs and on undermining their hold on their followers by sending out influential spokesmen to explain the Canadian case. In the end, the government recognized the dissidents when it publicly affirmed that the whole community was involved and that they had a respectable political motive in seeking to secure better terms for their entry into Confederation. This ultimate assessment was used to justify the government's negotiations with the Red River delegates.

These labelling shifts may be attributed to the persistence and political skills of the dissidents. Another factor was the initial unfamiliarity in Ottawa with Red River conditions and grievances. When these became known, they appeared moderate and reasonable in cost given the government's previous experience with the agitation that had accompanied the entry of Nova Scotia into Confederation and with making special allowances to appease the sensibilities of geographic or ethnic groups. Perhaps most important, however, was the government's need for the willing support of the people of Red River if it was to open the West for settlement, plus the great difficulty of getting a military force into the area. In contrast, by 1885, settlement was already well under way, and the virtual completion of the CPR line enabled the government to move troops quickly westwards. With conciliation no longer necessary and coercion a viable alternative, the government refused to recognize the rebels. Instead they were labelled criminals in order to justify their violent suppression.

It should be stressed again that the first Riel rising's negotiated settlement is exceptional in Canadian history. Generally, public opinion and a governmental assessment that a group is threatening, need not be conciliated, and is not amenable to persuasion, have prompted a reliance mainly on coercive control. But that this governmental coercion has been comparatively modest in scale and combined with other means of social control indicates that Canadian governments have recognized that coercion is neither a simple nor a total solution. It may be the "cheapest" means of control, but it too has its costs.

THE COSTS OF COERCION

Discussions of governmental violence seldom mention the costs involved. Major incidents of violence are expensive drains on governmental resources especially when they occur, as they often do, during periods of financial stringency or when resources have been diverted to some great national project. The Northwest Rebellion of 1885 is a good example, with the construction of the CPR line consuming every available dollar during a time of economic downturn. As far as Macdonald's government was concerned, the bill for sending the militia into the field against the rebels, an estimated $5 million, could scarcely have been presented at a less opportune time.

Besides the extraordinary costs incurred during an emergency, there are also the costs of maintaining the armed forces in anticipation of future trouble. A government fearful of disturbances to come may find a large share of its budget taken up in keeping under arms what it hopes will be a sufficient body of men and in granting them the prestige and resources deemed necessary to maintain their loyalty and morale. Providing citizens with routine security against private violence is also an expensive proposition, involving the upkeep for police forces, court systems, and prisons. Concerning prison costs, Gurr (1976: 178) remarks that only affluent societies can afford the wholesale incarceration of their offenders, especially in programs aimed at reform. Less wealthy societies tend to execute or maim their deviants or to use them as a source of cheap and expendable labour. Similarly, a large body of trained and efficient policemen, and courts that provide an accused with a full panoply of rights quickly add to the costs of the administration of justice.

Governmental violence is costly in ways other than the strictly financial. In particular it raises the possibility of a disastrous fall in the government's stock of legitimacy. This can happen in two ways. First is when a government tries to solve a problem with violence, but fails in the attempt. Such failures, which include defeats in international wars, are highly deleterious to governmental prestige and often precede the collapse of the regime. Second, in using violence, a government is walking a fine line between what is popularly acceptable and what is not. A government may initially have widespread support for putting down a rebellion, but if excessive amounts of violence are used, whether ordered by the government or not, or if innocent citizens are hurt by its indiscriminate acts of violence, then its legitimacy will again be called into question. This point is borne out in Gude's (1969) comparison of the response to insurrection by Batista in Cuba and Betancourt in Venezuela. The former overreacted with indiscriminate violence which alienated the final supportive segments of Cuban society for his regime, while Betancourt carefully gauged the level of governmental violence and was concerned throughout to maintain the legitimacy of his actions.

Gude makes the point that a government must not confuse legitimacy with legality. Even if technically legal, a government's use of violence may still be regarded as unjust or inappropriate, in which case it will serve only to transfer popular support from the government to the dissidents. However, the legal framework remains important, since illegal government actions will in all likelihood be considered illegitimate. Just as costs and the potential drain on legitimacy place constraints on a government's use of violence, so too does the law of the land.

THE LEGAL FRAMEWORK

Under the Canada Act, the "administration of justice," which includes the maintenance of public order, is a provincial responsibility. The provinces in turn require municipalities above a certain size to establish police forces. Provincial police forces work for the most part in the more sparsely populated areas. Ontario and Quebec have their own police forces; the other provinces contract with the federal government for the RCMP to provide provincial police services. In these cases the RCMP acts under the direction of the provincial Attorney-General, although recruitment, training, and other administrative matters continue to be handled by Ottawa. The contracts specify the number of detachments the RCMP must maintain in the province, although this may be varied during the term of the contract. The provinces pay for RCMP services according to a set formula.

Police reinforcements for special occasions are also paid for by the provinces. A provincial Attorney-General may request RCMP support from outside the province, and this will be provided if the Solicitor General of Canada approves. The latter's approval is by no means automatic. For example, the federal cabinet turned down a request for additional RCMP reinforcements from the Ontario government during the Oshawa strike of 1937 and delayed sending in the extra men sought by the Newfoundland government during the loggers' strike of 1959.

Further, although the RCMP acting in a provincial capacity is supposed to be under the direction of the provincial Attorney-General, there is a precedent for the federal government taking over control and summoning reinforcements on its own initiative. This occurred in Saskatchewan in 1935 during the On to Ottawa trek. Premier Gardiner of Saskatchewan telegraphed in exasperation to Prime Minister Bennett: "Throughout the whole course of this matter your government has acted without our knowledge, consent or concurrence and took complete charge of our police force and assumed the unquestionable functions of a provincial government" (Liversedge, 1973:

229). The federal government replied that the RCMP could act without provincial direction to enforce federal statutes such as the Railway Act. The constitutional dispute was never settled in the courts, and the Regina Riot Inquiry Commission specifically (and diplomatically) declined to comment on whether the federal government had exceeded its powers (Saskatchewan, 1936: 278).

The use of troops "in aid of the civil power" is also fraught with potential constitutional conflict. Under the present National Defence Act, the historical power of municipal officials to call for troops has been completely removed. The power now lies with the provincial Attorney-General, who may act on his own initiative or after receiving notice from a judge of a superior, county, or district court having jurisdiction in the troubled area. The Attorney-General sends a written requisition for aid to the Chief of the Defence Staff in Ottawa. The latter is required to act on this request, although he has discretion on how many men should be called out and the equipment they should have with them. Once called out, the men work under the command of their officers and stay on duty until the Attorney-General declares they are no longer needed. Costs are borne by the provincial government. There is one exception to this procedure: the warden of a penitentiary may apply directly to a local commanding officer for help in quelling a prison disturbance. This provision was used, for example, during the riot at Kingston Penitentiary in April 1971.

Troops have been used frequently to battle forest fires and floods, but we are dealing here only with their use in cases of civil disturbance. As the various police forces of the country have developed, the use of the military in this capacity has steadily declined. It has been used on only three occasions in the last half century: at Stratford, Ontario, in 1933; during the police strike in Montreal in 1969; and again in Montreal the following year during the October crisis. On each of these three occasions, the police were handicapped in some way. In 1933, the Ontario Provincial Police was badly understrength, and the provincial government felt reluctantly compelled to call on military aid (D. Morton, 1974: 84). In Montreal, in 1969 the police were on strike, and in 1970 they felt unable to handle the crisis on their own. The police are nowadays clearly the primary bastion against civil disturbance, with soldiers only being called in on rare occasions of police incapacity.

Apart from formal requisitions for troops in aid of the civil power, the armed forces may offer lesser forms of assistance. For example, a military plane was used to fly an emergency unit of the Quebec Police Force into Sept-Iles in May 1972.

The use of violence by police and military forces is subject to a number of legal restrictions. The position of a member of the armed forces acting in aid of the civil power has been outlined by Gellner (1974: 136-7):

Under Section 225 of the National Defence Act, he has the powers and duties of a constable, except that he acts only within "a military body" and is "individually liable to obey the orders of [his] superior officers." Then comes the snag. He must obey lawful commands (Section 74 of the National Defence Act), but he also must not obey those which are "manifestly unlawful" (Section 32(2) of the Criminal Code). The commander, on his part, must not use force if this is not necessary; and must not use more force than the situation demands. Both the officers who give the orders, and the men who execute them, are liable if they overstep these limits.

A senior police officer must accompany the soldiers and advise the commander when "force" should be used, but the final decision to use violence and how much rests with the military officer.

The Criminal Code sets out when violence may be used by police officers and others. Section 26 clearly states that any use of force in excess of the specifications is a criminal offence. The offender would also be liable to an action in a civil court for damages. The basic enabling provision is section 25(1) which permits a person administering or enforcing the law to use "as much force as is necessary for that purpose" if he is acting on "reasonable and probable grounds." However, under section 25(3) he may not use "force that is intended or is likely to cause death or grievous bodily harm unless he believes on reasonable and probable grounds that it is necessary for the purpose of preserving himself or anyone under his protection from death or grievous bodily harm." The various police forces are also governed by legal restrictions on their use of violence. For example, under the Ontario Police Act, an Ontario policeman is forbidden to discharge a firearm in the performance of his duty unless one of four conditions obtains: for the defence of life, to apprehend a person believed dangerous, to destroy a dangerous or suffering animal, or to give an alarm when no other means can be used (Kelly and Kelly, 1976: 174-81).

In dealing with a riot a policeman, acting in good faith and on reasonable grounds, may use or order as much force as he believes necessary to suppress the disturbance and which is not excessive having regard to the dangers to be apprehended from the continuation of the riot (section 32 (1)(b)). If the Riot Act (see below) is read, however, the policeman must, on pain of being prosecuted himself (section 70), disperse or arrest those not complying with the proclamation (section 33). Section 33 makes no mention of reasonable and probable grounds or excessive force, so that "the policeman is fully protected against criminal and civil proceedings even if serious injury or death occurs by reason of any resistance" (Kelly and Kelly, 1976: 188-90).

Citizens who use or threaten public violence face various charges. They may of course be arrested and tried for the full range of offences that are usually of a private nature, such as homicide, assault, arson, kidnapping, intimidation, causing a disturbance, and the misuse or possession of various weapons. But in addition there are a number of offences dealing directly with public violence.

An "unlawful assembly" involves three or more persons who are joined for a common purpose and who cause persons in the neighbourhood to fear, on reasonable grounds, that there will be a tumultuous disturbance of the peace (section 64(1)). A "riot" is an unlawful assembly that has begun to disturb the peace tumultuously (section 65). It is not the common purpose of the assembly that determines its lawfulness; the purpose may or may not be a lawful one. Rather it is the manner in which the assembly conducts itself that is the determining factor. A member of an unlawful assembly is punishable on summary conviction by a fine of up to $500, or imprisonment for not more than six months, or both. A convicted rioter faces imprisonment of up to two years.

Section 68 requires a justice, mayor, sheriff, or lawful deputy who receives notice of 12 or more persons disturbing the peace tumultuously and satisfies himself that this is the case to read the proclamation commonly known as the Riot Act "in a loud voice." This commands the rioters, in the name of Her Majesty, to disperse and warns that their refusal to do so renders them liable to life imprisonment. As noted above, this draconian measure also provides full legal protection for those called upon to quell the riot (Kelly and Kelly, 1976: 188-9).

Sedition is the offence of speaking or writing seditious words or taking part in a seditious conspiracy. Under section 60(4) "seditious" includes, but is not limited to, the advocacy of "the use, without the authority of law, of force as a means of accomplishing a governmental change within Canada." In *Boucher* v. *R.* (1951), the Supreme Court clarified the meaning of sedition. Boucher was a Jehovah's Witness who had published a pamphlet instancing police persecution of Witnesses in Quebec and alleging that Roman Catholic priests and public officials were behind the persecution. While noting that English legal textbooks include within the meaning of sedition an intention "to promote feelings of ill-will and hostility between different classes of [Her Majesty's] subjects" or an attempt to bring the administration of justice into hatred and contempt, the Supreme Court nevertheless ruled that for a charge of sedition to hold in Canada there must be as well evidence of an intention to incite to violence or resistance against a Canadian government. Boucher may have been trying to foment ill-will or disparage the administration of justice, but there was no evidence of him counselling anti-governmental violence, and accordingly the case against him was dismissed (Mewett, 1975: 160). A person found guilty of sedition is liable to imprisonment for 14 years. Seven leaders of the Winnipeg General Strike were convicted of seditious conspiracy in 1920.

Under section 51 it is an offence to intimidate by an act of violence the Parliament of Canada or a provincial legislature. Other public order offences include inciting members of the armed forces to mutiny or counselling members of the RCMP to desert.

Finally there are the offences of high treason and treason which cover a number of acts affecting the country's security. High treason carries a minimum punishment of life imprisonment, and includes attempts on Her Majesty's life and the levying of war against Canada (the charge against Riel in 1885). Treason, which carries a maximum sentence of life imprisonment, includes the use of, or conspiracy to use, "violence for the purpose of overthrowing the Government of Canada or a province."

Mention should also be made of the now defunct section 98, which came into effect after the Winnipeg General Strike. It was repealed in 1936. The section dealt with "unlawful associations" which were defined as those having as a purpose "to bring about any governmental industrial or economic change within Canada" by the use or threat of violence or which advocated the use of violence to secure such changes or any other purpose. The section was widely regarded as odious because it went on to make it easy for police to secure convictions for this offence: a person was to be presumed to be a member of an unlawful association, unless he could bring proof to the contrary, if he merely attended its meetings, spoke publicly at them, or distributed its literature. Conviction rendered the offender liable to imprisonment for twenty years. In fact, there were only three reported prosecutions under section 98 with two convictions. All three involved Communists (Manzer, 1974: 276). The section nevertheless had the effect of creating an atmosphere of governmental intimidation that compelled all radical groups to tread warily in the inter-war years.

All that has been said so far applies to the country during peacetime. However, the government of Canada, like that of most countries, possesses a reserve power for use in emergencies. It is embodied in "An Act to confer powers upon the Governor-in-Council in the event of war, invasion, or insurrection" – the War Measures Act. The Act has been invoked on three occasions: the First and Second World Wars and the October crisis of 1970. Conclusive legal evidence that there exists a state of war, invasion, or insurrection, "real or apprehended," requires simply a proclamation under the authority of the Governor-in-Council to this effect. Once the proclamation is issued, the Governor-in-Council may proceed by way of orders and regulations (as distinct from formal legislation passed through Parliament) to govern as if Canada were a unitary state and with no safeguards on civil liberties. The government's emergency powers would appear to be substantially unaffected by the new constitution and charter of rights.

Under the War Measures Act, the federal government has put troops into action at home without waiting for requests from provincial governments. On Ottawa's orders, troops were moved into Quebec City in 1918 to deal with the anti-conscription riots. They were armed with an order-in-council freeing them from all civil or criminal liability for their actions. During the Second World War troops were used during strikes to maintain uninterrupted war production, as in the Montreal tramway strike of August 1944 when the need to ensure that munitions workers got to work prompted the federal government to send in troops over "the point-blank refusal of the provincial government to step in" (Gellner, 1974: 136).

Various organizations regarded as detrimental to national security have been declared unlawful under the War Measures Act. Fifteen radical organizations were banned by order-in-council in 1918-19. During the Second World War communist and fascist organizations were treated similarly. And in 1970 the FLQ was outlawed. The most notorious case of coercion under the War Measures Act was the 1942 deportation of some 12,000 persons of Japanese origin from the British Columbia coast to the interior.

The extraordinary measures that a federal government can take to suppress violent dissent are exemplified by the order-in-council passed on 4 April 1918 after the Quebec City riots. The various provisions of the order were summarized by the Prime Minister, Sir Robert Borden:

(1) In case of riot, insurrection or civil disturbance the General Officer Commanding was authorized to order such intervention as would be reasonably necessary to quell such disturbance and to restore peace.
(2) [Martial law could be imposed and the civil courts replaced by courts martial.]
(3) [Suspension of habeas corpus.]
(4) Any male person who took part in any riot, insurrection or civil disturbance caused by way of opposition to the enforcement of the Military Service Act, if found guilty, was to be regarded as having been called out for Military Service whether or not he was within the class hitherto exempted. (Borden, 1969: 124-5)

Three conclusions emerge from this review of the legal framework. First the law of the land narrowly restricts the use of violence by citizens. If indeed Canadians are as law-abiding as commentators on the political culture allege, Canadian laws may help explain the relatively low levels of public violence. Presumably as well the greater restrictiveness of gun control legislation in Canada than in the United States is one factor in Canadian public violence being less lethal. The law also closely regulates the use of violence by government forces. If they overstep the mark they may face internal disciplinary proceedings, criminal charges, and civil suits for damages. The distribution of powers under the federal constitution provides some further check on the use of governmental violence.

Second, constitutional governments can and do change the law of the land. But they can only adapt within limits. They have to maintain a majority in the House of Commons, work with other elites including the provincial governments, maintain the loyalty of the police and armed forces, and respect popular conceptions of justice if they are to win the next election.

Third, despite these restrictions, Canadian authorities do have substantial powers of coercion, as evidenced by the Riot Act, the War Measures Act, and section 98 of the Criminal Code. (In any event, the restrictions are not absolute; the federal government has occasionally been prepared to take the political risk of disregarding public opinion and overriding the provinces.) Dissident groups advocating the use of violence face substantial penalties, while police and military forces are fully authorized to use violence against them. From a purely legal standpoint at least, the odds are heavily weighted against the dissidents. Coercion, however, is not always an effective means of control.

THE EFFECTIVENESS OF
GOVERNMENTAL VIOLENCE

Some theorists argue that governmental violence cannot suppress dissent over extended periods of time (Dahrendorf, 1959: 224). Analogies are drawn from the world of physics, where a head of steam must be vented sooner or later, or where rigid structures break explosively under pressure (Coser, cited in Johnson, 1964: 7). Yet these analogies seem to contain an element of wishful thinking and should be treated with caution. Governments today have such powerful forces at their disposal that, at least according to the literature, they cannot be violently overthrown unless the military is first incapacitated by defeat in foreign war or by internal divisions. Furthermore, there seems little doubt that governments with effective forces at their disposal can quell disturbances as and when they occur. Both the Tillys (1975: 84) and Gurr (1976: 131) note that forcible suppression can put an end to violent protest. One example in Canada is the ending of organized Métis protest, after government troops had put down the Northwest Rebellion of 1885. Another example is the dramatic decline in the number of demonstrations in Montreal in 1970, when government forces moved in after the FLQ kidnappings (Frank and Kelly, 1977: 150).

However, there would seem to be a number of conditions for the effective use of governmental violence. Foremost is the existence of loyal and efficient government forces. While doubts on this score have been occasionally voiced in this country, Canadian governments in comparison with most others have had few grounds for worry.

A government also requires the support of other elite groups. There is little use in the police arresting dissidents if judges refuse to convict them. The various municipal, provincial, and federal authorities also need to work in harmony for maximum effectiveness. In Canada such co-operation has frequently proved hard to obtain,[4] so that the branch or level of government

---

4 For example, the dispute between Ottawa and Regina over the handling of the On to Ottawa trek. See also D. Morton (1970: 409, 413) for examples of disagreements at the municipal level on the need for calling out the militia.

most determined to quell the dissidents has been forced to act on its own. Even an isolated authority can generally summon up the necessary troops or police for immediate success, but it may face heavy political consequences for its boldness, particularly in a subsequent election.

Next, some characteristics of the dissident group can facilitate governmental coercion against them. Suppression appears relatively easy in those cases such as 1885 when rebels foolishly venture into open battle with government forces of superior weight and are thoroughly trounced for their pains. By contrast, violent suppression is all but impossible when the military cannot bring the dissident group to battle. In particular conspiratorial groups are largely immune to legal governmental attack, as long as they maintain hit-and-run tactics and do not restrict themselves geographically, as the FLQ did in the 1970 kidnappings.

Goode (1972: 516) also proposes that governmental violence will be most effective against groups with low value consensus. Coser (1956: 92-3) suggests much the same thing in observing that, while generally outside conflict unites a group, it will lead instead to apathy and disintegration when the group is lacking in basic consensus. The Quebec City rioters in 1918, for example, found their actions condemned by the city's political, church, and press leaders even though sympathy was given to their motives and the presence of largely English-speaking troops in the city was widely resented. This lack of consensus over means, especially as it involved a division between elites and masses, helps explain why the rioters were effectively suppressed and there were no repeat performances in the city or elsewhere in the province. In contrast are the various governments' difficulties in handling the Sons of Freedom who long managed to maintain a fervent unity of purpose that enabled the group to present a largely unbroken front to governmental coercion.

Another set of conditions relates to the respective quality of government and rebel sanctions. The argument here is a psychological one, similar to that advanced with respect to crime prevention: that people learn not to resort to violent dissidence when punishment is certain to follow, or it is consistently or equitably or severely applied. Leites and Wolf (1969: 156), for example, argue that successful coercion, whether by governments or rebels, depends on: "(a) the degree of understanding on the part of the population as to what is intended and why; (b) the appropriateness of the penalties; (c) the extent of their enforcement through time; (d) the extent to which innocents are spared; and (e) the degree of protection available *if* compliance is forthcoming, in the face of countercoercion by the other side."

However Gurr (1970: 240-51) adds that, while appropriate governmental coercion can deter civilians, at the same time it angers them. Hence, for effective coercive control, a government has to maintain either high levels of coercion, so that deterrence restrains the expression of anger, or low levels, so that there is no anger needing to be deterred. Coercion is least effective at the intermediate stage, when governments use enough to anger but not to deter their populations. Gurr (1968) finds empirical backing for this curvilinear relation in his cross-national study: the countries with middling-sized military and internal security forces have the highest levels of strife. The Feierabends and Nesvold (1969: 660-3) arrive at a similar result using a concept of coerciveness that includes non-physical means of suppressing dissent (for example, press censorship, banning opposition parties, and restricting freedom of speech and assembly).

Both studies place Canada among the least coercive of nations (Feierabends and Gurr, 1972: 160, 219-22). Similarly, the *World Handbook* (Taylor and Hudson, 1972: 42-7) finds that Canada in the mid-sixties had the third lowest rate of internal security forces per adult population of 123 nations. The only international comparison that strikes a note in the opposite direction is that Canada in the early sixties had one of the highest rates of incarcerating people in penal institutions in the western world. However, there has since been a change in the sentencing practices of judges, with much greater resort to fines and probation, so that the rate in this country is now average in this respect (Hagan, 1977: 164-9). As a whole, these findings suggest that governmental coerciveness, and, by inference, governmental violence, are fairly effective in Canada because they are relatively light. (The curvilinear hypothesis will be examined further in the next section when I look at changing levels of coercion.)

Finally, to be effective, governmental violence has also to be accepted as legitimate. Some features of legitimate government violence are included in Leites and Wolf's prescription for successful coercion cited above. In addition, a government may have to convince the public (1) that it is only using violence in response to violence that was initiated by the dissidents or, more problematically, to their intended use of violence ("apprehended insurrections"); (2) that the dissidents' use of violence is illegal, illegitimate, unnecessary, and a serious threat that must be dealt with firmly; (3) that it is following prescribed procedures; (4) that it has tried and failed with non-violent methods or it has no alternative but to use violence; and (5) that governmental violence can solve the problem effectively. To retain public support, governments thus have to use the same normative and utilitarian justifications for violence as do rebels. This is not an easy task, even with their considerable powers of influencing public opinion.

Canadian governments have been able to draw upon the respect for constituted authority and support for peaceful conduct that have been identified in the country's political culture to garner strong public support at the height of disturbances. This support, however, has not necessarily been maintained after the crisis was over. The execution of Riel by Macdonald's government alienated Quebec support for the Conservative Party. Both the

Borden and Bennett governments were defeated in the general elections subsequent to their use of violence. Two years after the imposition of the War Measures Act in 1970, the Trudeau government lost a third of its seats and was reduced to minority status. There were many other reasons for these governments' loss of popularity. But it may be that, subsequent to the incident, overt displays of governmental violence come to be interpreted as a failure on its part – a failure in the sense of not having defused the conflict at an early stage through conciliation and in not avoiding a violent confrontation once the conflict had been allowed to develop. If the political culture enjoins citizens to respect and support their government, it also contains a corresponding expectation that the government will act so as to merit that respect and support.

On the whole, however, governmental violence would seem to have been an effective means of control in Canada. The Northwest Rebellion and the FLQ were suppressed, as were the various movements that culminated in riots involving a strong display of governmental violence – Quebec City, Winnipeg, Estevan, and Regina. When the Canadian government has made an effective use of violence, it can be attributed to the loyalty and efficiency of its police and military forces, the weakness and division of dissident groups along with their tactical folly in directly challenging superior government forces, the government's limited coerciveness, and the maintenance of governmental legitimacy at least during the crisis period. Nevertheless the impression of overwhelming and immediate effectiveness of governmental violence has to be qualified somewhat.

First, Canadian governments have not relied exclusively on violent means to quell dissidents. They have also used the various conciliatory gestures mentioned earlier, and these too have to be weighed in the balance in assessing the effectiveness of governmental violence. Second, where dissident groups like the Sons of Freedom have maintained their value consensus and avoided confrontation with government forces, coercion has not been immediately or conclusively successful. And third, improving economic and political conditions may have had as much or more to do with ending dissidence as the determined use of governmental coercion. For example, if there was no sequel to the 1918 Quebec City riots, a full explanation would have to embrace, not simply the use of government coercion, but the fact that the government's need for conscripted troops was declining and would soon vanish. This parallels Gurr's (1976: 134) conclusion that more efficient policing reduces crime when it reinforces improving socio-economic conditions but that it cannot on its own "counter the corrosive effects of ... economic dislocation, social fragmentation, and cultural decay."

Judging governmental violence simply as a means of social control (that is, whether it can effectively suppress dissident movements) is only one standard of comparison. Another criterion is whether a resort to violence or coercion by a government tends to raise or lower the overall incidence of violence in a country.

CHANGING LEVELS OF GOVERN-
MENT AND DISSIDENT VIOLENCE

The argument of the previous section was that Canadian governments have lowered the incidence of violence in the land through the use of limited amounts of violence that have effectively put an end to violent resistance. Yet in looking beyond the confines of individual incidents to patterns of coercion and dissidence over time, the picture becomes more complicated. An incident affects subsequent government policies, and these policies in turn affect the likelihood of subsequent incidents.

It seems fairly clear that as levels of dissidence rise, governments hasten to improve their coercive capacity. Gurr (1976: 130) reports in his historical analysis of urban conflict that 14 out of 16 abrupt increases in the ratio of police to population occurred after marked rises in the level of disorder. Several Canadian examples can be given, covering various parts of the government's coercive apparatus.

The origins of Canada's police forces owe much to the outbreak or anticipated outbreak of disorders. The NWMP was set up in response to the first Riel rising and to the general lawlessness in the West, including the massacre of Indians by American whisky traders in the Cypress Hills. There was also the consideration of possible future trouble among settlers, Indians, and railway workers. The Ontario Provincial Police was also founded in response to disorder in the unpoliced northern mining communities of the province.

Variations in the size of police and military forces and their budgets have yet to be compiled for the entire historical period with which we are dealing. However it does seem that they rose in troubled periods. The Browns (1978: 45-6) note the strengthening of the RCMP and militia after the First World War. At that time the minister in charge urged the reactivation of the non-permanent militia in order "to establish an organization throughout the Dominion to which, should attempts at subversion be made, the patriotic elements of the community could rally. Training in the militia would, without doubt, promote the cause of peace and order and be productive of better citizens." The Browns (1978: 58) also show that the RCMP grew rapidly in size and power during the Depression and cite the Prime Minister's justification for the increased strength on the grounds of the existing "threat to the social order."

Over the last 20 years the number of full-time police personnel per 10,000 population has grown from 17 in 1962 to 28 in 1981 (Statistics Canada,

Canada Yearbooks and Catalogue 85-204, various years; Catalogue 85-002, October 1981 and June 1982).[5] The growth was uneven, with most of it coming in the early seventies. Thus in 1970 and 1971 the rate stood at 23 but by 1976 it had increased to 28 at which level it has remained ever since. From what Jamieson (1979) and Jackson, Kelly, and Mitchell (n.d.) tell us about levels of disorder in the country, it would seem that policing rates did rise after an increase in the number of violent incidents during the 1960s, although they continued to rise even more substantially *after* the peak years of dissidence circa 1970.[6] (We shall return to the latter point below.)

A number of legal changes have followed on the outbreak of civilian dissidence. The most notorious case was the addition of section 98 to the Criminal Code in the aftermath of the Winnipeg General Strike. Another instance was the 1931 amendment to the Criminal Code which, in an attempt to deter the Doukhobors, provided for up to three years' imprisonment for nudity in a public place. In this same category we can also include the enforcement of laws that have been allowed to fall into desuetude, such as that against trespassing on railway property which, once applied, effectively put an end to the On to Ottawa trek.

Canadian judges appear to have particularly wide discretion in their sentencing (Hagan, 1977: 164). It is thus possible that harsher judicial penalties are handed down in troubled times. Again the historical statistics await compilation and analysis. Making sense of the statistics that are available is complicated by changing judicial philosophies concerning appropriate sentencing over the years and by the need to take into account the varying proportion of serious crimes the judges are called to pass sentence on. Table 7 assembles some data, but before turning to it one should note one other indication of greater coerciveness in troubled times: the percentage of convicted capital murderers actually executed for their crimes (which is more a decision of the executive than of the judiciary) reached an all-time high of 75 per cent during the Depression decade of 1930-40 (Solicitor General of Canada, 1972: 67).[7]

The first column in table 7 directly refers to the severity of judges'

5 Similar growth occurred in the U.K. and the U.S. and partly reflects the general expansion of government. Canada appears to be essentially similar to these countries in policing rates and expenditures (Statistics Canada, 1980: 164-6).

6 Rising police rates seem to have been more a response to public violence than to rising levels of crime. Canadian criminal and court statistics reached the depths of disarray for the very period – around 1970 – that is at issue. For what they are worth, however, they do not indicate any marked increase in crime before the 1972-6 growth of policing rates. See the discussion on crime rates in chapter 6.

7 Gurr (1976: 151-2) notes that the disorderly 1830s and 1840s in the United Kingdom were accompanied by temporary increases in executions. "The arguments against capital punishment were not enough to dissuade officials under stress from stepping up reliance on the older methods."

TABLE 7

Levels of Judicial Severity, Canada, 1896-1979

Years	Severe sentences[1] as per cent of all sentences for indictable offences	Number in penitentiaries per 100,000 population	Number in penitentiaries per 100 convictions for indictable offences
1896-1900	10.2%	26.8	25
1901-1905	9.1%	23.2	21
1906-1910	8.8%	23.4	15
1911-1915	7.2%	25.0	11
1916-1921	6.1%	22.0	10
1922-1925	8.7%[2]	26.4	15[2]
1926-1930	9.4%	26.0	12
1931-1935	8.3%	37.7	12
1936-1940	8.0%	30.4	8
1941-1945	6.7%	27.5	8
1946-1950	8.9%	29.0	9
1951-1955	7.0%	32.4	11
1956-1960	7.9%	32.7	10
1961-1965	7.6%	38.2	10
1966-1970		36.0	
1971-1975		37.6	
1976-1979		39.9	

Note 1: "Severe sentences" are those involving two or more years in the penitentiary, as opposed to suspended sentences, probation, fines, or lesser terms of imprisonment. Sentences of life imprisonment or the death penalty (comprising less than 1 per cent of all sentences) are ignored, as they mainly reflect the number of homicide cases brought before the courts rather than any judicial propensity to severity.
Note 2: After 1921, the figures refer only to adult offenders.
Sources: Sentences, 1896-1952, are from Statistics Canada, Catalogue 85-201, 1946: 168 and 1952: 149. For sentences 1953-65, the percentages are calculated by author from figures given in Statistics Canada, Canada Yearbook, various years. For penitentiaries, the rates are calculated by author from figures given in Leacy, 1983: series Z224 and in Statistics Canada, Catalogue 85-207, various years. For convictions, see table 5.

sentences. Since the turn of the century, the proportion of severe sentences has been tending downwards, though there are some interesting anomalies. The war years are particularly notable. Surprisingly enough, judges were less severe in these years of Durkheimian restraint. The same is true for another restraint period already identified, the early fifties. However, it is not altogether clear that judges hand down stiffer sentences during periods of turmoil. It is true that the proportion of severe sentences rose in the two turbulent post-war periods, even relative to pre-war levels, as if the judiciary was trying to get the country back on an even keel after the disruptions of the war years. But the other turbulent periods – before the First World War, the Depression years, and the sixties – are simply not times when judges were being severe. Indeed, ten individual years which Jamieson (1979) has identified as being peak years of industrial conflict and violence show no relation between violence and judicial severity. In the peak conflict years, the average proportion of severe sentences was 8.1 per cent; in the year following the peak years, it was 7.5 per cent; but in the non-peak years, it was 8.4 per cent. (I have left aside the anomalous war years in these calculations.)

Another method of gauging judicial severity is to examine the size of the population held in penitentiaries – the institutions that customarily hold those sentenced to two or more years' imprisonment. These figures are rather more difficult to interpret. First, they partly reflect sentencing practices at an earlier point in time; and second, they are the product not simply of judicial severity but also of the number of cases brought before the judiciary. Their main advantage lies in their availability for more recent years.

The second column of table 7 reveals three periods of exceptionally high rates of incarceration: 1931-5, 1961-5, and 1976-9. The first two of these periods are times of heightened civil disturbance, the last is not. Nevertheless the first two also follow preceding periods of judicial severity and come at a time when an unusually large number of cases are before the courts. Indeed, with the standardization of the incarcerated population by the conviction rate (the third column in table 7), these two periods no longer stand out. The court statistics that would help interpret the unprecedented penitentiary population for the years 1976-9 are unavailable. The crime rate figures, however, suggest that the number of cases coming before the courts is a major reason for the currently overpopulated penitentiaries.

All these indicators of judicial severity have to be taken only conditionally, particularly until it is determined whether the courts are taking cases more seriously or whether the cases themselves are actually more serious. Nevertheless court and penitentiary statistics would seem to indicate that judges do not respond to troubled times by increasing the severity of their sentences.

One semi-judicial process that has been frequently used is the deportation of "troublesome" immigrants. During the Winnipeg General Strike the scope of the Immigration Act was enlarged to permit for the first time the deportation of British immigrants, although it seems that only non-British immigrants who participated in the strike were actually deported (Masters, 1950: 126). During the thirties, the government almost succeeded in deporting Peter the Purger, a Doukhobor leader. It failed because Peter had influential contacts and the resources to hire lawyers. Few others were so fortunate, and they were rendered all the more helpless by the secrecy surrounding deportation proceedings. During the Depression, the rate of deportations rose rapidly, reaching 7000 in 1931 alone, some seven times the average annual rate for the years 1903 to 1928. Many were deported to their homelands for being "public charges." Others were radicals and deported for political reasons; "even a conservative estimate would put them in the hundreds during the 1930-1935 period" (Browns, 1978: 64-5).

If rising levels of dissidence lead to increasing coercion (with the possible exception of the courts), the two do not necessarily rise and fall in simple lockstep. A government may improve its coercive capacity before civilian resistance emerges if it anticipates trouble (for example, the NWMP was formed prior to the arrival of settlers and the railway in the West). As well, Canadian governments have typically increased their ability to coerce after incidents were resolved. Thus Borden's order-in-council under the War Measures Act was devised in the week after the Quebec City riots were quelled and section 98 came into force some months after the Winnipeg General Strike was over. More recently, policing rates in the country continued to rise after the disorders peaked circa 1970.

Lags and leads, then, would have to be built into any model explaining governmental coercive capacity in terms of civilian levels of dissidence. However such a model only tells half the story: it also requires an arrow circling back from coercion to civilian dissidence. The question is whether that arrow should be marked to indicate a causal relationship in which rising coercion leads to rising dissidence (indicated by a plus sign) or whether increased coercion causes a decline in dissidence (a minus sign).

The proponents of a plus sign are numerous and offer several mechanisms explaining the linkage, some of which have already been noted. Johnson's power deflation argument postulates a sequence of loss of community integration, signalled by a refusal of citizens to comply willingly with the law, which is followed by an increased reliance by the government on violence, which is followed in turn by increasingly violent civilian resistance to governmental demands. Marx and Engels started from the alternative initial assumption – that society is riven with class conflict and is not a value-co-ordinated community – but nevertheless see a similar sequence: incipient revolt leading to increased state violence leading to greater working-class solidarity and the revolutionary overthrow of the capitalist system. Coser parallels the latter argument with his contention that conflict with external forces raises a group's morale and solidarity. Gurr's curvilinearity hypothesis suggests that as governmental levels of coercion rise from low to moderate, angry but undeterred citizens resort more frequently to violence.

Others lay stress on how governments and their agents create violence. According to Oberschall (1973: 334), "violence is more often initiated by the authorities and the agents of social control than by the protesters." Governments are also primarily responsible for any escalation in the extent and intensity of the violence. Tilly (1978: 177; 1979: 110) uses the same argument: governments have a choice of tactics, and an incident generally turns violent when they make the decision to stop an illegal but nonviolent protest. Thus in periods of rising coerciveness we can expect more violence-fomenting decisions from the government quite simply because of the greater availability of military and police personnel to engage in confrontations with the protesters, but also because governments may become confident in their strength and ability to coerce a group into quiescence. Once they have built up their coercive control, they may well attack from a position of strength (Gamson, 1975: 82) and thereby provoke or escalate violent civilian resistance. It is when governments lack confidence in their ability to coerce that they are more likely to explore conciliatory means of control (Turner, 1969: 827-8).

Other mechanisms linking rising governmental coercion to increased dissidence lie in the realm of ideas. As a government becomes more coercive, it provides its citizens with more justification for their own resort to violence. Moral sensitivities against the use of violence may also become blunted.

In particular, there is the power of example. When a government uses violence to get out of its difficulties, citizens may also come to consider it a legitimate and effective tactic. The effect of wars on rates of public and private violence was discussed in chapter 6. Another form of governmental violence that is sometimes said to create more violence by offering a bad example is capital punishment. However, the growing body of data comparing countries or American states with and without the death penalty, or comparing homicide rates before and after the abolition of capital punishment, indicates no consistent pattern. In Canada the removal of the death penalty in 1967 for some homicides but not others was followed by increased rates for non-capital murder and also, most confusingly, for capital murder as well (Teevan, 1972: 162). In 1976 the death penalty was totally abolished. Since then the number of homicides has fallen steadily. These recent figures support the notion that capital punishment has no deterrent effect and indeed if the government stops using violence others will follow its example. However such a conclusion would be brash in the light of the earlier contradictory evidence and the fact that most murders are unpremeditated.

Another linking mechanism is similar to the structural argument often used to explain rising crime rates. A modest rise in crime, or even a single spectacular case, produces demands that police forces be expanded and given more powers and that the judicial system deal more harshly with those caught in its net. More policeman are able to find more criminals from the reservoir of previously unreported or unsolvable crimes; judges and juries are more likely to convict; and suddenly the crime and conviction rates leap upwards. McDonald (1969), for example, has found that one of the best predictors of increasing crime rates is a growth in size of police forces. (It was noted in chapter 6 that Canadian crime rates tend to jump sharply in the years after a period of public disorder. A partial explanation of this phenomenon would now appear to be that the governments' response to the disorders involves strengthening the police force which, as the disorders ebb, then has the resources to pursue criminals more actively.)

Analogously, for levels of dissidence one could anticipate a process whereby an initial governmental malaise leads to the strengthening of police and military forces and their powers. More governmental agents are then busily seeking out sedition. Rumours and wild talk are taken seriously. The government becomes increasingly alarmed. More and more resources are diverted into the coercive apparatus, and techniques and habits of conciliation become rusty from disuse. The government thus becomes boxed into a policy of repression. Violence escalates both because the government refuses to conciliate and because police and military forces are ordered to intervene more actively against protesters. Further, quelling the dissidence becomes such a priority to the government that pressure on its agents to get "results" leads to their use of illegal and often violent tactics (burglaries and, in one notable case, a barn burning).

Once again the absence of reliable historical data and the joint effects of the several factors that affect the outbreak of violence make it difficult to judge the validity of this sequence. However, something like it can be observed in Canada around the end of the First World War, at the start of the Depression, and during the late sixties and early seventies. Undoubtedly, given the discontent of these times, there would have been violent civilian protest whatever the governments' actions. The argument is that once the governments had started increasing their coercive control and become locked into a policy of repression, much more civilian violence was created than otherwise would have been the case.

From all this, it would seem that there would be no question but that increasing levels of governmental coercion produce increasing levels of civilian violence. There are, however, some arguments in favour of placing a minus sign on the linkage. First of all, in pouring more resources into its coercive apparatus, a government may be as much concerned to improve the quality as the quantity of its personnel. It is quite clear that violence blossoms when poorly equipped, trained, disciplined, and organized forces enter the fray (Oberschall, 1973: 337-9). Conversely, violence is less likely to erupt or escalate when police and military forces have non-lethal weaponry at their disposal, when they are trained in the techniques of crowd control, when they maintain discipline in the face of provocation, when they act with professional impartiality, and when they are fully accountable for their actions to higher authorities, preferably to external ones such as the courts or citizens' review boards. Large national police forces are more able to meet these standards than local or amateur forces. The growth of national and provincial police forces which replaced the militia as the primary bastion of civil order, along with the extension of the RCMP's jurisdiction after the First World War and during the Depression, could thus be seen as raising the quality of coercion in Canada and hence as an influence for declining levels of violence.

Second, there is some evidence that civilian violence rises not when coerciveness waxes, but when it wanes. The other side of Gurr's curvilinear hypothesis points to rising civilian violence when governmental coercion falls from high to moderate as people formerly deterred now express their anger. Oberschall (1973: 76, 163) comes to a similar conclusion by arguing that declining coerciveness lowers the risks of, and hence encourages, participation in social movements. A prudent government enacts socio-economic reforms before relaxing its coercive grip. The Quebec violence in the 1960s could be attributed in part to the loosening of church and state control before the reforms of the Quiet Revolution could take effect.

The converse of Gurr's and Oberschall's arguments is that rising levels of coercion at some stage pass the point when they become great enough to deter expressions of anger or make participation in protest movements too risky for any possible rewards. Once this threshold is reached, civilian violence drops off. Yet a government caught up in a period of turmoil may well have difficulty gauging just when its coerciveness has risen sufficiently and thus may continue to increase its coercion for a period of perhaps three or four years, not only to satisfy its felt need for greater security, but also until it is able to assume with confidence that the crisis is over.

Indeed, such seems to have been the typical pattern in Canada: that is, (1) civilian dissidence prompting rising coercion, (2) leading to more dissidence and yet more coercion, (3) dissidence then falling off, (4) while coercion continues to rise for a while. At other times and places, the third and fourth stages have been replaced by ever expanding dissidence leading to the fall of the regime. Which scenario will be followed depends on the factors considered in previous chapters, such as the depth of discontent and its organizational base, and also on the factors raised in the discussion on the effectiveness of governmental violence: which side runs out of resources first, whether the government retains its legitimacy and control over the armed forces, and whether the government has the benefit of improving economic conditions and is able and willing to introduce reforms that will defuse the tension.

In short, increasing levels of governmental coerciveness will probably raise the number of violent incidents over the short term as the government engages in more confrontations with protesters. Over the longer term, the overall level of violence will fall if coercion reaches the threshold of deterrence or tilts the risk:reward ratio against participation in dissident movements. However, violence will increase to the point of governmental collapse if the government cannot maintain superior, effective powers of coercion.

CONCLUSION

Canadian governments have treated violent incidents as matters of grave concern. They have repeatedly and emphatically stated that their first duty is the preservation of order. The duty was not one they have taken lightly. In their own estimate, they would be unfit for office if they flinched from it or let considerations of electoral popularity stay their hand (Torrance, 1977: 478-9).

As well, "there is practically no Canadian legislative debate on the militia and national defence," says McNaught (1975: 170), "that does not include references (often central) to the armed forces as elements necessary to the preservation of law and order inside the country." Indeed for the militia this was regarded as their "principal object" (Minister of Militia, 1909, cited in D. Morton, 1970: 407). The same has been true for the country's various police forces. Macleod (1976: 114-15, 118) describes the priorities of the NWMP:

The police operated on the assumption that their first duty at all times was the maintenance of peace and order. This meant that crimes of violence were always accorded top priority ... Violence which had the effect of leading to further violence or which undermined respect for the law was not taken lightly. The police recognized that to prevent all fights and quarrels was not humanly possible; their concern was to prevent the public from accepting violence as a normal way of life ... Mob action was considered by the police to be the most potentially dangerous of all manifestations of violence.

Why should Canadian governments and their agents be so concerned with the preservation of order? Undoubtedly the peaceable kingdom idea provides part of the answer. As well McNaught (1975a: 138) refers to the traditional political ideas of the country. In particular, "the basically British belief that both liberty and justice are impossible without order lies at the heart of the Canadian political tradition." Furthermore:

In Canada the positive aspects of politics seem more clearly to belong to the political parties, the legislatures, and the press. A corollary of this is that political action outside the party-parliamentary structure tends automatically to be suspect – and not least because it smacks of Americanism. This deep-grained Canadian attitude of distinguishing amongst proper and improper methods of dealing with societal organization and problems reveals us as being, to some extent, what Walter Bagehot once called a 'deferential society.' We have certainly showed deference to the concept of *established* authority and procedures and even to the legal idea that valid authority flows downward from the crown. (1975a: 138)

McNaught (1975a: 139) also suggests, notwithstanding the conventional wisdom, that "we have had somewhat more confidence in the validity of our institutions and our whole national experiment than have the Americans in theirs." It is this confidence that has enabled Canadians and their governments to assert without equivocation that conflict must be channelled through party-parliamentary institutions.

As pointed out in chapter 5, political ideas such as these remain strong only so long as they serve a useful purpose. Elite groups obviously favour a deferential society, but this holds true in any country. For public order to be given the primacy it has achieved in Canada, recognition of the idea's usefulness must extend beyond the elite. I would suggest again that the country's vulnerable economy has made a strong government seem necessary and that the heterogeneity of the country's population has convinced many that freedom is only possible as long as a government is able to force conflict to remain within the bounds of established institutions. Neither the liberal fear of tyrannical governments, nor the Marxist view of the state as the ugly coercive arm of the bourgeoisie, has received much currency in Canada.

Hence, with strong popular encouragement, Canadian governments have been quick to suppress violent challenges to their authority. Civilian violence is irredeemably illegal and illegitimate. The governments have raised their coercive capacity in anticipation of civilian violence or after incidents were over in order to retain a position of strength. However, confidence in the propriety of party-parliamentary institutions has permitted considerable leniency towards repentant rebels: "Few countries have witnessed the repentance of such a high proportion of political rebels. It is not impossible that a major reason for this has been the combination of firm action and succeeding lenience which seems to characterize our basically conservative political-judicial tradition" (McNaught, 1975a: 139). Blaming incidents on leaders manipulating their misguided followers and some awareness that coercion is neither necessarily the sole, the least costly, nor the most effective means of control have produced prompt but limited recourse to violent means.

Challenging groups in Canada have thus been in a dilemma. If they sought attention from the government and the media, there was no surer way of gaining it than to threaten or engage in violence. Yet if they took this step, they were calumniated in the media, and the government refused to recognize them and instead promptly sent forth a riot squad or militia company to meet them. Recognition only came when they turned from direct action to the party-parliamentary system. Groups believing this system immoral, ineffective, or barred to them have had nowhere to turn but to the violence that ultimately destroyed them.

CHAPTER TEN

Conclusion

Violence has been used in many different ways in Canada. Examples of the the public varieties include: intimidation of election opponents; attacks on public property in protest against conscription; police firing on illegal demonstrators to clear the streets; soldiers using their weapons in self-defence against a hostile crowd; soldiers trying to win the field of battle; rival religious or union groups clashing to advance or protect their group; attacks on strike-breakers to coerce solidarity; looting during a police strike; a group of Doukhobors destroying the property of another to bring them closer to God; stealthy bombings to gain public notice; and the murder of Pierre Laporte because his captors apparently did not know what to do with him. This range of violent action is diverse in motivation and form. No single theoretical approach to understanding violence (let alone any one variable within an approach) can possibly capture its complexity.

There are a number of useful ideas among the approaches we have examined. Together they help to answer three key questions: Why is the incidence and severity of public violence relatively low in Canada? Why has the Canadian pattern of public violence differed from that of the United States? And how can we account for the times and places of high violence in Canada?

In chapter 3 I compared the incidence, intensity, and form of public violence in Canada to that in 17 other western democracies. Canada was not among the least violent nations, but given that the country was ranked during one of its peak episodes of violence, the size of its population, and the heterogeneity of its people, it was clear that it had emerged from the comparison as well as, or better than, might be expected. A number of factors can help to explain this relatively low incidence and intensity.

Perhaps the most important has to do with the different risks and rewards of violent action faced by governments and protesters. Canadian governments benefit from laws that sanction their own coercive violence and threaten that of protesters. They have been quite prepared to increase the legal risks of violent protest as the occasion warranted. They have generally enjoyed the support of the public in using violent coercion, while protesters resorting to violence have lost public support. The resources Canadian governments command have been far superior to those of the often divided groups confronting them. The superiority has extended to manpower, weapons, organization, the ability to impose their own interpretation on events and to justify their resort to violence, and a willingness to use these resources in order to uphold what they have considered their prime duty, the preservation of law and order. Another extremely important factor has been the loyalty and efficiency, by international standards, of Canada's soldiers and police.

I would suggest that Canadian governments have been less tolerant of public disorder than American ones, which is one reason why there has been less turbulence in this country. The difference reflects the political cultures of the two countries. The justification for civilian violence stemming from historic public events that positively shape the nation's destiny is lacking in Canada. As well, the United States has attached greater importance to the freedom of the individual, including his or her right to bear arms. Canada has emphasized "peace, order and good government" and upheld British traditions that clearly distinguish proper and improper political conduct. These differences are epitomized in the two countries' gun control legislation. The more restrictive Canadian laws may be plausibly associated with the less lethal character of Canadian public violence.

The myth of the peaceable kingdom affirms and celebrates such distinctions. To quote Underhill (1960: 12) again: "In Canada, we have no revolutionary tradition; and our historians, political scientists, and philosophers have assiduously tried to educate us to be proud of this fact." The myth reinforces the notions of proper political conduct and the impropriety of violence by summoning up the element of nationalism. The Canadian national identity encompasses the shunning of violent protest.

The myth also has played a part in restraining Canadians from violence. It is most apparent in the awareness of protest leaders that violence alienates public support and invites repression. As well, the use of violence by Canadian governments has usually been careful, controlled, and legalistic, both in the sense of limited amounts of violence being used to uphold the law or bring malefactors to justice, and in the sense of close legal regulations hedging the police and military. I would suggest that Canadian police and military forces have been more subject to discipline and control by their political masters than have American ones. If this is so, the greater restraint Canadian forces operate under would help to curtail the amount of violence.

The myth as well as the broader political culture also support a strong, interventionist government that regulates conflicts effectively. The location of conflicts in a society affects the form these conflicts take. As long as trade unions were not recognized by governments, conflicts between employers and employees were carried on, often enough with considerable violence, outside established political and economic institutions. Because Canada industrialized later than the United Kingdom or the United States, its unions did not have to undergo a comparable period when they were dismissed outright as illegal combinations. Canadian governments early sought to regulate industrial disputes. Even if these regulatory attempts favoured employers, and perhaps because they did so, Canadian employers were forced to accept at least some union activity and were restrained from hiring private armies and engaging in the warfare that scarred certain industries, especially coal-mining, in late nineteenth-century America.

One effect of the political culture and myth may have been self-reinforcing. I have used the concept of public violence to stress that what are objectively termed civil disturbances or acts of political violence may be interpreted as private deviancy, that where one observer sees persons acting for the common good to raise valid political issues, another will see only traitors, criminals, or ruffians at work. Given the emphasis on keeping conflicts within the party-parliamentary system and the conception of violence as an un-Canadian activity, the barriers to achieving public status may be especially high in Canada. There may well have been much more violence than Canadians and their historians recall, but it has been dismissed as not worth memorializing. The myth consequently has been sheltered from challenge.

The myth is also sheltered by another mechanism. Richly endowed protagonists in conflicts of interest have the ability to shape public perceptions of their actions. Often enough they will seek to have their violence excluded from the conventional definition of the word, so that only the actions of weaker groups are labelled violent. Governmental violence, for example, is usually disguised by euphemisms such as "force," "protection," and "upholding law and order." Similarly the injurious acts of other powerful groups in industry and the professions are simply not recognized as violence. A good deal of conflicting evidence is thus not weighed when the myth of the peaceable kingdom is being assessed. The discrepancy between real and perceived levels of violence is rendered all the more germane by Gamson's (1975) argument that violence is often the product of strong groups "moving in for the kill" against weak opponents. Chapter 8 suggested that a good deal of Canadian violence – in particular, the violence of Canadian governments – did fit this pattern. A good deal of Canadian violence, consequently, will be affected by the tendency of strong groups to hide their violence by calling it something else.

Macleod puts forward a suggestive argument in his discussion of attitudes towards crime and class. He points out (1976: 88) that both the NWMP and the public assumed that "criminality was largely a lower class phenomenon and that it was important that law enforcement officers be the social superiors of those who broke the law." The frontier was expected "to be lawless not because of its physical or economic characteristics, but because it was peopled initially by the lower social groups. Hence Sir John A. Macdonald's expectation that the need for the police would disappear once large-scale settlement took place." What shocked Canadians about the American West, according to Macleod (1976: 130), was not its violence so much as the fact that the violence "sometimes occurred among social and economic groups which in Canada would have fallen into the category of the respectable middle class."

I think much the same could be said about Canadian attitudes towards public violence and class. Civil disturbance is expected to be largely a lower-class phenomenon and its occurrence of little significance; Canadians also expect those called upon to quell the violence to be the social and moral superiors of the protesters. The American practice of filling police and judicial posts on the basis of electoral popularity, evidence of brutality and indiscipline among American public and semi-private security forces, and the fact that the American historical incidents of public violence, if no others, were the work of the middle class: all these affronted Canadian sensibilities.

The middle class has long been the champion of the progressive extension of order in this and other countries, including the United States. The myth of the peaceable kingdom is really a middle-class myth. That the myth should be Canadian and not American suggests that the middle class has been more homogeneous and more powerful relative to other groups in Canada than in the United States, and conversely that Canadian dissident groups have been more divided and more remote from the centres of power than have American ones.

Among the peculiarities of Canadian violence noted in chapter 3 was the high proportion of Conspiracy events relative to Turmoil ones during the 1960s. A possible reason for this may be the weakness and isolation of Canadian dissident groups. Weak groups who do not know how to turn the workings of the political system to their advantage and who lack the resources to organize, if they opt for violent tactics, typically choose stealthy attacks on selected, usually governmental properties in order to voice a protest or garner public support. This course of action requires few resources, and it has proved effective on occasion. But not in Canada. Here the resort to conspiratorial violence seems to have had the effect of further isolating the group from the mainstream and of swinging support towards the government.

Historically the main fault line in Canadian society has been understood to be the division separating French-speaking and English-speaking Canadians. Nevertheless there has been little violence emerging from this division over the years. Until the arrival of the FLQ, the country largely managed to channel the conflict into established political institutions. This has been due to the sheer size of the francophone minority and its concentration within one of the major provinces. It has consequently been able to control salient positions in the political system. In comparison are the relatively small and more dispersed minorities in the United States.

Another reason for Canadian peacefulness may be the relative contentment of its citizens by worldwide standards. Like other advanced democracies, Canada has sufficient resources for reallocation, stability, and openness of political channels to keep a majority of its people happy for most of the time. It is also among the least coercive of nations as measured by both the size of its security forces and infringements of civil liberties.

There are, then, several good explanations for Canadian peacefulness. Singled out for mention have been the resources available to the government as opposed to challenging groups; the political culture which is intolerant of extra-parliamentary opposition and violence, and supports an interventionist government stepping in to regulate conflicts; the definition of what constitutes violence; the structure of French-English relations; and low levels of discontent by international standards. Canada, however, is only relatively peaceful. Canadians have resorted to arms on many occasions, and what remains to be explained is when and where they have been most prone to do so.

Several concentrations of Canadian public violence were tentatively identified in chapter 3. Violence seems to have been higher than usual in the 1880s, around the turn of the century, after the First World War, during the Depression, and in the 1960s. Among the provinces, Quebec and British Columbia (at least up to the Second World War) have been the most violent. Small centres appear to have been overrepresented. The most affected industries have probably been primary resources, transport and communications, and textiles and clothing.

The various theories offer a number of explanations for these concentrations. Among the breakdown variables, the age structure of the population and social or geographic isolation seem most helpful. Young males aged 15-24 years formed an unusually large proportion of the population in both the Depression and the 1960s. In Quebec, they have historically been somewhat overrepresented in the population compared to the national average, and this was probably also true in early British Columbia. Isolation helps to explain the concentration of incidents in early British Columbia, the small centres, and the three industrial sectors.

Discontent theories suggest that nationalism serves to deepen the discontents of Quebeckers. Relative deprivation would also be a prime factor in Quebec, where the people could compare their position unfavourably to that enjoyed by people in most other provinces and, even more tellingly, to that enjoyed by the Anglophone minority within their own province. Across Canada at least some of the most affected industries are particularly unstable and are carried on in the remote centres where discontent in company-dominated towns is exacerbated by want of alternative opportunities. To some extent we can also see the peak periods of violence in the country as a whole as times when individuals have had multiple discontents and when different sectors of the community have had reason for discontent.

Solidarity theories offer some suggestions. They point to social or geographic isolation as a factor facilitating mobilization. If the number of contending parties affects the likelihood of violence, then Quebec has been a prime candidate with its organizations perennially divided on ideological, linguistic, and religious grounds.

Solidarity theories emphasize that violence involves two parties, and that one of these parties is usually the government. In explaining the episodicity of Canadian violence, one must consider when governments have been more willing to resort to coercion than conciliation. Perhaps Canadian governments have been more impatient with opposition movements and more fearful of them, and hence more willing to engage in coercion, during the peak periods. Their fears have been various: concern for the fate of great national projects; for the extent of dissatisfaction; over the apparent novelty and revolutionary implications of the ideas that are circulating; and for a movement's contagiousness. Willingness to use coercion probably raised the level of violence over the short-term, at least until the threshold of deterrence was reached. After this point violent protests declined in number, although crime rates continued to climb, probably as a result of the heightened level of policing.

In highlighting some features of the explanatory theories, I have ignored others which, while often central to these theories, have not proved helpful in explaining the Canadian experience. For instance, breakdown theories contribute to our understanding of the country's periods of restraint but are generally unhelpful with respect to the so-called anomic periods. The factors identified in these and the other theories – for example, crime rates, immigration, rapid socio-economic change, business cycles, J-curves, trade union membership, and the resources available to a government for reallocation – are not or are only inconsistently linked to Canadian public violence. The peak periods have had rising and stationary crime rates, high and low immigration, boom conditions and depression, rapid change and no change, expanding and contracting governmental resources, and trade union growth and decline.

I have argued throughout that we need better data, both for the incidence of violence and to measure the concepts used in the various theories. The theories themselves also need refinement. Perhaps when these tasks are done some of the confusion will be sorted out.

Another peculiarity of Canadian public violence is the prevalence of mixed-context incidents. The heterogeneity of the population explains the presence of communal overtones in so many incidents. The frequency of political overtones is not so readily explained. It can be partly attributed to the government's willingness to intervene in communal and economic disputes in order to avoid disruption and to protect the rights of one side or the other. Another factor is the labelling of violence as public or private. If a political element cannot be found, an incident tends to be written off as private deviancy that can be safely ignored.

As well, there have been some occasions in Canada of the "politicization" of issues. Examples include major incidents such as the Northwest Rebellion and the FLQ campaign where the movements asserted their discontents were the result of, and could not be remedied under, existing political arrangements. These are the occasions of what in chapter 5 were called periods of ideological effervescence and in chapter 6 the anomie of social ferment. The politicized perspective is also essentially that of the solidarity theorist who argues that injustice can only be remedied by a group accumulating enough power to compel an elite to concede. It seems clear that the incidence and intensity of violence is associated with the politicization of issues. But it is rather more difficult to explain the circumstances under which a movement espouses a politicized perception of the world.

The study of discontents in chapter 7 indicates that the facts of the case have a bearing. One needs to know whether discontents are actually multiple and whether the government has been impermeable, insensitive, or standing in the way of a group's progress. Yet, insensitive governments and multiple discontents do not invariably add up to the widespread politicization of discontents (for example, the late 1970s in Canada), and there have been politicized discontents when governments have not been notably insensitive (surely the Pearson government was not insensitive to the needs of French Canada).

Indeed, on this point, the explanatory theories, singly or in combination, are not very helpful. Admittedly the process can be understood well enough once it is underway, but its onset cannot be predicted with any reliability. It is this failure that renders inadequate any explanations of the peak periods of public violence, especially the 1960s. Taking the Quebec political violence of the sixties as an example, one needs to know why the FLQ, students, and trade unionists attributed their discontents to the basic institutions of their society at this particular time. Factors to be considered as partially responsible include the age structure of the population, the revolutionary ideas that were circulating elsewhere, the rise of the new middle class, the uneven growth in different sectors of the economy some of which were stagnant while others were spurred by spectacular construction projects, contracting governmental resources for reallocation, the relaxation of church and state control, and so on. The very multiplicity of explanations casts doubt on their individual value, and each is open to the objection that they have not created politicized discontents at other times and places.

Perhaps the onset of politicized discontent is so complicated a phenomenon that all these factors and more could comprise an equation that would predict its occurrence. Yet there is the suspicion that a simpler explanation exists though it is not immediately obvious. This lack constitutes a critical gap in our understanding of violence.

By way of a summary, here are the eight factors that should be taken into account when seeking to explain an incident or pattern of violence. First, the motivations of the violent must be considered. They may be expressing their frustrations, seeking to coerce others, acting in self-defence, or trying to draw attention to their cause. Acts included within the scope of public violence are generally those designed to achieve some purpose. On occasion this purpose may be difficult to pin down. Motives can be mixed, and the trigger or precipitating cause – which characteristically involves the behaviour of specific opposing individuals – must be distinguished from the remoter, underlying causes. The incident may even have been the product of misunderstanding, and the violence unintentional.

Second, there must be some notion of societal disequilibrium – of changes that strain the society's integrative mechanisms or some failure in these mechanisms themselves. A bulge in the youthful population, migration to sparsely settled areas, and disruptions of the economy are challenges that can be responded to creatively and justly by a society's institutions and elites. It is when internal divisions, rigidity, or preoccupation with other matters prevent a creative and just response that the scene is set for violence.

Third, the idea of using violence has to come from somewhere. I believe that violence is learned behaviour (that is, it is neither instinctual nor a necessary outcome of frustration). Consequently the more there is of it, the more readily people will resort to it rather than to some other method of dealing with their problems. The use of violence may be suggested by the cultural repertoire of collective actions, by the government using violence to get out of its difficulties, and by the actions of others at home and abroad.

Fourth, the use of violence has to be justified. Normative justifications may be provided by the culture or by an ideology. Utilitarian justifications involve judgments on the risks and rewards of violent action: the belief that violence can be used with impunity; that there is no other choice; that it will achieve desired ends; or that the intended victim is an acceptable and vulnerable target.

Fifth, public violence is nearly always a collective action. The apathetic, the truly anomic, do not engage in it. There is thus a need to consider the conditions for solidarity and mobilization by which previously isolated individuals are brought together and into confrontation with other groups. As well, the dissidents' perception of the world around them will determine the type of organization that they create, which in turn affects the type of violence that will be used.

Sixth, there is the behaviour of the other party. They may simply pack up and leave or concede to all demands. They may arm themselves and deter anyone from taking violent action against them. Or they may initiate the violence by making a pre-emptive strike.

Seventh, governments using violence are affected by the above factors, but they also have a special role of their own. In choosing to conciliate or coerce a challenging group, governments have to be mindful of such considerations as the effect of their actions on the legitimacy of the regime, the maintenance of law and order, the loyalty of police and military forces, the raising of expectations that cannot be satisfied, and the power of their example. Having decided to coerce, a government can raise the level of violence in a society if it fails to deter the justifiable anger of its citizens or to tilt the risk:reward ratio for violent action in its favour.

Finally, the essentially political process by which violence is accorded public status must be accounted for. The amount of empathy towards themselves and their cause that the violent can muster, their own political status and that of their sympathizers, and their ability to disseminate and enforce their own version of events will determine which of the competing interpretations of an incident will predominate.

This list draws on all the explanatory approaches that have been examined in this study. It is difficult to pick out any one approach as being the most important. Each has something to offer in the search to understand the many varieties of violent behaviour. Moreover, as I explained at the outset, I have not devoted space to those theories that I believe contribute little or nothing to our knowledge of violence (the various theories based on the study of animals, for example).

Some readers will argue that I have given too much space to subjective factors. However, in my opinion, other studies have tended to neglect them unduly. Even more importantly, there is the evidence that Canadians often fail to behave in accordance with the predictions of the various theories. This suggests that the theories may be ethnocentric – that is, they work very well in the theorist's own culture (usually that of the United States), but they are less effective when applied to people operating under different cultural conditions. The forces that are supposed to lead to anomic breakdown and the discontent theories, including the predicted linkage between frustration and aggression, seem to be most affected by this problem. Solidarity theories are rather less affected. The concepts of risks, rewards, and resources are sufficiently general to embrace most cultural and societal differences. For instance, Canadian popular distaste for public violence can be entered under the heading of an additional risk run by Canadian protest groups.

Indeed, solidarity theories probably provide the most promising framework for the retrospective analysis of particular incidents. Yet I think such theories are relatively weak in providing an understanding of the incidence of violence. In looking for the similarities between legitimate and challenging groups and stressing that challenging groups engage in normal, everyday political behaviour, solidarity theorists fail to account adequately for the non-everyday resort to violence. Perhaps their sympathy for these groups makes it hard for them to examine extensively the use of tactics that they know are widely regarded as deviant or abnormal. Whatever the reason, there is a tendency among them to dismiss too quickly the question of why and when there are peaks of violence, including especially that of unorganized groups or those poorly endowed with resources. As noted in chapter 9, these peaks cannot be simply attributed to acts of governmental coercion or the resources available to governments for reallocation. Solidarity theories thus do not supplant the other explanations of violence; they supplement them.

Violence, in short, is a complex phenomenon requiring an eclectic approach. However, the effort invested in its study is well worthwhile. If it is ignored, as Canadians have so often done, an imperfect understanding of a country and its history results. Thus Canadians can learn about their culture by examining the reactions of their society and government to incidents of violence. The very failure of challenging groups reveals much about the distribution of resources and power in Canadian society. The incidents show that there are other sources of division in the country than that between French and English. They can act as tracers for movements of protest in the historical record and help Canadians focus their attention on the aspirations and changing conditions of the "little people." They call into question any notion of straight-line and unchallenged progress.

Furthermore Canadian violence deserves to be taken seriously. With regard to the uses of governmental violence, there are critical questions on the nature of power, legitimacy, and social order that must be addressed. With regard to the violence of challenging groups, if people are going to risk life and limb, governmental coercion, and popular opprobrium, then surely they should receive attention, no matter how eccentric or disreputable they appear to be or how little success attends their efforts.

In devoting more attention to Canadian violence, the pendulum should not be swung too far in the opposite direction in an attempt to redress the balance. Canadians and their governments are not violent in comparison with most other nations. This conclusion, however, should not cause Canadians to bask in a sense of ineffable moral superiority. Canadians have not found "a better way" with which to teach the rest of the world to mend its manners, so much as they have benefitted from a unique and non-exportable combination of societal, economic, and historical circumstances.

Appendix

References to the less well known incidents are provided. I have counted only the deaths directly attributable to the violence itself. This includes those who died subsequently of injuries sustained during the incident, but not, for example, the victim of a heart attack during the course of the *La Presse* riot of 1971.

Incidents marked with an asterisk are those which are not clearly of a public nature. The 1971 prison riot, for instance, had public elements in the inmates' organization and call for reforms, but the death associated with it involved the sadistic murder of a sexual offender. The 1982 prison riot is even more of a borderline case. In other incidents, the assailant's motives were unclear or his mental stability was in doubt.

Year	Place	Victims	Form
1868	Ottawa	1	Assassination of D'Arcy McGee
1870	Kildonan, Man.	2	Attack during mustering of Canadian party
1870	Fort Garry	1	Execution of Thomas Scott
1870*	Fort Garry	1	Attack on a Métis
1877	Montreal	1	Riot during Orange parade
1878	Quebec City	1	Strike clash, only person killed by militia (D. Morton, 1970: 416, 421)
1878	Quebec City	2	French-Irish attack (Latouche, 1971: 181)
1880	Lucan, Ont.	5	Vigilante attack on Donnelly family
1883	near Lytton, B.C.	1	Attack on Chinese workers (Berton, 1971: 200)
1885	Saskatchewan	c. 200	Northwest Rebellion
1903	Vancouver	1	Attack on union organizer (Jamieson, 1968: 112)
1906	Buckingham, Que.	3	Strike clash (Jamieson, 1968: 94-5)

Year	Place	Victims	Form
1918	Quebec City	4	Clash, conscription riots
1918	U.K.	7	Riots by Canadian troops in demobilization camps
1919	Winnipeg	2	Clash during general strike
1924	B.C.	9	Explosion in railway car carrying Doukhobor leader
1925	Nova Scotia	1	Strike clash (Jamieson, 1968: 202)
1931	Estevan, Sask.	3	Strike clash
1935	Regina	1	On to Ottawa trek clash
1938	Sorel, Que.	1	Municipal election "battle" (Jamieson, 1968: 503)
1944	B.C.	1	Sons of Freedom arson
1958	Murdochville, Que.	1	Striker killed by own bomb (Jamieson, 1968: 364)
1958	B.C.	1	Sons of Freedom, killed by own bomb
1959	Badger, Nfld.	1	Strike clash (Jamieson, 1968: 367)
1962	B.C.	1	Sons of Freedom, killed by own bomb
1963	Kapuskasing, Ont.	3	Strike attack (Jamieson, 1968: 414)
1963	Montreal	1	FLQ bomb
1964	Montreal	2	Clash during FLQ arms theft
1966*	Ottawa	1	Chartier killed by own bomb in House of Commons
1966	Montreal	1	FLQ bomb
1966	Montreal	1	FLQ, killed by own bomb
1969	Montreal	1	Attack during police strike
1970	Ottawa	1	FLQ bomb
1970	Montreal	1	FLQ kills Pierre Laporte
1971*	Kingston, Ont.	1	Prison riot
1972*	Sept-Iles, Que.	1	Car runs into demonstrators
1982	Ottawa	1	Turkish diplomat assassinated
1982*	Montreal	5	Prison riot, Archambault Institute
1982*	Toronto	2	Sikh community attack
1984*	Quebec City	3	Lortie's attack on National Assembly

Bibliography

Abella, Irving, ed.
  1974 *On Strike: Six Key Labour Struggles in Canada, 1919-1949*. Toronto: James Lewis and Samuel.
Adams, O.B.
  1981 *Health and Economic Activity: A Time-Series Analysis of Canadian Mortality and Unemployment Rates, 1950-1977*. Ottawa: Statistics Canada, Catalogue 82-539 E Occasional.
Allen, Sir Carleton Kemp
  1953 *The Queen's Peace*. London: Stevens.
Allport, Gordon W.
  1964 *Personality and Social Encounter: Selected Essays*. Boston: Beacon.
Archer, Dane, and Rosemary Gartner
  1976 "Violent acts and violent times: a comparative approach to postwar homicide rates." *American Sociological Review*, 41, 937-63.
Arendt, Hannah
  1965 *On Revolution*. New York: Viking Press.
  1969 *On Violence*. New York: Harcourt, Brace and World.
Armstrong, Elizabeth H.
  1967 *The Crisis of Quebec, 1914-18*. New York: AMS Press.
Armstrong, Jill
  1972 "Canadians in crisis: the nature and source of support for leadership in a national emergency." *Canadian Review of Sociology and Anthropology*, 9, 299-324.
Beck, J.M.
  1968 *Pendulum of Power: Canada's Federal Elections*. Scarborough, Ont.: Prentice-Hall.
Bell, David V.J.
  1970 "The loyalist tradition in Canada." *Journal of Canadian Studies*, 5, 22-33.
  1973 *Resistance and Revolution*. Boston: Houghton Mifflin.

Bell, David V.J., and Lorne Tepperman

1979   *The Roots of Disunity: A Look at Canadian Political Culture*. Toronto: McClelland and Stewart.

Bell-Rowbotham, Beverly, and Craig L. Boydell

1972   "Crime in Canada: a distributional analysis," pp. 93-116 in C. Boydell, C. Grindstaff, and P. Whitehead, eds., *Deviant Behaviour and Societal Reaction*. Toronto: Holt, Rinehart and Winston.

Bercuson, David J.

1974   "The Winnipeg general strike," pp. 1-32 in I. Abella, ed., *On Strike: Six Key Labour Struggles in Canada, 1919-1949*. Toronto: James Lewis and Samuel.

1975   "Western labour radicalism and the One Big Union: myths and realities," pp. 244-56 in S.D. Clark, J.P. Grayson, and L.M. Grayson, eds., *Prophecy and Protest: Social Movements in Twentieth-Century Canada*. Toronto: Gage.

Berton, Pierre

1971   *The Great Railway, 1881-1885: The Last Spike*. Toronto: McClelland and Stewart.

Blumenthal, Monica D., Robert L. Kahn, Frank M. Andrews, and Kendra B. Head

1972   *Justifying Violence: Attitudes of American Men*. Ann Arbor: Institute for Social Research, University of Michigan.

Borden, Henry, ed.

1969   *Robert Laird Borden: His Memoirs, Vol. II: 1916-1920*. Toronto: McClelland and Stewart.

Bowen, Don R., and Louis H. Masotti

1968   "Civil violence: a theoretical overview," pp. 11-31 in L. Masotti and D. Bowen, eds., *Riots and Rebellion: Civil Violence in the Urban Community*. Beverly Hills: Sage.

Brady, Alexander

1958   *Democracy in the Dominions: A Comparative Study in Institutions*. 3rd ed. Toronto: University of Toronto Press.

Breton, Raymond

1972   "The socio-political dynamics of the October events." *Canadian Review of Sociology and Anthropology*, 9, 33-56.

Brinton, Crane

1965   *The Anatomy of Revolution*. Revised ed. New York: Vintage Books.

Broadfoot, Barry

1973   *Ten Lost Years, 1929-1939: Memories of Canadians Who Survived the Depression*. Toronto: Doubleday.

Brooks, Robin

1979   "Domestic violence and America's wars: an historical interpretation," pp. 307-27 in H. Graham and T.R. Gurr, eds., *Violence in America: Historical and Comparative Perspectives*. Beverly Hills: Sage.

Brown, Lorne, and Caroline Brown

1978 *An Unauthorized History of the RCMP*. Toronto: James Lorimer.

Bull, William Perkins

1936 *From the Boyne to Brampton, or John the Orangeman at Home and Abroad.* Toronto: The Perkins Bull Foundation, George J. McLeod.

Bwy, Douglas P.

1968 "Dimensions of social conflict in Latin America," pp. 201-36 in L. Masotti and D. Bowen, eds., *Riots and Rebellion: Civil Violence in the Urban Community*. Beverly Hills: Sage

Cairns, Alan C.

1968 "The electoral system and the party system in Canada, 1921-1965." *Canadian Journal of Political Science*, 1, 55-80.

Campbell, Sir Alexander

1885 *In the Case of Louis Riel Convicted of Treason and Executed Therefor, Dated 25 November, 1885*. Memorandum prepared at the request of the Committee of the Privy Council. Ottawa: Maclean, Rogers.

Campbell, Angus, and Howard Schuman

1968 "Racial attitudes in fifteen American cities," pp. 3-67 in *Supplemental Studies for the National Advisory Commission on Civil Disorders*. New York: Praeger.

Camus, Albert

1960 "Preface to Algerian reports," pp. 81-93 in *Resistance, Rebellion, and Death*. Translated by Justin O'Brien. New York: Random House.

Chesnais, Jean-Claude

1981 *Histoire de la violence en Occident de 1800 à nos jours*. Paris: Editions Robert Laffont.

Clark, S.D.

1962 *The Developing Canadian Community*. Toronto: University of Toronto Press.

Cobb, R.C.

1970 *The Police and the People: French Popular Protest, 1789-1820*. London: Oxford University Press.

Cole, G.D.H., and Raymond Postgate

1961 *The Common People, 1746-1946*. London: Methuen.

Coser, Lewis A.

1956 *The Functions of Social Conflict*. New York: Free Press.

Cromwell, Jerry

1977 "The size distribution of income: an international comparison." *Review of Income and Wealth*, 23, 291-307.

Cross, Michael S., ed.

1970 *The Frontier Thesis and the Canadas: The Debate on the Impact of the Canadian Environment*. Toronto: Copp Clark.

Currie, Elliott

1971 "Violence and ideology: a critique of the final report of the violence commission," pp. 452-69 in A. Platt, ed., *The Politics of Riot Commissions, 1917-1970: A Collection of Official Reports and Critical Essays*. New York: Macmillan.

Dahrendorf, Ralf
  1959 *Class and Class Conflict in Industrial Society*. Stanford: Stanford University Press.

Davies, James C.
  1962 "Toward a theory of revolution." *American Sociological Review*, 27, 5-30.

Debray, Régis
  1967 *Revolution in the Revolution? Armed Struggle and Political Struggle in Latin America*. Translated by Bobbye Ortiz. New York: Grove Press.

de Tocqueville, Alexis
  1955 *The Old Régime and the French Revolution*. Translated by Stuart Gilbert. Garden City, N.Y.: Doubleday Anchor.

Dietz, Mary Lorenz
  1978 "The violent subculture: the genesis of violence," pp. 13-39 in M. Gammon, ed., *Violence in Canada*. Toronto: Methuen.

Durkheim, Emile
  1951 *Suicide: A Study in Sociology*. Translated by John A. Spaulding and George Simpson. New York: Free Press.

Easterlin, Richard A.
  1980 *Birth and Fortune: The Impact of Numbers on Personal Welfare*. New York: Basic Books.

Eckstein, Harry
  1964 "Introduction: toward the theoretical study of internal war," pp. 1-32 in H. Eckstein, ed., *Internal War: Problems and Approaches*. New York: Free Press.

Edelman, Murray
  1971 *Politics as Symbolic Action: Mass Arousal and Quiescence*. Chicago: Markham.

Edelman, Murray, and Rita J. Simon
  1969 "Presidential assassinations: their meaning and impact on American society." *Ethics*, 79, 199-221.

Edwards, Lyford P.
  1970 *The Natural History of Revolution*. Chicago: University of Chicago Press.

Feierabend, Ivo K., Rosalind L. Feierabend, and Ted Robert Gurr, eds.
  1972 *Anger, Violence, and Politics: Theories and Research*. Englewood Cliffs, N.J.: Prentice-Hall.

Feierabend, Ivo K., Rosalind L. Feierabend, and Betty A. Nesvold
  1969 "Social change and political violence: cross-national patterns," pp. 632-87 in H. Graham and T.R. Gurr, eds., *Violence in America: Historical and Comparative Perspectives*. A report submitted to the National Commission on the Causes and Prevention of Violence. New York: Bantam.

Flanagan, Thomas
   1979   *Louis 'David' Riel: 'Prophet of the New World.'* Toronto: University of
          Toronto Press.
   1983   *Riel and the Rebellion 1885 Reconsidered.* Saskatoon, Sask.: Western
          Producer Prairie Books.
Flanigan, William H., and Edwin Fogelman
   1970   "Patterns of political violence in comparative historical perspective."
          Comparative Politics, 3, 1-20.
Fogelson, Robert M.
   1968   "Violence as protest," pp. 25-41 in R. Connery, ed., *Urban Riots: Violence
          and Social Change*. Proceedings of The Academy of Political Science, 29
          (1). New York: The Academy of Political Science, Columbia University.
Fogelson, Robert M., and Robert B. Hill
   1968   "Who riots? A study of participation in the 1967 riots," pp. 221-48 in
          *Supplemental Studies for the National Advisory Commission on Civil
          Disorders*. New York: Praeger.
Frank, David
   1976   "Class conflict in the coal industry: Cape Breton, 1922," pp. 161-84 in G.
          Kealey and P. Warrian, eds., *Essays in Canadian Working Class History*.
          Toronto: McClelland and Stewart.
Frank, J.A., and M. Kelly
   1977   "Etude préliminaire sur la violence collective en Ontario et au Québec,
          1963-1973." *Canadian Journal of Political Science*, 10, 145-57.
   1979   "'Street politics' in Canada: an examination of mediating factors." *American Journal of Political Science*, 23, 593-614.
Friedrich, Paul
   1972   "Political homicide in rural Mexico," pp. 269-82 in I. Feierabend, R.
          Feierabend, and T.R. Gurr, eds., *Anger, Violence, and Politics: Theories
          and Research*. Englewood Cliffs, N.J.: Prentice-Hall.
Frye, Northrop
   1971   *The Bush Garden: Essays on the Canadian Imagination*. Toronto: Anansi.
Galtung, Johan
   1964   "A structural theory of aggression." *Journal of Peace Research*, 2, 95-119.
Gamson, William A.
   1975   *The Strategy of Social Protest*. Homewood, Ill.: Dorsey.
Garver, Newton
   1969   "What violence is," pp. 5-13 in T. Rose, ed., *Violence in America: A
          Historical and Contemporary Reader*. New York: Random House.
Gellner, John
   1974   *Bayonets in the Streets: Urban Guerrilla at Home and Abroad*. Don Mills,
          Ont.: Collier-Macmillan.
Gerth, H.H., and C. Wright Mills, eds. and trans.
   1958   *From Max Weber: Essays in Sociology*. New York: Oxford University Press.

Giffen, P.J.

1976 "Official rates of crime and delinquency," pp. 66-110 in W.T. McGrath, ed., *Crime and Its Treatment in Canada*. 2nd ed. Toronto: Macmillan.

Gillespie, W. Irwin

1976 "On the redistribution of income in Canada." *Canadian Tax Journal*, 24, 419-50.

Goode, William J.

1972 "The place of force in human society." *American Sociological Review*, 37, 507-19.

Goranson, Richard E.

n.d. "Television violence effects: issues and evidence," pp. 2-30 in Royal Commission on Violence in the Communications Industry, *Report, Vol. V: Learning from the Media*. Toronto: Queen's Printer for Ontario.

Gordon, Mary

1978 "The predicament." *New York Review of Books*, 20 July, 37-9.

Graham, Hugh Davies, and Ted Robert Gurr, eds.

1969 *Violence in America: Historical and Comparative Perspectives*. A report submitted to the National Commission on the Causes and Prevention of Violence. New York: Bantam.

Grant, George

1965 *Lament for a Nation: The Defeat of Canadian Nationalism*. Toronto: McClelland and Stewart.

Gray, James H.

1966 *The Winter Years: The Depression on the Prairies*. Toronto: Macmillan.

Grimshaw, Allen D.

1959 "A study in social violence: urban race riots in the United States." Ph.D. thesis, University of Pennsylvania.

1968 "Three views of urban violence: civil disturbance, racial revolt, class assault." *The American Behavioral Scientist*, 11, 2-7.

Gude, Edward W.

1969 "Batista and Betancourt: alternative responses to violence," pp. 731-48 in H. Graham and T.R. Gurr, eds., *Violence in America: Historical and Comparative Perspectives*. A report submitted to the National Commission on the Causes and Prevention of Violence. New York: Bantam.

Guevara, Ernesto Che

1969 *Guerrilla Warfare*. Harmondsworth: Penguin Books.

Guindon, Hubert

1975 "Social unrest, social class and Quebec's bureaucratic revolution," pp. 337-46 in S.D. Clark, J.P. Grayson, and L.M. Grayson, eds., *Prophecy and Protest: Social Movements in Twentieth-Century Canada*. Toronto: Gage.

Gurr, Ted Robert

1968 "A causal model of civil strife: a comparative analysis using new indices." *American Political Science Review*, 62, 1104-24.

1969 "A comparative study of civil strife," pp. 572-632 in H. Graham and T.R. Gurr, eds., *Violence in America: Historical and Comparative Perspectives*. A report submitted to the National Commission on the Causes and Prevention of Violence. New York: Bantam.

1970 *Why Men Rebel*. Princeton: Princeton University Press.

1976 *Rogues, Rebels, and Reformers: A Political History of Urban Crime and Conflict*. Beverly Hills: Sage.

1979 "Political protest and rebellion in the 1960s: the United States in world perspective," pp. 49-76 in H. Graham and T.R. Gurr, eds., *Violence in America: Historical and Comparative Perspectives*. Revised ed. Beverly Hills: Sage.

1979a "On the history of violent crime in Europe and America," pp. 353-74 in H. Graham and T.R. Gurr, eds., *Violence in America: Historical and Comparative Perspectives*. Revised ed. Beverly Hills: Sage.

Gurr, Ted Robert, and V.F. Bishop

1976 "Violent nations, and others." *Journal of Conflict Resolution*, 20, 79-110.

Hackney, Sheldon

1969 "Southern violence," pp. 505-27 in H. Graham and T.R. Gurr, eds., *Violence in America: Historical and Comparative Perspectives*. A report submitted to the National Commission on the Causes and Prevention of Violence. New York: Bantam.

Hagan, John

1977 *The Disreputable Pleasures: Crime and Deviance in Canada*. Toronto: McGraw-Hill Ryerson.

Hanson, S.D.

1974 "Estevan 1931," pp. 33-77 in I. Abella, ed., *On Strike: Six Key Labour Struggles in Canada, 1919-1949*. Toronto: James Lewis and Samuel.

Harris, Paul

1973 "The concept of violence." *Political Science*, 25, 103-14.

Health and Welfare Canada

1981 "Patterns in Canadian suicide mortality." *Chronic Diseases in Canada*, 1, 37-40.

Hibbs, Douglas A.

1973 *Mass Political Violence: A Cross-National Causal Analysis*. New York: Wiley.

Hiller, Harry H.

1976 *Canadian Society: A Sociological Analysis*. Scarborough, Ont.: Prentice-Hall.

Hoar, Victor

1970 *The On to Ottawa Trek*. Toronto: Copp Clark.

Hobbes, Thomas

1960 *Leviathan*. Edited by M. Oakeshott. Oxford: Basil Blackwell.

Hobsbawm, E.J.

1965 *Primitive Rebels: Studies in Archaic Forms of Social Movement in the 19th and 20th Centuries*. New York: W.W. Norton.

Hobsbawm, E.J., and George Rudé
  1969   *Captain Swing*. London: Lawrence and Wishart.
Holt, Simma
  1964   *Terror in the Name of God: The Story of the Sons of Freedom Doukhobors*.
          Toronto: McClelland and Stewart.
Hopkins, J. Castell
  1919   *The Canadian Annual Review of Public Affairs, 1918*. Toronto: Canadian
          Annual Review.
  1920   *The Canadian Annual Review of Public Affairs, 1919*. Toronto: Canadian
          Annual Review.
Horowitz, Gad
  1966   "Conservatism, liberalism and socialism in Canada: an interpretation."
          Canadian Journal of Economics and Political Science, 32, 143-71.
Jackson, Robert J., Michael J. Kelly, and Thomas H. Mitchell
  n.d.   "Collective conflict, violence and the media," pp. 228-314 in Royal
          Commission on Violence in the Communications Industry, *Report, Vol. V:
          Learning from the Media*. Toronto: Queen's Printer for Ontario.
Jamieson, Stuart
  1968   *Times of Trouble: Labour Unrest and Industrial Conflict in Canada,
          1900-66*. Studies of the Task Force on Labour Relations, No. 22. Ottawa:
          Supply and Services Canada.
  1973   *Industrial Relations in Canada*. 2nd ed. Toronto: Macmillan.
  1979   "Some reflections on violence and the law in industrial relations," pp.
          141-54 in D.J. Bercuson and L.A. Knafla, eds., *Law and Society in
          Canada in Historical Perspective*. University of Calgary Studies in History,
          No. 2. Calgary: University of Calgary.
Jervis, Robert
  1968   "Hypotheses on misperception." *World Politics*, 20, 454-79.
Johnson, Chalmers
  1964   *Revolution and the Social System*. Hoover Institution Studies, No. 3.
          Stanford: The Hoover Institution on War, Revolution and Peace, Stanford
          University.
  1966   *Revolutionary Change*. Boston: Little, Brown.
Johnstone, John C.
  1969   *Young People's Images of Canadian Society: An Opinion Survey of
          Canadian Youth 13 to 20 Years of Age*. Studies of the Royal Commission
          on Bilingualism and Biculturalism, No. 2. Ottawa: Information Canada.
Kealey, Gregory S.
  1976   "The Orange order in Toronto: religious riot and the working class," pp.
          13-34 in G. Kealey and P. Warrian, eds., *Essays in Canadian Working
          Class History*. Toronto: McClelland and Stewart.
Kelley, Thomas P.
  1974   *The Black Donnellys*. Toronto: Pagurian Press.

Kelly, William, and Nora Kelly
1976   *Policing in Canada*. Toronto: Macmillan.
Kerr, Clark, and Abraham Siegel
1954   "The inter-industry propensity to strike," pp. 189-212 in A. Kornhauser,
        R. Dubin, and A.M. Ross, eds., *Industrial Conflict*. New York: McGraw-
        Hill.
Kilbourn, W., ed.
1970   *Canada: A Guide to the Peaceable Kingdom*. Toronto: Macmillan.
Kirkham, James F., Sheldon G. Levy, and William J. Crotty
1970   *Assassination and Political Violence*. A staff report to the National Com-
        mission on the Causes and Prevention of Violence. New York: Bantam.
Kohn, Melvin L.
1977   *Class and Conformity: A Study in Values*. 2nd ed. Chicago: University of
        Chicago Press.
Kopkind, Andrew
1971   "White on black: the riot commission and the rhetoric of reform," pp.
        378-91 in A. Platt, ed., *The Politics of Riot Commissions, 1917-1970:
        A Collection of Official Reports and Critical Essays*. New York: Macmillan.
Kornhauser, William
1959   *The Politics of Mass Society*. New York: Free Press.
Latouche, Daniel
1971   "Violence, politique et crise dans la société québécoise," pp. 175-99 in L.
        Lapierre, J. McLeod, C. Taylor, and W. Young, eds., *Essays on the
        Left: Essays in Honour of T.C. Douglas*. Toronto: McClelland and
        Stewart.
Laurendeau, André
1973   *Witness for Quebec*. Essays selected and translated by Philip Stratford.
        Toronto: Macmillan.
Laurendeau, Marc
1974   *Les Québécois violents: un ouvrage sur les causes et la rentabilité de la
        violence d'inspiration politique au Quebéc*. 2nd ed. Québec: Boréal
        Express.
Leacy, F.H., ed.
1983   *Historical Statistics of Canada*. 2nd ed. Ottawa: Statistics Canada.
Leiden, Carl, and Karl M. Schmitt
1968   *The Politics of Violence: Revolution in the Modern World*. Englewood
        Cliffs, N.J.: Prentice-Hall.
Leites, Nathan, and Charles Wolf, Jr.
1969   *Rebellion and Authority: An Analytic Essay on Insurgent Conflicts*.
        Chicago: Markham.
Lipset, Seymour Martin
1970   *Revolution and Counterrevolution: Change and Persistence in Social
        Structures*. Revised and updated ed. Garden City, N.Y.: Anchor.

Liversedge, Ronald

1973   *Recollections of the On to Ottawa Trek, With Documents Related to the Vancouver Strike and the On to Ottawa Trek.* Edited by Victor Hoar. Toronto: McClelland and Stewart.

Lodhi, Abdul Qaiyum, and Charles Tilly

1973   "Urbanization, crime, and collective violence in 19th-century France." *American Journal of Sociology*, 79, 296-318.

Mackenzie, Alexander, ed.

1882   *The Life and Speeches of Hon. George Brown.* Toronto: Globe Publishing.

MacLennan, Hugh

1970   "After 300 years, our neurosis is relevant," pp. 8-13 in W. Kilbourn, ed., *Canada: A Guide to the Peaceable Kingdom.* Toronto: Macmillan.

Macleod, R.C.

1976   *The NWMP and Law Enforcement, 1873-1905.* Toronto: University of Toronto Press.

Manitoba

1919   Royal Commission to Enquire into and Report upon the Causes and Effects of the General Strike which recently existed in the City of Winnipeg for a Period of Six Weeks, Including the Methods of Calling and Carrying on such Strike. *Report.* H.A. Robson, Commissioner. Winnipeg: Province of Manitoba.

Manzer, Ronald

1974   *Canada: A Socio-Political Report.* Toronto: McGraw-Hill Ryerson.

Marchak, M. Patricia

1975   *Ideological Perspectives on Canada.* Toronto: McGraw-Hill Ryerson.

Masters, Donald Campbell

1950   *The Winnipeg General Strike.* Toronto: University of Toronto Press.

McDonald, Lynn

1969   "Crime and punishment in Canada: a statistical test of the 'conventional wisdom.'" *Canadian Review of Sociology and Anthropology*, 6, 212-36.

1976   *The Sociology of Law and Order.* Montreal: Book Centre.

McKellar, Peter

1968   *Experience and Behaviour.* Harmondsworth: Penguin Books.

McKenzie, Robert

1971   "Trouble in Quebec." Toronto *Daily Star*, 23 October.

McNaught, Kenneth

1970   "Violence in Canadian history," pp. 66-84 in J.S. Moir, ed., *Character and Circumstance: Essays in Honour of Donald Grant Creighton.* Toronto: Macmillan.

1975   "Collective violence in Canadian history: some problems of definition and research," pp. 165-76 in *Report of the Proceedings: Workshop on Violence in Canadian Society.* Toronto: Centre of Criminology, University of Toronto.

1975a "Political trials and the Canadian political tradition," pp. 137-61 in M. Friedland, ed., *Courts and Trials*. Toronto: University of Toronto Press.

McNeill, William H.

1982 *The Pursuit of Power: Technology, Armed Force, and Society since A.D. 1000*. Chicago: University of Chicago Press.

Mealing, S.R.

1965 "The concept of social class and the interpretation of Canadian history." *Canadian Historical Review*, 46, 407-25.

Mewett, Alan W.

1975 "Legal defences against violence," pp. 159-62 in *Report of the Proceedings: Workshop on Violence in Canadian Society*. Toronto: Centre of Criminology, University of Toronto.

Moore, Jr., Barrington

1966 *Social Origins of Dictatorship and Democracy: Lord and Peasant in the Making of the Modern World*. Boston: Beacon Press.

Morf, Gustave

1970 *Terror in Quebec: Case Studies of the FLQ*. Toronto: Clarke, Irwin.

Morgan, Henry J.

1886 *The Dominion Annual Register and Review, 1885*. Toronto: Hunter, Rose.

Morrison, Donald J., and Hugh M. Stevenson

1971 "Political instability in independent black Africa: more dimensions of conflict behavior within nations." *Journal of Conflict Resolution*, 15, 347-68.

Morrison, Jean

1976 "Ethnicity and violence: the Lakehead freight handlers before World War I," pp. 143-60 in G. Kealey and P. Warrian, eds., *Essays in Canadian Working Class History*. Toronto: McClelland and Stewart.

Morton, Desmond

1970 "Aid to the civil power: the Canadian militia in support of social order, 1867-1914." *Canadian Historical Review*, 51, 407-25.

1974 "Aid to the civil power: the Stratford strike of 1933," pp. 79-91 in I. Abella, ed., *On Strike: Six Key Labour Struggles in Canada, 1919-1949*. Toronto: James Lewis and Samuel.

1980 "'Kicking and complaining': demobilization riots in the Canadian Expeditionary Force, 1918-19." *Canadian Historical Review*, 61, 334-60.

Morton, W.L.

1965 *The Canadian Identity*. Toronto: University of Toronto Press.

1967 *Manitoba: A History*. 2nd ed. Toronto: University of Toronto Press.

Naegele, Kaspar D.

1961 "Canadian society: some reflections," pp. 1-53 in B. Blishen, F. Jones, K. Naegele, and J. Porter, eds., *Canadian Society: Sociological Perspectives*. New York: Free Press.

Nardin, Terry

1973 "Conflicting conceptions of political violence," pp. 75-126 in C.P. Cotter,

ed., *Political Science Annual: An International Review*. Vol. 4.
Indianapolis, Indiana: Bobbs-Merrill.

Nieburg, H.L.

1962   "The threat of violence and social change." *American Political Science Review*, 56, 865-73.

1969   *Political Violence: The Behavioral Process*. New York: St Martin's Press.

Oberschall, Anthony

1973   *Social Conflict and Social Movements*. Englewood Cliffs, N.J.: Prentice-Hall.

Olsen, Dennis

1977   "The state elites," pp. 199-224 in L. Panitch, ed., *The Canadian State: Political Economy and Political Power*. Toronto: University of Toronto Press.

Olson, Jr., Mancur

1968   *The Logic of Collective Action: Public Goods and the Theory of Groups*. New York: Schocken Books.

1971   "Rapid growth as a destabilizing force," pp. 215-27 in J. Davies, ed., *When Men Revolt – and Why: A Reader in Political Violence and Revolution*. New York: Free Press.

Ormsby, Margaret A.

1971   *British Columbia: A History*. Toronto: Macmillan.

Payne, James

1965   "Peru: the politics of structured violence." *Journal of Politics*, 27, 362-74.

Pelletier, Gérard

1971   *The October Crisis*. Translated by Joyce Marshall. Toronto: McClelland and Stewart.

Pickersgill, J.W., and D.F. Forster

1968   *The Mackenzie King Record, Vol. II: 1944-1945*. Toronto: University of Toronto Press.

Piven, Frances Fox, and Richard A. Cloward

1977   *Poor People's Movements: Why They Succeed, How They Fail*. New York: Pantheon Books.

Pope, Sir Joseph

n.d.   *Correspondence of Sir John Macdonald*. Toronto: Oxford University Press.

Porter, John

1965   *The Vertical Mosaic: An Analysis of Social Class and Power in Canada*. Toronto: University of Toronto Press.

Preston, Richard A.

1964   "The transfer of British military institutions to Canada in the nineteenth century," pp. 81-107 in W.B. Hamilton, ed., *The Transfer of Institutions*. London: Cambridge University Press.

Provencher, Jean

1971   *Québec sous la loi des mesures de guerre, 1918*. Montréal: Boréal Express.

Robin, Martin
1968   *Radical Politics and Canadian Labour, 1880-1930*. Kingston: Industrial
       Relations Centre, Queen's University.
Roseborough, Howard, and Raymond Breton
1971   "Perceptions of relative economic and political advantages of ethnic groups
       in Canada," pp. 401-25 in B. Blishen, F. Jones, K. Naegele, and J. Porter,
       eds., *Canadian Society: Sociological Perspectives*. Abridged 3rd ed.
       Toronto: Macmillan.
Rubenstein, Richard E.
1970   *Rebels in Eden: Mass Political Violence in the United States*. Boston:
       Little, Brown.
Rudé, George
1964   *The Crowd in History: A Study of Popular Disturbances in France and
       England, 1730-1848*. New York: Wiley.
Rummel, R.J.
1966   "Dimensions of conflict behavior within nations, 1946-59." *Journal of
       Conflict Resolution*, 10, 65-73.
Russett, Bruce M.
1964   "Inequality and instability: the relation of land tenure to politics." *World
       Politics*, 16, 442-54.
Russett, Bruce M., Hayward R. Alker Jr., Karl W. Deutsch, and Harold D. Lasswell
1964   *World Handbook of Political and Social Indicators*. New Haven: Yale
       University Press.
Safarian, A.E.
1970   *The Canadian Economy in the Great Depression*. Toronto: McClelland
       and Stewart.
Sartre, Jean-Paul
1968   "Preface," pp. 7-31 in Frantz Fanon, *The Wretched of the Earth*. Translated
       by Constance Farrington. New York: Grove Press.
Saskatchewan
1936   *Report of the Regina Riot Inquiry Commission*. Regina: Queen's
       Printer.
Senior, Hereward
1978   *The Fenians and Canada*. Toronto: Macmillan.
Shearing, Clifford D.
1981   "Subterranean processes in the maintenance of power: an examination of
       the mechanisms coordinating police action." *Canadian Review of Sociology
       and Anthropology*, 18, 283-98.
Siegfried, André
1966   *The Race Question in Canada*. Toronto: McClelland and Stewart.
Silver, Allan A.
1968   "Official interpretations of racial riots," pp. 146-58 in R. Connery, ed.,
       Urban Riots: Violence and Social Change. Proceedings of The Academy

of Political Science, 29 (1). New York: The Academy of Political Science, Columbia University.

Skelton, O.D.
1965 *Life and Letters of Sir Wilfrid Laurier*. Toronto: McClelland and Stewart.

Skolnick, Jerome K.
1969 *The Politics of Protest*. A report submitted to the Task Force on Violent Aspects of Protest and Confrontation of the National Commission on the Causes and Prevention of Violence. New York: Simon and Schuster.

Smiley, Donald V.
1976 *Canada in Question: Federalism in the Seventies*. Toronto: McGraw-Hill Ryerson.

Smith, Michael D.
1975 "The legitimation of violence: hockey players' perceptions of their reference groups' sanctions for assault." *Canadian Review of Sociology and Anthropology*, 12, 72-80.

Sorel, Georges
1961 *Reflections on Violence*. Translated by T.E. Hulme. New York: Collier Books.

Stanley, George F.G.
1961 *The Birth of Western Canada: A History of the Riel Rebellions*. Toronto: University of Toronto Press.

Statistics Canada
1980 *Perspectives Canada III*. Edited by H.J. Adler and D.A. Brusegard. Ottawa: Supply and Services Canada.

Steele, Samuel B.
1972 *Forty Years in Canada: Reminiscences of the Great North-West With Some Account of his Service in South Africa*. Toronto: McGraw-Hill Ryerson.

Stewart, Walter
1976 *But Not in Canada!* Toronto: Macmillan.

Tanter, Raymond
1969 "International war and domestic turmoil: some contemporary evidence," pp. 550-69 in H. Graham and T.R. Gurr, eds., *Violence in America: Historical and Comparative Perspectives*. A report submitted to the National Commission on the Causes and Prevention of Violence. New York: Bantam.

Taylor, Charles L., and Michael C. Hudson
1972 *World Handbook of Political and Social Indicators*. 2nd ed. New Haven: Yale University Press.

Teevan, Jr., James T.
1972 "Deterrent effects of punishment: the Canadian case," pp. 153-65 in C. Boydell, C. Grindstaff, and P. Whitehead, eds., *Deviant Behaviour and Societal Reaction*. Toronto: Holt, Rinehart and Winston.

Tepperman, Lorne
  1975   *Social Mobility in Canada*. Toronto: McGraw-Hill Ryerson.
Thorner, Thomas
  1979   "The incidence of crime in southern Alberta, 1878-1905," pp. 53-88 in
         D.J. Bercuson and L.A. Knafla, eds., *Law and Society in Canada in
         Historical Perspective*. The University of Calgary Studies in History, No.
         2. Calgary: University of Calgary.
Thorner, Thomas, and N. Watson
  1981   "Patterns of prairie crime: Calgary, 1875-1939," pp. 219-56 in L.A. Knafla,
         ed., *Crime and Criminal Justice in Europe and Canada*. Waterloo,
         Ont.: Wilfrid Laurier University for the Calgary Institute for the
         Humanities.
Tilly, Charles
  1978   *From Mobilization to Revolution*. Reading, Mass.: Addison-Wesley.
  1979   "Collective violence in European perspective," pp. 83-118 in H. Graham
         and T.R. Gurr, eds., *Violence in America: Historical and Comparative
         Perspectives*. Revised ed. Beverly Hills: Sage.
Tilly, Charles, Louise Tilly, and Richard Tilly
  1975   *The Rebellious Century, 1830-1930*. Cambridge, Mass.: Harvard Univer-
         sity Press.
Torrance, Judy
  1975   "Cultural factors and the response of governments to violence: the case of
         Canada." Ph.D. thesis, York University, Toronto.
  1977   "The response of Canadian governments to violence." *Canadian Journal
         of Political Science*, 10, 473-96.
Trudeau, Pierre Elliott
  1972   Speech to the National Newspaper Awards dinner. *The Globe and Mail*, 10
         April.
Turner, Ralph H.
  1969   "The public perception of protest." *American Sociological Review*, 34,
         815-31.
Turner, Ralph H., and Lewis M. Killian
  1972   *Collective Behavior*. 2nd ed. Englewood Cliffs, N.J.: Prentice-Hall.
Underhill, Frank
  1960   *In Search of Canadian Liberalism*. Toronto: Macmillan.
United States
  1968   National Advisory Commission on Civil Disorders. *Report*. Otto Kerner,
         chairman. New York: Bantam.
  1970   National Commission on the Causes and Prevention of Violence. *Final
         Report*. Milton S. Eisenhower, chairman. New York: Bantam.
Vaz, Edmund W.
  1965   "Middle-class adolescents: self-reported delinquency and youth culture
         activities." *Canadian Review of Sociology and Anthropology*, 2, 52-70.

Wade, Francis W.

1971   "On violence." *Journal of Philosophy*, 68, 369-77.

Waite, P.B.

1962   *The Life and Times of Confederation, 1864-1867: Politics, Newspapers, and the Union of British North America*. 2nd ed. Toronto: University of Toronto Press.

Walter, Eugene V.

1969   *Terror and Resistance: A Study of Political Violence*. New York: Oxford University Press.

Ward, Norman, ed.

1960   *A Party Politician: The Memoirs of Chubby Power*. Toronto: Macmillan.

Wedge, Bryant

1972   "Students and political violence: Brazil, 1964, and the Dominican Republic, 1965," pp. 295-313 in I. Feierabend, R. Feierabend, and T.R. Gurr, eds., *Anger, Violence, and Politics: Theories and Research*. Englewood Cliffs, N.J.: Prentice-Hall.

Westley, William A.

1953   "Violence and the police." *American Journal of Sociology*, 59, 34-41.

Wolff, Robert P.

1969   "On violence." *Journal of Philosophy*, 66, 601-16.

Wolfgang, Marvin E., and Franco Ferracuti

1967   *The Subculture of Violence: Towards an Integrated Theory in Criminology*. London: Tavistock.

Wolin, Sheldon S.

1963   "Violence and the western political tradition." *American Journal of Orthopsychiatry*, 33, 15-28.

Woodcock, George, and Ivan Avakumovic

1977   *The Doukhobors*. Toronto: McClelland and Stewart.

Zay, Nicolas

1963   "Gaps in available statistics on crime and delinquency in Canada." *Canadian Journal of Economics and Political Science*, 29, 75-89.

Index